OUR EXPERIENCE OF LANGUAGE

For in this above all do we excel the beasts, that we speak to one another, and by speaking can communicate meaning—Cicero

> *Let them leave language to their lonely betters*
> *Who count some days and long for certain letters.*
> *We, too, make noises when we laugh, or weep;*
> *Words are for those with promises to keep.*
> —W. H. Auden

OUR EXPERIENCE OF LANGUAGE

by

Walter Nash

ST. MARTIN'S PRESS, NEW YORK

Preface

This book is not about linguistics. It is about language, as the medium, the determinant, the substance, even, of much of our experience; as something we use and respond to, rather than as an object for definition and analysis. Indeed, in its emphasis on our performance as speakers rather than on our competence to speak, my book may seem to many to be alien to the proper concerns of the linguist.

I am therefore bound to say that I am by no means indifferent to what modern linguistics has to offer, and would hope that the spirit of its common teachings might be felt in these chapters as a benevolent presence. If I have refused to give that spirit the embodiment of some particular doctrine or linguistic model, it is because the proposed course of my book forbade entry into polemic and the long corridors of theory. By thus refusing commitment, I may well have laid myself open to specialist criticism on matters of presentation and terminology. It may appear that some matters are presented in conservative, not to say old-fashioned, terms; that I bring a common-tongue casualness to my use of certain expressions which a linguist might regard as terms proper to his craft (a colleague has suggested that my freedom with words like *symbol, code* and *norm* is to be criticised on this count); and that occasionally I have been enticed into the apparent absurdity of inventing a terminology in order to avoid technicalities. I acknowledge these defects, but will venture to hope that they may not grossly impede the common reader's understanding of what I have to say.

Naturally, I hope that the book may please and in some measure instruct any adult reader about to succumb to that most potent of all obsessions, a curiosity about language and its use. I realise, however, that in effect my audience will probably consist of students of English at some quite early stage of their careers. There are many students, destined as a rule for the teaching profession, who have no immediate interest in scientific linguistics, and who are unlikely to be coaxed into such an interest, but who, in the normal course of their professional lives, will be involved in an intense traffic of language, possibly as the medium of literature, certainly as the conductor of personal relationships. I had such students very much in mind as I wrote my book, and this may explain why I pay so much attention to dialogue in social contexts, and why the longest chapter of the book is devoted to the subject of literary language.

At the end of the book there is a select bibliography, with numbered items arranged in annotated sections. Wherever possible, footnote references in my text indicate bibliographical items by author's surname, section number, and item number. Where the reference is to a book not listed in the bibliography, full details are given.

Among the people who have given me help and encouragement, I have particular reason to be grateful to Mr Peter Kemmis Betty and to my colleague Dr R. K. K. Hartmann. I need hardly say that their extremely useful criticism, which I have tried to act upon, does not involve them in any responsibility for stylistic blemishes and organisational defects which are now, alas, beyond purgation. One further, and final, acknowledgement I make with great joy: to my wife, D. M. Nash, who has never allowed me the luxury of losing heart.

Walter Nash
Nottingham, December 1970

Contents

In cradle-time, when a shape came lurching
Out of the imbecile sky (a star? an apple? a face?),
    You might even pause to crow,
Then your gums and sightless fists would get on with their searching;
Being wordless to put a world in its place
You were hardly abashed by a heaven you couldn't know.

Then words discovered you, and you taught them
The discernments of your eye, and your hands' unending to-do.
    You gave them errands to run;
If there were secrets for sale, they willingly bought them,
And they put on their game little acts for you—
'Cheese please', 'Thou art fair, my love', 'X equals one'.

It was immense, till one bed-time, turning
Absently into a blind alley of sleep, you kicked
    Against an unbiddable wall,
And started awake, your throat full of fear and yearning;
But syntax had you barred and bricked,
And the strict white words were there, within easy call.

Then you understood how you lay in prison,
How your kindly attentive guards on the parapet beneath
    Would lend you names for things,
Would comfort you in the brilliant cell of reason—
An idiot breaking idiom in his teeth,
A gargoyle spouting steeples, passions, wings.

1 Code and Environment

A man comes home from work, greets his family, goes through the motions of shrugging off the day, switches on TV, settles down to his evening meal. Presently, the screen fills with the image of the weather-forecaster, who announces that a trough of low pressure is moving in over the Atlantic, that there will be rain in western Scotland before late evening, reaching the north of England and the Midlands by morning. The man makes a wry comment to his wife, but she is only half attentive. She is listening to the noises from next door, where a less peaceably-disposed couple are quarrelling violently, belabouring each other with a high-pitched abuse which almost disturbs the composure of the mother in the house beyond, who is reading a story to her children. Across the street, an old lady is reading a letter from her son in Canada; marks on the paper make the shape of his voice. Her other son sits at the half-cleared table, speechlessly struggling with the task of completing his income-tax form. All over the city, people come home, eat, talk, read, watch the evening unfold its tale of distractions or obligations. A young teacher comes back to his rented room and begins to coax onto paper a lecture, which next week he will try to read aloud as though it were a grand effusion of unpremeditated speech. Beyond his room, beyond the prattling circles of the pub, beyond the newsboys shouting their chalked headlines, there is the football ground, where twenty-two players and three officials provoke the cheers, catcalls, imprecations, objurgations, enthusiasm, disparagement, of twenty thousand spectators. In the small house a mile away, a man sits quite alone, while in his mind a voice re-creates problems and grievances. Having no one else to talk to, he is talking to himself; for as Cicero reminds us, it is above all as talkers that we excel the beasts.

Imagine these, and many kindred scenes, on any evening, in any town; they represent the experience of language, as it occurs in connection with the diverse experience, trivial or profound, of our lives-at-large. Our handful of examples may suggest that the experience of language is changeable and many-sided. Some of our projected characters experience language in solitude, remote from any partner in discourse other than the imagined form, the whispering *alter ego*. For others, language is a shared property, a lively face-to-face exchange – or even a form of collective expression. For some, the experience of language means recognising, passively, certain ranges of symbolism; language 'happens *to*' them. There are others for whom the experience is active; they create it, it 'happens *through*' them, as they themselves produce linguistic symbols. For many, language is an experience in which 'happening to' and 'happening through' follow each other in turn-and-turn-about: an ordinary conversation involves both passivity, or recognition, and activity, or production. For some, the produced or recognised symbolism takes the form of speech, while for others it appears as writing. In one of our imagined instances, speech is transmitted through an especial medium (i.e. via television), one of a range of technical devices which are commonplaces of our time and which impose particular conditions on language. For some of our actors, the experience of language is not associated with any strength of feeling; for others it is bound up with powerful emotions. In some cases, physical gesture and facial expression are likely to be associated significantly with the experience; in other instances, they are immaterial.

It is clear that if we think of language as an experience, we can make a number of distinctions as to the forms this experience may take. We can also make one distinction of major importance, concerning the relevance of the experience of language to the experience of life. A review of the actors who make up our opening paragraph might suggest that there are some for whom language is a relatively minor, or peripheral, element in the experience of the moment. The man in the grandstand, for instance, does not have to avail himself of the experience of language in order to have the experience of a football-match; it happens that the ability to make noises adds to his pleasure, and that the shouting of slogans and directives – to say nothing of the abuse that serves to discharge violent emotions – is therefore a component of the football-watching sensation. On the other hand, for the old lady silently perusing her letter, or for the children listening to their mother's reading, language is much more than a component or peripheral element. It is something central, something tantamount to the experience itself – a proponent of life, if we will. For the old lady, for the children, the essentials of the moment's experience are mediated through language. Language and experience are one – the love of a son, the excitement of strange events, exist by virtue of language alone; in effect, language becomes a surrogate experience. This is even true of the quarrellers, who, at this imagined moment, are seen demonstrating their civilisation by fighting in phrases rather than by battling with brickbats. They are living a part of their lives at the symbolic level.

It is an enormous achievement of mankind, to have learned to manipulate experience symbolically. We outface the beasts not merely because we speak, but because by speaking we make things happen, or even make happenings without things. We make words lever our world, in doing so we manifest the fact that our language and the social environment (or environments) in which it is exercised are governed by conventions of usage which we all recognise, and on which we rely as prerequisites to communication and to the continuity of our experience. We take a great deal for granted about the world we are brought up in, and about the conventions of symbolism which give us our guidance and purchase in that world. If, for example, I take a bus-ride, and ask the conductor for a 'sevenpenny, please', I expect my words to produce a certain effect. They initiate on the conductor's part an action, the central and significant element in which is the handing to me of a small piece of paper called a ticket. The handing over of the ticket and my continued possession of it during the time that I am on the bus, are socially important. I waste no time in offering my sevenpence to anybody and everybody on the vehicle. I keep it for the person whose special dress and equipment mark him out as the official called the conductor; and it is to him that I speak the words that begin the ritual of ticket-issuing. I know what to do and what to say and what will happen, because I have long since learned the conventions of language and situation that pertain in my society. If the conventions were to change every day, if tomorrow it should become necessary to say 'three and a half rapid haddocks', upon which the conductor would hand over a plastic rose, and if the day after tomorrow the form were to be 'an eggcupful' and the response the marking of my forehead with coloured chalk – then obviously life would become unendurably various, and I could rely on nothing, learn nothing, assume nothing, do nothing of any importance, because of the unpredictability of commonplace situations. But situations, on the whole, are not unpredictable, and the conventions of language and behaviour do not change so violently and absurdly.

Perhaps this is all too obvious; but it cannot be said too emphatically or too often that language depends, for its working power, on the existence of two conventions, the one social or environmental, the other having to do with the symbolism and structure of language itself. It is sometimes hard for people not trained to the study of language to accept fully the principle that the symbols of language are conventional, and that the conventions are at bottom quite arbitrary. We do not use a particular set of vowels (for example) because they are proper to right-thinking people, or a certain tense-system because it embodies the robustness of the national character. Of course it would be absurd to suppose that language is like that; and of course there should be no need to say (but there always is) that it is not an immutable ordinance of heaven. Englishmen order their affairs with the help of a symbolic system which is neither superior nor inferior to, but merely different from, the one used by Frenchmen. It is also different from the system used by Englishmen living a thousand years ago. Symbolic systems vary, and change. At the moment, we accept a certain system as a matter of convention, and put it into daily operation as a *code*. The image of our activity in language as a process of encoding and decoding signals may be a little too machine-like, and may especially repel those who look to language for the stuff of poetry, for the medium of all that is startling and sweet in human thought. Let us insist, therefore, that the word *code* is simply a useful metaphor. Its implication of a design in the production of words need cast no coldness on our desire for the Word.

A basic component of the code is *sound*. We are able to make noises – and on the basis of this fact empires have arisen and technological marvels have been established. But the sound of speech is something different from raw noise-making. Noise-making is a demonstration of our fellowship with the animals. As W. H. Auden says, ' We too make noises when we laugh, or weep '; but he continues, ' Words are for those with promises to keep '.* Our use of sound transcends the instinctive cries of pain, fear, warning, etc. which are our animal heritage. We have used speech-sounds to create an

---

* The quotation is from Auden's poem ' Their Lonely Betters ' printed in the collection *Nones*, (London: Faber and Faber, 1962). This poem is also the source of the Auden quotation on the title page.

elaborate symbolism through which the relationships, purposes, obligations of a complex society are established and discharged. This could not have happened without design, pattern, system; and pattern could not be achieved if we used an endless variety of sounds in endless permutations. English-speakers use nothing like the total number of speech-sounds produced by man in the hundreds of languages spoken throughout the world. Like the speakers of any other single language, they use a limited number of sounds, which acquire significance in our speech by virtue of the fact that A is not B, that each sound in the restricted range may be contrasted with other items in the range. The operation of sound-contrasts is not the least of the many things we take for granted in our experience of language. When a foreigner confuses the words *bitch* and *beach*, when a child constructs *swing-swang* on the model of *sing-sang*, when a flu-bound invalid pronounces *doze* for *nose*, when a faulty telephone-line leaves us wondering whether we have been told to ' get *seeds* for the garden ', or ' get *seats* for the Garden ', when puns exasperate us and poetic assonances please us, we show, by our various responses, that we are fundamentally aware of meaningful contrasts resting upon oppositions of sound.

Our awareness of speech-sounds belongs, as a rule, to the domain of instinctive response rather than that of rational analysis. We use the complex instrument of language with automatic skill, but when, as untrained observers, we try to describe its componency or operation, we often become childish or naïve. Phoneticians are sometimes irritated by the fumbling intrusion into their domain of the layman who insists on the ' correct ' way of pronouncing ' letters '; forgetting, as often as not, that in the early stages of their training they themselves had to be conditioned to know language by hearing rather than by sight. The most remarkable fact of western culture as it has developed since the Middle Ages is the primary equation of language and letters. The consequences of this are seen over and over again in our daily life. We continue to use sounds with astonishing skill and precision, while our common notions about standards in language are related to writing. This is not as disruptive of our culture as we are sometimes urged to believe, but it does affect our consciousness of speech; we ' unconsciously ' discriminate and act upon stimuli which, ' consciously ', we have to be specially trained to identify!

For example, a good deal of information in language is carried by the progressive variations of pitch and accent which we call ' intonation patterns '. Our speech is not a monotone, but has melodic characteristics, at least to the extent of rising and falling in more or less rhythmic pulses. This periodic rising and falling which we call intonation is harnessed to various tasks in language, tasks which we carry out daily, even though we may think of intonation as no more than a free variation of pitch which we use to make our voices pleasant and interesting. To some extent intonation patterns are used to mark out the shape of our utterances; they indicate the phrasing and basic structure of spoken sentences, they lay special emphasis on the part or parts of an utterance to which some priority of meaning is to be assigned. Moreover, they may play an important part as indicators of whatever operation an utterance is intended to carry out. In English, for example, there is a basic distinction between intonations closing to a fall in pitch and those which end with a final rise; this distinction can be loosely related to the operations called ' statement ', ' command ', ' question ', ' request ', etc. A further, and very important, role of intonation is to express attitudes and emotions. There are, of course, other features in language through which we can convey our feelings. We can reveal them through our choice of vocabulary, and we may even indicate them by choosing a special grammatical construction which is by implication contrasted with some more or less ' neutral ' form – e.g. by saying *What a mistake that was* instead of *That was a mistake*. But intonation and accent are the commonest, the most immediately apparent, and perhaps the most powerful manifestations in language of our emotions and attitudes. They often baffle systematic description, but the fact remains that in practice we are usually able to identify the attitudinal import of intonations occurring in the stock situations of our environment. Such identification is spontaneous and, as it were, pre-logical. A categoric recognition of speech-sounds is a hard-won thing, and brings with it a sense of amazement at the latent efficacy of language; students often show great pleasure and surprise on making their first conscious discovery of some simple sound-contrast.

Sound is the primary substance of language. We have a secondary, or parallel, medium in the form of graphic symbolism, i.e. of writing. Our writing system has developed as a more or less adequate means of translating phonic data into visual terms, and our phonic and graphic conventions are thus in a large measure interrelated – though we should beware of regarding writing as a simple derivative of speech; there are many instances in which the graphic convention operates independently, using its own special forms of visual stimulus, not necessarily reinforced by an implied phonic model. In fact a case could be made for regarding speech and writing from the outset as different methods of encoding our thoughts, suitable for different purposes and circumstances, related as parallels, so to speak, rather than as interdependents. Such view forestalls the layman's habitual error of confusing letters and sounds – an error which will not pass out of currency until we abandon the hoary old doctrine that ' the English language has five vowels, *a, e, i, o,* and *u,* and one semi-vowel, *y* '; or until schoolteachers stop urging their pupils to distinguish between the ' long and short sounds of the letter *a* ' and not to ' drop the final g ' in words like *hunting* and *fishing.* The fact is, that the twenty-six letters of our alphabet are merely conventional representations of a rather larger number of speech-sounds. It follows inevitably that some of our letters have to do duty for several sounds, while some sounds can only be indicated by a combination of letters. The word *shooting* ends with a sound which we represent alphabetically by the letters *-ng.* It is inappropriate, in such a case, to talk about ' dropping the final g ', since the sequence of letters, *ng,* is merely a visual representation of a single sound. Our six symbols, *a, e, i, o, u,* and *y* function either singly or as compound symbols graphically representing some twenty or more vocalic sounds. The letter *a,* for example, represents different sounds in *plate, pass, wash,* and *passage,* and occurs in combination with other letters to form graphic compounds representative of various sounds, e.g. *quay, gauge, cause, heart, aisle, etc.* All this can be summed up with the commonplace observation that English spelling is unphonetic. A phonetic spelling would demand a distinct symbol for every significantly contrastive sound in the language – and the alphabet we have is not rich enough to meet such a demand. This is well known; and yet people go on talking about ' the sound of letters ' as though each letter bore a unique relationship to a single, distinct sound.

As a method of phonetic transcription, our graphic system is a mere makeshift. However, its efficacy as a communication device is not related entirely or even primarily to its sound-transcribing powers. The visual symbols of writing purport, certainly, to have a phonic reference, i.e. to be reflective of underlying sounds or patterns of sound. But they also provide direct stimuli, for the benefit of the eye alone rather than on behalf of the eye-working-for-the-ear. The capacity to perceive and interpret these stimuli rapidly and without re-creating a phonic reference varies a good deal from person to person. Some people silently mouth the words as they read, or lose track of printed symbols so easily that they have to keep a finger in the text. Others become so skilled at decoding written language that they can take in whole stretches of text at a sweep. In such cases it seems likely that the reader shuts off the phonic channel, so to speak, and concentrates on the eye-language of strokes, curves, clusters and spaces which make up our graphic system. The most casual study of our handwriting convention – or of the typographical forms which have emerged from it – might suggest that letters have developed certain shapes because these make for easy identification. If I run my eye over a page of text, I notice immediately that there are some letters which are ' elongated ', with strokes projecting above or below an implied middle track, and others which are ' compact ', being contained within the line of the imaginary track. Letters of the elongated type are distinguished by different means of treating their elongated stroke – sometimes it is above the middle track, sometimes below, sometimes it is vertical, sometimes oblique, sometimes marked with a bend, sometimes with a dash, etc. Letters of the compact type also have their distinguishing features – although the history of English spelling affords examples which suggest that it has always been possible to confuse some of these compact forms – e.g. *m, n, u, w, i, v.** In reading foreign handwritings we may be confused, not only by the occurrence of curves where we would expect strokes, and vice versa, but also by a different distribution of elongated and compact types. German handwriting, for instance, uses a ' long *s* ' in some positions, whereas *s* in English orthography is a compact letter – though, indeed a long form was used in eighteenth-century typography, and is easily mistaken for *f* by present-day readers.

We are so well trained to our own manuscript conventions that we unconsciously direct our attention to those parts of our graphic

---

* Cf. Bruce Dickins and R. M. Wilson, *Early Middle English Texts* (Cambridge; Bowes and Bowes, 1951), pp. 137-8, where the authors discuss the development of certain spellings during the Middle English period as a consequence of scribal attempts to avoid the confusions resulting from the formation of adjacent letters by similar pen-strokes. They have a footnote which is worth quoting: ' As an example of the confusion which this spelling was designed to avoid, cf. Sir Henry Newbolt's historical novel *The New June* which centres round the London house of one of the great magnates of the late fourteenth and early fifteenth century. The name appears to be due to the misreading of capital *I* and *J* and of *nn* as *un*. The building was really called *The New Inne*, a much more probable name for a medieval house.'

symbols which carry essential and distinguishing characteristics. Portions of our writing are redundant, in the sense that they are not utterly necessary to the successful transmission of a message (slovenly clerks take no comfort from this – the redundancy decreases sharply with poor performance). The reader can test the degree of redundancy in English script by writing a sentence in a careful, fairly large hand, and then by covering half the script with a card, the edge of the card running along an imagined line laid horizontally through the middle of the 'compact' letters. He will find that, with careful writing, his covering of either portion of the script, upper or lower, does not greatly impair legibility; though a reader invited to decipher the half-covered text will probably do so a little more easily when the upper portion is exposed than when he is asked to read from the lower half. In our handwriting system, the tell-tale distinctive features seem often to be associated with the upper end of the letter-sequence. It is necessary for us, when we read, to perceive and interpret these features quickly and accurately. If the handwriting is careful we need no more than about half the strength of the signal to confirm our inference of essential clues. The rest of the signal is peripheral and complementary; as a conveyor of essential information it is redundant. But if the letters are badly formed, then more and more of the total substance of writing has to be scrutinised in order to interpret the message fully and accurately, and in such cases the redundancy drops sharply.

There is redundancy and clue-giving in sound as well as in writing; in listening we only need to perceive essential acoustic features in order to identify meaningful sound-elements. But the clue-giving of sound is naturally quite different from the clue-giving of writing, and the clues of writing for the most part do not reflect or translate the clues of sound. The different media of writing and speaking bring different devices and perceptions into play; and so it might be said that writing is a communication channel operating co-existently with, though quite separately from, speech. However, this would be an over-simplification, since writing, while in some ways independent and sovereign, does in others provide rough reflections of the devices of speech, equating, for example, space with pause or punctuational conventions like the comma, the hyphen, the exclamation mark, the question mark, etc. with variations of pitch and accent. It would be more appropriate to say that writing and speech are casually inter-dependent. Speech has an influence on the conventions of writing;

and writing, at any rate in our culture, has some effect on speech. But the media are essentially distinct, and each has it own possibilities which cannot be developed or reflected in the other.

The existence of writing has supplied us with a good many of our notions of what language is. We have to remember that, until very recent times, any kind of linguistic description and analysis depended on the existence of the written word. Unless you have a tape-recorder, or some similar device, you cannot easily describe and analyse speech – it runs away, and you have no guarantee that you have remembered it correctly. But writing puts language before your eyes, bids it hold still, allows you to discuss it, ponder on it, refer back to it, often as though it were a specimen in the laboratory and not an aspect of human behaviour. This has had more than a little effect on the study of language, and on our attitude to language. To take a small example, we may ask ourselves how we should define the term sentence – if, indeed, the notion could occur to us – were it not for the fact that somewhere in our minds we carry the memory of a visual pattern. Typographically, the sentence is fairly easy to define: it is a stretch of text running between conventionally indicated bounds – the indicators we use being (a) spaces at either end of the text, rather longer than the spaces we set between the units called words, and (b) a capital letter at the beginning of the text, following the space, and a full stop at the end, preceding the space. Once we have marked off a specimen of text in this way, we can proceed to discuss its structure, the order of words, the relationship of its parts, the functioning of different elements suggesting certain theoretical categories, etc. But analysis, demonstration, discussion cannot take place without transcription, without fixing the specimen of text between its agreed termini. Hence, writing represents a procedural stage in our study of language which we can hardly dispense with; most of our ideas about grammar, for example, are undoubtedly derived from the study of texts. A consequence of this for many laymen, if not for scholars, is that written language acquires authoritative status; it represents a standard of correctness, which is conservative, prohibitive, prescriptive, often manifestly artificial, yet extremely persistent and powerful. Graphic symbolism has a very considerable influence on our concepts of linguistic communication. So far from being the complete servant and derivative of a sound-system, it makes use of devices for which there is no precedent in speech. The paragraph, for example, is a unit belonging wholly to the written code. Nobody speaks in paragraphs, nobody, as yet, has tried to present the paragraph as a grammatical unit; yet it is an important unit of visual communication, and paragraphing is a fine art, especially in such fields as journalism and copywriting.

The capacity to make significant sounds and create graphic symbols is almost a condition of human civilisation. Yet speech-sounds and graphic symbols are of themselves no more than the basic substance or raw material of language. They can communicate little or nothing, until we arrange them in forms obeying principles of internal organisation and relationship – i.e. until we make a grammar – and until we assign to these forms symbolic values expressive of the notions and realities of our culture – i.e. until we devise a *lexicon*. Sounds (or, as the case may be, graphic symbols), grammar and lexicon thus constitute three great areas or levels of organisation in our code. Each of these levels is of great interest in its own right, and we shall have much to say about them in later chapters. Our object, for the moment is to make some general observations about the character and function of these broad constituents of the code.*

The ability to make a range of distinct sounds enables us to devise vocal gestures labelling the objects and percepts of our experience. We create sound-sequences (e.g. those represented by the written forms *fire, strike, good, quickly, but, not*) which identify the separable elements and operations in our experience. We are also able to translate this labelling into graphic terms, so that we have visual stroke-sequences which fulfil the same purpose of identification. However, the identification of pertinent elements in our experience is merely a primitive or baby-stage in language. True experience begins when we are able to perceive connections and relationships, when it occurs to us that A is not merely A and B only B, but that A in some way operates on B, that B is contingent upon C, etc. Our world is a perceptual map. The primary, identifying forms of language, the labelling apparatus of particles and words, provide the stations on the map, but the stations remain apart until we devise a system of routes and connections. In language, the business of routing and connecting makes up a set of organisational principles which we describe as grammar. The grammatical map of experience is not something

---

* My presentation here of a series of 'constituents', proceeding from *sounds*, through *grammar*, to the *lexicon*, and my discussion of these 'constituents', is conservative, but convenient to my purpose. See however my bibliographical comments, Appendix 3, VI.

we make for ourselves, though we may during the course of our
lives contribute to its correction and revision. We inherit it from our
predecessors, and with it we inherit the shape of a good deal of our
experience. We think we are free to experience the real world, but
in many cases we are free only to experience the possibilities and
limitations of grammar. In English, for example, it is 'possible' to
produce an expression like *It is fast getting slower*. We might think,
privately, that we as individuals would never use such an expression,
but it lies well within the compass of our common grammar, and
describes a relationship which we can not only visualise, but could
quite easily plot on graph-paper as a simple deceleration curve. If
someone were to say *It is getting slower faster*, it would perhaps be
less easy to visualise and draw the indicated relationship, for such
constructions are not, so to speak, grammatically central.* It might
even appear that *It is getting slower faster*, and *It is fast getting slower*
amount to much the same thing. Nevertheless, if we study them
closely, we can see that there is a distinction within the sameness, a
distinction which has to do with the actual rate of change of deceleration. Kinetic changes are physical realities, but because they are not
main-highway-mapped in our grammar, we find them difficult to
grasp. It would be extremely difficult to visualise the curve of change
referred to in such an expression as *It is getting slower faster slower*.
No doubt there is such a 'thing' as getting slower faster slower; but
the kind of grammar we have does not readily permit us to experience
that 'thing'. We know best the territory which the large-scale map
opens up for us.

The standard map-form of grammar is the sentence; we have noted
above the probability that deference to written forms has dictated
the acceptance of the sentence as the grammatical standard. Within
this form all the connections and relationships that are possible in
the language may be demonstrated. The concept 'sentence' is notoriously difficult to define, other than typographically, because the word
is used to indicate any isolable utterance, from the most complex

---

* 'Grammatically central' is perhaps rather vague. I mean that whilst the
construction *comparative adjective + comparative adverb* is perfectly possible in English, it is yet sufficiently unusual to attract the attention of eye or
ear. The fact that in advertisements we may meet with such injunctions as
Get slimmer sooner or *Feel fitter faster*, suggests that such constructions are
good eye-and-ear catchers—i.e. not 'grammatically central'. I suspect, moreover, that as a rule we would be concerned to make explicit the adverbial
role of *faster*, i.e. by re-phrasing, *It is getting slower more quickly*.

proposition down to rudimentary responses like *maybe* or *oh*. But the perplexities of theoretical definition have never interfered with the empirical acceptance of the sentence as the major working unit of grammar, the ultimate component, any example of which must contain one or more lesser components. A practical exploration of English grammar would not begin with the question ' What is a sentence?' but with the examination of scores of examples of utterances or pieces of text accepted by English-speaking people as possible English sentences. Such analysis would reveal the existence of certain units of form showing variations of patterning and function. It would appear, for example, that *apple, ripe, give, soon, but,* all as a rule exemplify the same kind of unit – we call them all ' words '* – but that they do not function in the same way; we have labels like ' noun ', ' verb ', ' adjective ', ' adverb ', ' conjunction ', to help us distinguish functionally between types of word. In the same way, *the white clouds, turning black, move rapidly,* can all be regarded as exemplars of different types of a particular unit, the ' phrase ', just as *he eats meat* and *although he shouldn't* can be supposed to exemplify different classes of another unit, the ' clause '. Looking at the make-up and function of words, phrases, and clauses, as revealed through their operation in English sentences, must be a major part of the task of anyone seeking to compile a grammar of English.†

Another part of this task would be to consider the importance, in English, of the ordering and integration of words, phrases and clauses. To the investigating grammarian, a page of text is a sequence of events, the events being the grammatical units in their various classes; more accurately, it might be said that the page is a sequence of sequences of events. Close examination of any text will suggest that the construction of sequences follows laws or methods which in some cases are applied with rigour, and in others more freely, with some possibility of alternative choices. Sometimes word-order may be shown to derive from a powerful ruling pattern based on the principle of successively delimiting choices – e.g. in nominal phrases like *that very charming little blue hat,* or *some rather well-worn brown leather walking shoes.* In other cases, the order of units may appear to be freely, but in some way significantly, changeable – e.g. in the positioning of

---

* Prudence naturally demands that I should emphasise the qualification ' as a rule '; they might in due place exemplify other categories.

† But of course his terms of reference will be conditioned by the kind of grammar he is trying to write. See the bibliographical note, Appendix 3, VI.

adverbial phrases such as *on Thursday* in the contrasted expressions *He rests on Thursday* and *On Thursday he rests*. Or again, the integration of units into sequences may be managed by means of the connectives and hook-words which we call ' conjunctions ' and ' prepositions ', and which we use to link word to word, phrase to phrase, clause to clause, and even sentence to sentence. In studying such connective devices the grammarian has to ask whether they merely provide links and transitions, or whether they also indicate some relationship between items, of priority, subordination, qualification, ratio, etc.

The grammarian must also be concerned with the fact that some components in language change shape, as it were, according to their position and role in a sequence; most languages avail themselves of the possibility of selecting from among certain alternatives and of contriving formal agreements between the items operating the selection. In English, for instance, we have the alternatives *boy* and *boys* which relate to the concepts ' one ' and ' more than one '; we say, in grammatical terms, that our nouns have a number-system, which works quite simply, in the overwhelming majority of cases, by adding an –s (or its phonic equivalent in speech) to the base form of the noun when ' more than one ' is intended, i.e. when we wish to form a plural. This number-system ties in with a system of formal variation for number which we apply to demonstratives like *this* and *that,* so that when such demonstratives occur in construction with nouns, we expect to find an agreement of number choices, e.g. *This wild little boy, These wild little boys, That smelly old cat, Those smelly old cats.* Again, when native speakers of English use sentences of the type *He beats his son* and *His son detests him,* they are well enough aware that *he* and *him* are related items, *he* being used in a position grammatically known as ' subject ' and *him* in the position of ' object '. We can say, if we like, that some items in our language have a range of alternative forms, from which we make an appropriate selection when we have to indicate that the item functions in a certain capacity. We should be much more aware of this principle of selection if English were an inflected language like German, in which not only personal pronouns, but also nouns, adjectives, and even articles have forms appropriate to different grammatical roles. As it is, the problems of selection in English are relatively simple; we have to make only a few formal or inflectional choices expressive of the categories ' subject ', ' object ', ' person ', ' number ', ' tense ', etc.

In some respects, these choices unite two aspects of language, its internal organisation and its external reference. They remind us that our grammar is not a formal structure existing in and for itself, but that it is an attempt to give symbolic coherence to some of the notions we have derived from our environment: it reflects our way of looking at the world. We have certain ideas about time, and place, about the scope of our actions, about agency itself, about the one and the many, the specific and the general, the actual and the possible – in fact about the problems which our experience and our culture have forced upon us: and these ideas are ultimately preserved in the grammar of our language, not in such a way as to reveal a national or racial character (linguistic racialism is neither more valid nor more venial than any other kind), but perhaps a faint impress, a sort of fossilisation, of the experiences which, collectively, we have found to be of central importance in our struggle to cope with our environment.

Grammar enables us to convert the naming of things into the mapping of experience; with the result that more and more things are named as the map-making grows more detailed and assured. The naming of things yields us the mass of material known in linguistics as the *lexicon*. The term is not unfamiliar to the layman, to whom it is a more or less learned synonym for ' dictionary '; however, there might be some variance between layman and linguist as to the sort of ' thing ' the lexicon can be expected to name. There is no difficulty in understanding that items like *boat* or *temperature* or *envious* are part of the lexicon; we recognise them as ' words ', having a ' meaning ' which we expect to be clarified by definition or citation when we look them up in dictionary. But the linguist's ' dictionary ' also includes items which we would not necessarily expect to find separately listed in the useful companions we keep at hand on our writing-tables. Suffixes like *-dom* or *-escent* or *-ish* or *-ster* or *-wards* are structurally bound to certain word-classes and so may be said to indicate functional ' meanings ' like *noun, adjective, adverb,* etc. But they have more than a structural importance; they bear a certain content, a complementary reference which in most cases may be roughly defined. Similarly, prefixes such as *ab-, dis-, for-, in-, pre-, trans-, un-,* etc. have some kind of lexical meaning, perhaps not in themselves but certainly in relationship to the word-bases to which they are affixed; they modify or complement the base-meaning in much the same way as adjectives and adverbs modify or extend the meanings of the items to which they are attached. We are accustomed to think that only 'whole words' can have the symbolising power which we call meaning, but it is easy to show that this power may exist residually in fragments or constituent particles of words.

Another kind of item which we would not expect to find separately listed in the dictionary is exemplified by common phrases and tags such as *a raw deal, a red herring, the last straw, on top of the world, at sixes and sevens, to look daggers*, etc. These collocations of words are not quite like the free collocations we can devise in the ordinary business of phrase-making. *A raw deal* is not the same sort of item as *a raw fish, a red herring* is lexically different from *a fresh herring, on top of the world* has a different sort of reference from *on top of the chimney*, etc. The difference lies in the fact that we are here comparing true phrases with what are in effect single items; the tags *a raw deal, a red herring*, etc. have phrasal construction, but are susceptible to the same processes of definition (including the use of one-word synonyms) and citation which we might employ in dealing with single items. These set phrases might in fact be regarded as a special kind of compound word. In addition to these fixed collocations, we find in our language a great many expressions in which certain word-choices occur so regularly as to lead us to expect them, or even to regard them as the natural and correct idiom. For example, we say *She heaved a sigh, The train gathered speed, We must proceed with caution, This is a burning question, Caught in the act, This needs a woman's touch, He rides an old bicycle*, but not *She hoisted a sigh, The train amassed speed, We must go along with caution, This is a flagrant question, Caught in the deed, This needs a female's handling, He drives an old bicycle*. Our language is full of time-honoured collocations which we are by no means bound to respect – indeed, some spirit of fun or angel of poetry may now and then prompt us to flout or upset the accepted idiom of our native tongue; but in general practice we place a lot of reliance on lexical commonplaces which answer the expectations of those who share our oral and literary culture. In many cases, the ease with which we grasp a verbal message depends to a great extent on our ability to anticipate word-choices before they are made explicit; and therefore the use and study of idiomatic collocations is an important aspect of the lexicon.

The lexicon is the sum of our attempts to label the material and psychological realities of our culture. Its size is not necessarily a testimony to the richness and variety of our material possessions or the subtlety of our intellectual life, but the density of lexical items referring to particular areas of experience might at least be taken as a clue to the material circumstances and prevalent attitudes of a culture. It is well known that in some languages there is a relatively large number of words relating to certain facts or notions, while in other languages the same phenomena may be rather thinly represented in the lexicon; we might perhaps venture to express this greater or lesser density of lexical labelling as ' high differentiation ' or ' low differentiation '. Thus, it is a text book commonplace that the Eskimo languages have a number of different words for *snow,* distinguishing between falling snow and snow on the ground, drifting snow, crusted snow, etc. This high differentiation is natural enough, in view of the fact that snow plays an important part in the life of the Eskimo; it is a principal feature of his environment, and he makes use of it as a housebuilding material and as a road surface. Yet since the English differentiation of *snow* is much less high, it seems to us noteworthy, even odd, that the Eskimo should have so many snow words. He in his turn might be a little surprised by the extent to which in English we have evolved a high differentiation of terms relating to emotions and states of mind – for instance, we distinguish between *love, affection, devotion, liking, partiality, fondness, regard,* etc. The centre (so to speak) of high differentiation may tell us something about a culture, its dominant institutions, its artefacts, its modes of livelihood, its attitudes. In a complex society, however, in which people are pursuing differing forms of livelihood (or even different leisure activities) at various levels of affluence, the centres of high differentiation may shift a good deal. In a fishing community, we might expect the differentiation of the word *boat* to be high – so high, in fact, as to make the mere word *boat* a generalised and rather imprecise term. On the other hand it is quite possible that fishermen, whilst certainly possessed of all ordinary human feelings, would find relatively little use for such differentiations as *intuition, apprehension, inkling, foreboding, misgiving, intimation,* etc., which have distinct values in literary currency. The distinction may be brought out by postulating the statement *I have a boat* and trying to imagine a fisherman's response, which is likely to be *What sort of boat?;* just as, in response to *I have a funny feeling,* the intellectual is likely to demand *What sort of feeling?*

It must be noted that the purpose of these examples is by no means to suggest that Eskimos and fishermen are exclusively possessed of one kind of vocabulary, a vocabulary of materials and artefacts, while the affluent and the intellectual are exclusively possessed of another, a vocabulary of notions. Of course we all have need of both kinds of vocabulary, whatever our professions and pursuits may be; but employment and avocation do play some part in determining what are here called the centres of differentiation. In some cases, the pursuit of a hobby or sport may extend the individual's power of differentiation. When a judge, for example, takes up yachting, he adds to the common vocabulary of the educated and the technical vocabulary of his profession, another set of differentiations, akin to those observed by fishermen. Every trade and every sport has its specialised vocabulary, and it is by extending our activities beyond our normal professional and domestic routine and into the realm of some speciality that we help, unconsciously, to enrich the general vocabulary of the language by bringing many words and expressions out of the special and into the public domain.

The lexicon allocates names to our various experiences, but it is important to realise that these experiences must relate to two worlds, the world of observed phenomena and events, and the inner world of thoughts and feelings. Many items in our vocabulary have reference to things which are apparent to our senses, which we can use or modify, which present us with data which we can assess by some physical means – e.g. *apple, fire, steel, hammer, black, round, run, kill, quickly.* Others are culturally standardised abstractions, words which do not refer to objects which can be measured or felt in any material way, but which relate to institutions or concepts which we all have resort to, and about which there is some general measure of agreement – e.g. *government, temperature, judicial, scientifically.* Others again relate wholly to the world of private judgements and emotions, to attitudes and opinions which are not directed through the standardising form of an institution and so are felt to lie within the domain of private experience – e.g. *happiness, savagery, acceptable, properly, sneer.* The items thus range from a complete outer-world state which we might call *external* or *declarative* to a complete inner-world state which could be called *internal* or *evaluative.*

It is a common, and unfortunate, fact of linguistic experience that we are not always in agreement with each other, or quite clear in our own minds about the place certain items should occupy on the declarative-evaluative scale. For example, we may use the word *justice* as though it were a ' culturally standardised abstraction ', that is to say as though the meaning of the word were a matter of common and manifest agreement; and all the time we might be using the word in some fairly private, evaluative way. Even words like *round* or *run* may be vulnerable to this kind of interpretative confusion, which sometimes becomes apparent when one of a pair of interlocutors exclaims *That's not what I call round,* or *Is that what you mean by run?* In some instances we are well aware of using an item declaratively in one context and evaluatively in another. This frequently happens when a standard word has a secondary, slang, meaning, or when it is used metaphorically; for instance, we talk about *a blue coat* (declarative) and about *a blue film* (evaluative), or, again, we might say *the yacht sailed in yesterday, full of contraband* (declarative) and *the youngster sailed in yesterday, full of confidence* (evaluative). Obviously, there must be many items and usages about which we can never be certain or fully agreed (for instance, how ' declarative ' or ' evaluative ' is *long* in *a long piece of string, a long walk, a long chat, a long wait?*) but it is useful to have some sort of terminology enabling us to reflect on the distinctions, implied in our lexicon, between the public, communal, ' objective ' parts of our experience, and the private, personal, ' subjective ' areas. These are obviously not inviolably distinct territories; the traffic between them is busy and constant, so busy and so constant that we are all guilty, at one time or another, of losing our semantic bearings, of using evaluative words as though they had public validity and of relating to a private standard terms normally dependent on social consensus. The inner-and-outerness of our vocabulary is potentially a danger to clear thought and social responsibility; it is also a source of self-expression for the individual, a facility for the poet, a field for the cultivation of language which can help us to develop new insights into our experience.

Our ' code ' thus uses the primary media of sound and writing, evolving forms which are related in grammatical patterns expressing lexical values. These values obviously do not derive from the code itself; they relate to the environment in which the code is employed and developed. The word ' environment ', as used here, may be taken to refer not only to material features of geography, climate, technological achievement, etc., but also to sociological factors of custom, institutions, and inherited attitudes. In fact, for the word environment, we might substitute ' society ', except that it is difficult to say what society is, or even what *a* society might be supposed to include. We know that terms like ' society ' and ' culture ' refer to complexes of institutions, customs, activities, products, etc., all related to an economy and a political system of cooperation and co-existence. On the other hand, we cannot possibly assert that certain institutions and customs are universal, and are therefore to be taken as basic characteristics of society. We cannot even assert that the institution of the family, which seems to be so natural and widespread, is common to all societies. We can, however, make the obvious assertion that all societies have a material environment, which influences behaviour and modes of livelihood, and so comes to influence customs and beliefs. Furthermore, we are entitled to suppose that all societies have customs, however they are derived, and whatever forms and institutions they are directed into, and that these customs affect the individual profoundly, perhaps more profoundly than he knows. As Ruth Benedict has put it, ' The life-history of the individual is first and foremost an accommodation to the patterns and standards traditionally handed down in his community. From the moment of his birth the customs into which he is born shape his experience and behaviour. By the time he can talk, he is the little creature of his culture, and by the time he is grown and able to take part in its activities, its habits are his habits, its beliefs his beliefs, its impossibilities his impossibilities.*

It is important to remind ourselves that in language as in other things, man is ' the little creature of his culture '; otherwise, our reflections on man as a *speaker* tend to change insensibly into reflections on man as a *spokesman*. We are naturally inclined to think of language in terms of the individual's voluntary and freely-directed response to the stimuli that present themselves to him in the course of his experience. We suppose, in other words, that, given the elements of the code, the conventional symbolism by means of which the common ground of experience may be interpreted, baby may thereafter please himself. But of course he cannot please himself; a good deal of his time is spent in behaviour which is acceptable to his environment and the traditions of his tribe – and this includes language-behaviour. It is a mistake to suppose that language is a form of behaviour in which we have freedom, once the conventions of symbolism have been accepted and mastered. In a good deal of our language we are socially shackled. A child in our society learns very early in life that the process of making its wishes known is related inexorably – and even on pain of punishment – to certain formulae (*Say please!*); it learns likewise that gifts are acknowledged in some ways and not in others. These are but two of the many, many lessons

---

* Ruth Benedict, *Patterns of Culture*, reprinted in the Routledge Paperbacks series (London; Routledge and Kegan Paul, 1963), p. 2.

we have to learn, as we go through life, about language as social behaviour. Naturally, the individual struggles for his freedom to speak for himself – to be spokesman, not merely speaker; and this struggle is important to the life and art of language. But here, as elsewhere in our lives, there is a conflict of social demand and individual reaction which asks for a compromise, a compromise which we can reach, as a rule, by learning to recognise and accept the situations of life in which our behaviour is governed by custom, and governed to our benefit and convenience. We are not necessarily zombies because we submit our behaviour to the *mores* of our society; we may in fact be surrendering our capacity for folly to the proven forms of traditional wisdom.

The individual is custom-trained in two ways. Firstly, he accepts as a condition of self-expression and communication with others, the necessity of using the same set of symbols as others round him use, in the same way that they use them. This is one obvious way in which man is linguistically the creature of his environment, an effect of custom with which we are not, however, primarily concerned here. The other way in which his language-habits are directed by custom is seen in his readiness, in all circumstances other than those in which a powerful emotional commitment turns him into a rebel, to use the language the situation requires. The English phrase ' the done thing ' might be thought to include, as a sub-species of proper behaviour, ' the said thing '. In the overwhelming majority of situations in which we find ourselves, we produce the ' said thing '; our linguistic behaviour follows the demands and traditions of our culture. Our apparent puppetry under such conditions is offset by the fact that while custom and tradition demand of us certain *kinds* of behaviour, the actual manifestations leave us some possibility of choice. In any case, the pressure on the individual to behave in a certain way, is only by numerous byways and removes the pressure of the organisational complex known as a ' culture '. If I think, speak, and act in certain ways, this is not the *immediate* consequence of Christianity, concepts of chivalry, the development of the English class-system, the industrial revolution, the demography of the British Isles, our system of government, or any of the numerous factors which no doubt have an ultimate bearing on my behaviour. I behave in such-and-such a way because my family or my friends or my colleagues or the people whose services I require look for and rely on the occurrence of certain forms of behaviour. Behaviour at this personal level, however customary, can rarely if ever be felt to be merely automatic, simply the product of an immanent cultural power. If I am able to feel that my behaviour pleases my family, obliges my friends, creates pleasant relationships with tradesmen, I am unlikely to feel that I am a linguistic automaton, even though I may rarely say anything that has not been said hundreds of times before.

We may perhaps imagine the individual's relationship to his culture as follows. He is imprisoned within successive confines, the outermost of which is the palisade of ethnic tradition, institutions, and attitudes we call a 'culture'. Nearer to him than this outer ring, there is a second confine, representing the totality of the activities, locations, and pursuits that make up his daily life – his work, his township, his clubs, hobbies, etc.; this confine we might call 'community'. 'Community' is a product of 'culture'; while for the individual, culture is no doubt remote, theoretical, numinous, community represents actual experience. Within the ring of community, we might then draw a third ring, representing the individual's community life in its personal enactments, his contacts and transactions with his own circle of kinsfolk, friends and acquaintances. This confine, – the confine of Bobby and Jane and Old Wilkinson and Mr Jobbs the grocer – is the ring of immediate realities; it is in personal contacts within this limit, which we may call 'company' that the individual encounters, and exercises, the forces of custom deriving ultimately from his culture. We can thus imagine the individual as an agent contained by a sort of

hierarchy of social confines. This is symbolised in the accompanying diagram.

Of course this presents an oversimplified account of environmental pressures on the individual. The ring called ' community ' should really be several overlapping rings; a factory, an office, a school, can be institutions with customs and traditions of their own, placing on the individual special demands differing from those put upon him when he visits his club, or when he goes shopping. A culture is made up from various sub-cultures, which increase in number as a society grows more populous and more complex economically and politically. These sub-cultures would each draw an especial arc in the ring called ' community '. Furthermore, within each especial community ring, there would be one or more company rings, representing X as related to his wife and family, X as related to his boss, X collaborating with colleagues, X relaxing among his friends, etc. We could not effectively reproduce all this in a simple diagram; but it is worth trying to visualise this complexity, because the effort will serve to remind us that, as far as his culture-conditioned behaviour is concerned, the so-called individual is apparently several persons. In the comings and goings of our daily life we are actors, hypocrites, wearers of masks. The masks we wear vary in accordance with the company we encounter and the segment of community in which we encounter it. This play-acting is forced upon us as a matter of social convenience. It is expected of us that we should enact certain roles, and we soon discover that life runs most smoothly when we fulfil this expectation.

In the enactment of our social roles, we assume postures of activity and passivity (speaking-listening, command-obedience, stimulating-reacting, informing-learning, etc.) in relationship to the hierarchies of rank and personal relationship which are effective in our society. As a rule, we have little doubt as to what our roles should be in the changing situations of daily life; from childhood onwards, our minute observations of the community life around us have bred in us the social sense, the instinctive recognition of required behaviour. Moreover, social organisation often presents us with quite specific and concrete indicators of role. One such indicator is dress. Bus-conductors, for example, or hotel porters, or attendants of various kinds, wear a distinctive uniform. The social value of this is not simply to make it easy to identify these people. The wearing of special dress also indicates that the wearer is in a certain phase of his social activity – a role –

which places him in a specific (usually subordinate) relationship with
other people, a relationship which conditions both his behaviour and
theirs. A theatre commissionaire in uniform is expected to use the
polite forms, *sir, madam, miss,* in his encounters with members of the
general public, but when he has doffed his uniform at the end of his
period of duty, this obligation need no longer trouble him. A uniform
may guarantee social protection as well as imposing social obligations.
In British society it is tacitly accepted that one must not seem to
bully or take verbal advantage of a uniformed servant discharging his
public duties. Those who do so may find their fellow-citizens looking
suddenly embarrassed and withdrawn. A scene has been made, and
at the expense of someone manifestly not in a position to answer back.
It is possible that the marked class-stratification of British society
and the British horror of ' making a scene ' are frequently connected.
The class-boundaries impose roles, and the scene-maker steps out of
his role. Roles can even be indicated by objects. In our society, one of
the commonest role-indicators is the desk or counter. If we meet
somebody stationed behind a counter, we approach him with a different set of attitudes and behaviour forms – different tones of voice,
different gestures, different word-choices, even a different facial
expression and physical bearing – than those we should manifest if we
met him under less rigidly defined circumstances. The counter is very
largely responsible for this rigid definition – it indicates that A is
here and B is there, that one is superior and the other is subordinate,
and that the roles cannot be reversed as they might be in the course
of other exchanges.

Even the garden gate or the front door can be considered a sort of
role-indicator since it fairly obviously marks the transition from one
kind of relationship or behaviour pattern, which we call ' private life ',
to another known as ' public life '. Our lives are a constant shuttling
back and forth between the private and the public domain, and we
take these alternatives for granted. There is perhaps one phase of our
experience, however, when the transition is painful and fraught with
problems, this being in the very early years of our lives, around the
time when we are first sent to school. Then it seems to us that while
family life is free and easy, public life is bafflingly ritualised; that at
home one can do and say as one pleases, while in life at large one
has to follow prescribed courses of action and speech. In fact, home
life can be as ritualistic as public life, the fact being that we come
to accept the rituals with which we grow up as definitions of freedom.

Nevertheless, it is possible to maintain a distinction between 'ritual-ised' and 'free' situations, our behaviour (including, of course, our language-behaviour) in the one case being prescribed by common usage, even by explicit formulation, whilst in the other case we have some freedom, subject to the general conditions of the situation, of action and speech. A courting couple discussing the possibility of mar-riage are in a 'free' situation as far as their intonations, grammar, lexical choices, etc. are concerned;* when the same couple actually go through the wedding ceremony, they are in a 'ritualised' situation, one in which their actions are prescribed and the language they use written down for them. Obviously, the words 'free' and 'ritualised' are relative terms. The wedding ceremony is an extreme example of the ritualised situation, but in life at large there are many situations which, though substantially 'free', have something of ritual in them. It is hard to say to what extent one's behaviour in making a purchase, or one's responses to fellow-guests at a cocktail party, are character-istic of 'free' situations. There may be a good deal of freedom of verbal behaviour in, for example, one's argument with a fellow-guest on the merits of Mozart or Manchester United; on the other hand, the processes of greeting and taking leave of one's host and hostess are marked by much verbal ritual. Our childhood impressions of public life as something inexplicably ritualised, in contrast with the freedom of home life, may not be entirely unjustified. Ritual intervenes in public life where chaos is to be avoided, where uncertainties are to be resolved, where efficient cooperation is to be brought about, where it is desirable, for one reason or another, that the individual should sur-render to the collective. It is also a means of negotiating the artifice of public life.

Not a few of our corporate activities are artificial, not necessarily in any pejorative sense, but in the sense they are not obvious or natural consequences of our economic or biological needs. What vital necessity

---

* But of course their freedom is limited. For instance, they may have at their disposal at least three lexical choices (there are certainly more), *get married, get spliced, be joined in the bonds of holy matrimony*. Their free-dom to choose between these is really illusory. The third is appropriate only to the special style of the ritual situation, and would not be used here other than facetiously. The second is possible as a piece of whimsy which might be in character with one or the other speaker, or which might be used to cover embarrassment. The first is the only expression of the three which in this context would not be allusive or humorous; hence it is almost the inevitable choice, if we assume that the subject is to be discussed calmly and seriously, with no intrusion of embarrassed frivolity.

dictates that a group of smartly-dressed people, male and female, should gather together between the hours of 5 and 7 p.m. (or thereabouts) to stand in a crowded room, drink quantities of alcohol, consume sundry delicacies, blow smoke in each others faces, and attempt, with uncertain success, the arts of conversation? We could theorise a great deal about the cocktail party as a social form, but always we should have to conclude that it is not an institution with a primary and indispensable function in answering our social and spiritual needs – in short, that it is an artifice, one of a number of artifices we have produced because we have leisure. To incorporate these artifices into the normal round of our life we require ritual actions and ritual language. A cocktail party has no obvious biological or social motivation; we do not attend one because we are hungry, or because we have business to transact. There is not a 'natural' time for such a thing to begin and end, and it is not the sort of pursuit that can be drifted into and drifted out of. Its introduction into the circuit of our activities is negotiated by ritual; by the sending of a ritually-worded invitation requiring a ritually-worded reply, by the use of ritual formulae of greeting and leave-taking, etc. The uses of ritual behaviour and language are not confined to situations governed by political and religious institutions. Our public life is full of situations in which 'free' behaviour occurs within the confines of socially useful ritual.

In emphasising the importance of a social and cultural environment, we ought not, of course, to underestimate the importance of man's physical surroundings and of his direct experience of natural and material phenomena. The development of a language may certainly be influenced by geographical and climatic factors working on the lives of the speakers of that language. If, however, we give some priority in these pages to a consideration of the social environment, it is because a great deal of our experience, even of the physical circumstances of our lives, is acquired through social contacts and exchanges. It may be said that a man's experience is acquired in one of two ways: he picks up life like a hot coal, and so learns directly about the pain of burning, or he sees someone else pick it up, and so acquires his knowledge indirectly. It is likely, to say the least of it, that a very great number of our experiences are initially indirect, and it is probable that many will remain indirect, and be nonetheless valid for that.

The likelihood that our experiences will be preponderantly

indirect is increased by the existence of language. With language at our service, we no longer have to *see* somebody else picking up a hot coal. We can be *told* about the experience by somebody who has suffered it in the past, or who has seen yet another person undergoing it. Now to be told about something implies involvement in a relation- ship, enacted in a social context; and it may therefore be said that a very large proportion of our experience is socially mediated. The use of writing has greatly extended the domain of indirectly-acquired experience; and the media of our own day, notably the film and tele- vision, may be thought so to have increased the dimensions of our environment that it now embraces a great deal of the world. The effect of communication-media on language is a question which is taken up at greater length in the next chapter.

Diverse though our experiences may be in specific details they yet resolve themselves into broad patterns, or archetypes, which we are able to recall at will, or at any rate to recognise whenever they recur. This ability is central to our powers of learning and survival, and it is an ability which affects language as much as anything else. We may suppose that the usefulness of language as a tool for survival depends mainly on two things. Firstly, we must be able to recognise the association of certain forms in the code with given types of event in the environment; and secondly, we must be able to assume that the people among whom we live associate form and event in much the same way. The specific experiences which are peculiar to us as individuals are in this regard irrelevant, though in other respects highly interesting; what is important is our ability to assume that we share the archetypes of experience and acknowledge a common sym- bolism. Between the pattern of symbolism, the code, and the pattern of experience, the environment, there is a relationship which is rather more subtle and complex than the relationship between a set of sym- bolic devices and a set of things symbolised. The distinction between the one thing and the other is really no more than a convenient arti- fice. In effect, the code is part of the environment, and the environ- ment is a determinant of the code; when we speak, we reveal the pressures of custom and tradition, the inherited assumptions of our culture, the coherence of our social system. The principle that our environment is a determinant of our language is nowadays something of a commonplace. It is not so very long, however, since Bronislaw Malinowski found it necessary to remind us that ' . . . the *situation* in which words are uttered can never be passed over as irrelevant to the linguistic expression ',* and if there were no other reason for the priority given in these pages to an environmental view of language, Malinowski's authority would be justification enough. In the chapters which follow, the interaction of code and environment will be illustrated as fully as possible, but we cannot escape the necessity of choosing a standpoint, of viewing language always from one or other of the two ' sides ' considered in this chapter. It can only be hoped that in working through these limited and changing perspectives, the reader may sometimes have glimpses of the rounded world of words and things.

* B. Malinowski, *The Problem of Meaning in Primitive Languages;* printed as *Supplement 1* to C. K. Ogden and I. A. Richards, *The Meaning of Meaning,* 10th ed. (London: Routledge and Kegan Paul, 1953), p. 306.

2 *The Pattern of Communication*

'Communication', unfortunately, is one of the Great Overstretched Words of Our Time, and has come to mean so many things that it is difficult to say exactly what it *does* mean. It can have a specialised reference to a body of scientific knowledge, and particularly to what we call 'information theory'. It can denote what happens when man feeds data into a machine, or subsequently retrieves information which the machine has processed. It can even, I suppose, mean the transference of data from mechanism to mechanism, in the stages of the computer process. In our day, men communicate with machines, and machines communicate with each other.

But these technological applications of the word need not concern us here. In this chapter we are to be concerned with some very simple factors governing communication between persons. We may think of such communications as taking place either in direct face-to-face conference, or else through one or other of the common media which facilitate long-distance and wide-range communication. The oldest of the long-distance media is, of course, writing; to which we now have to add the audio-visual media of our time, i.e. the telephone, films, radio, TV.

Linguists, like other academics, are not averse to convenient borrowings from neighbouring sciences. From communication theory they have derived the following representation, which, in this or some kindred form, is now virtually a standard proposition, a paradigm:

The 'sender' produces or encodes a 'message' which is processed through a suitable 'channel', and is decoded by the 'receiver'. In communication theory, the channel is of course a matter of central interest; sound engineers, for example, are concerned with measuring the signal-bearing capacities of a channel, with estimating its distortions, with calculating the degree of redundancy that could therefore be tolerated in a signal passing through the channel. The use of this image to the linguist is not so much that it reminds him of the importance of the channel (although of course he attaches great importance to it), as that it represents language to him as a tripartite manifestation; it reminds him that his descriptions of language must take into account the characteristics of a sender and a receiver as well as the nature and capacities of a channel. Adapted to linguistic descriptions, the communication model might be presented thus:

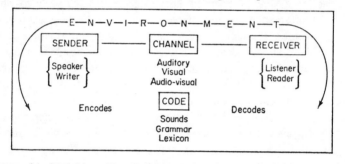

In considering this self-explanatory diagram, we might take note of the assumption that sender and receiver share a common environment. This is a conventional, wide-range, *generalising* assumption about language. When, for instance, we talk about 'the English language', we postulate a stable, uniform, environment which is shared by all speakers and which supports the operation of the code. Matters look different when we come down to cases. There is the obvious case of communication across cultures; as in, let us say, a conversation, held in English, between a Londoner and a native of Karachi. This might be represented by the diagram at the top of the following page. The code is here 'unsupported', and carries most of the burden of communication, without the informing energies of inference, common assumption, knowledge of institutions, etc., which proceed from a shared environment. Some indeterminate elements of general experience, as indicated by the dotted line, may provide helpful overlaps or analogies, but the vital interaction of code and environment is no

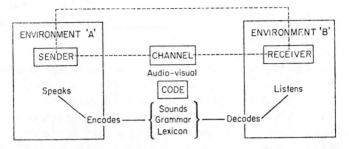

longer to be presumed. This much is obvious when the case is that language is used across cultures. But might it not equally well be the case when usage extends across communities within one and the same culture? It might even be true of linguistic contacts across the minor social groupings we have called ' companies '; the little environment of my family, for example, constitutes a climate of experience, custom, principle, prejudice, in many ways different from that of any other family.

Most communication models generalise about language at its widest – at the breadth of a culture. It is quite natural that they should do so. All models must abstract and generalise; that is their valued property as models. However, let us try to propose a somewhat smaller model, envisaged at the company level. This model would keep the tripartite view of language, but would tend to emphasise the ' what ' rather than the ' how ' of communication, thus:

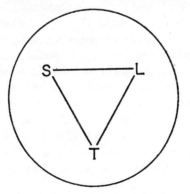

S here stands for Speaker, L for Listener, and T for Theme, the latter being a ' message ', the nature of which we must presently discuss. The enclosing circle suggests the setting, the location-somewhere, of the speaker-listener conference; furthermore, it excludes other parties and influences and so represents an intuitive supposition that the intricacies of personal communication can be reduced to the simplicities of a sort of primary cell. However, what is described and drawn here is obviously an over-simplification that begs many questions. Above all else, there is the question of what is involved in the element labelled Theme. Asked what it is that we use language for, common wisdom would almost certainly reply that we use it to convey information and emotions. Now the word 'information' may be variously applied. (Of course it has a precise scientific meaning, but this is not in question here.) We take it that in common usage, information is 'about' what we call 'facts'. But facts are various. There are facts of physical experience, such as we communicate in remarks like *It's raining, The bath has overflowed, Look, the cat's been sick on Uncle Joe's waistcoat,* or *Grandma is double-trenching the garden.* There are abstractions drawn from systematic observation of the facts of experience – mathematical, philosophical, or moral observations which are not 'facts' in the crude concrete sense, but are of such proven validity that we proceed upon them as on a factual basis. Then again, there are 'facts' about a speaker's mental states and inclinations – e.g. *I'm low today, I'm wondering what to do, It seems to me we need a plan, Here's my view of the problem.* It is apparent that in such cases the speaker is giving information about psychological facts, or, to put it more generally, that he is talking about his 'feelings'.

This challenges our original too-easy supposition that language communicates (a) information and (b) emotions. The content of our messages cannot be partitioned in this way; it must be fairly obvious that 'feeling' is frequently involved with 'fact', especially in observations that have to do with our personal relationships or our individual engagement with the world. We may in some instances assume that feeling and fact are distinctly expressed, as in *I despise that fellow* (I report my feeling) or *He sleeps in his socks* (I report the fact which prompts the feeling). It is likely, however, that in speech the second half of this assertion would be tinged with manifestations of the feeling which informs the first half. In any case, we can equally well convey fact and feeling together by saying, with the appropriate intonation of scorn, *He's the sort of fellow who sleeps in his socks,* or even simply *He sleeps in his socks.* Our examples lead us to suppose that in considering the varieties of 'feeling' that may be communicated, we ought to distinguish between the reporting of feelings as a species of personal ' fact ', e.g. *I am angry with him,* and the expression of feelings as a concomitant of fact, e.g. *Why, he's stolen my watch!* In the latter example, the ' feeling ' is manifested through the pattern of intonation and emphasis which accompanies the reporting of the fact; and it is the reporting *plus* an attitude towards what is reported which in this case make up the package called ' information '.

Clearly, our ' rudimentary image ' or ' primary cell ' oversimplifies the process of interpersonal communication in at least one very important respect. It does not reflect the circumstance that we not only speak *about* objects or events or ideas, that we not only speak *about* feelings, but that our speech itself may be a manifestation of feeling, may convey an attitude to the thing it mediates. There is another way in which the effects of this personal emanation we call ' attitude ' are not accounted for in our basic sketch. Description and diagram seem to imply that our speaker and listener have no history, no social background, no motivation for coming together in a specific situation, no personal relationship, that they are blanks who have come out of nowhere to enter into an abstraction. Of course this can never be the case. The pattern of communication is complicated by a play of attitudes, not the least important of which are those which exist between the partners in discourse – the *interlocutors,* if we may use that handy term without bringing Mr Bones and the nigger minstrels too vividly to mind. These interpersonal attitudes are (or may be) socially predicated, e.g. in encounters between representatives of different social classes, different stages of education, or different professional rankings; they may seem to be called for in connection with the discharge of particular intentions in specific situations; or they may ultimately be simple personal responses of liking or disliking, not produced by special situations, perhaps not motivated by any particularly convincing reason. My attitudes in any encounter may well be a blend of the social, the situational, and the personal. If, for example, I have invited a professional superior to lunch at a fashionable restaurant, where we are incompetently served by a waiter for whom I have already conceived a strong personal dislike, tempered only by my knowledge that he is the sole support of an ageing mother – then I am bound to feel the various pressures of general social relationships, of situational demands, and of purely personal inclinations; in such circumstances my attitudes would probably be so complex and conflicting, that I might well be reduced to paying up with a smile, and saying nothing.

It is difficult to think of any situation, any experience of life shared with another human being through the medium of language, that is not to some extent complicated by personal attitudes. We can readily bring to mind any number of daily encounters in which it seems that our personal interest is best described as ' indifferent ' or ' neutral ', but even in such situations there is some traffic of socially-conventional attitude between the persons engaged, and towards the objects of their discourse. A clerk may neither like nor dislike his employer as a person, but social convention demands that he shall assume an attitude of deference when he approaches him in a work-situation, and that he shall display an appropriate gravity and formality in discussing whatever topic may be at issue between them; so that he will speak of *the spread of Mr Boodle's investments* rather than *the dodges old man Boodle gets up to with his cash*. The clerk's involvement in situations of this sort may not be very great, but there is a general cultural demand upon him to enact a certain role, with its appropriate attitudes expressed in appropriate language. The requirements of role yield to the pressures of self-interest as the factors which shape our attitudes become more specific, i.e. when we get down to particular situations and particular personal relationships, enacted as ' free ', not as ' ritual ' exchanges. In representing to a colleague his claim to take a summer holiday during a certain fort-night, our clerk would no doubt show freely a warmth of attitude rather more convincing that the ritual gestures demanded of him during his exchanges with his employer. Quite obviously there are degrees of personal involvement in various situations, and quite obviously there are fluctuations in the control which environment imposes on this involvement and its expression in language. Our clerk may feel a personal contempt for his employer, while his profes-sional role demands a show of respect; under these circumstances his language may be conditioned in such a way as to convey personal attitude without breaking the requirements of role – he can say *As you please sir*, or *Very well, Mr Brightside*, or *You can leave that to me, sir*, etc., with as much of the intonation and wry face of scorn as he dare project into the situation. His involvement at the social, ' ritual ' level is so superficial, that he can turn its forms to his advantage in expressing his deeper involvement at the personal level.

The diagram on p. 37 inevitably but falsely conveys the suggestion that communication is a one-way process, and hence that the attitudes conveyed and the involvement established are entirely properties of the speaker. Only under especial circumstances, discussed below, is communication one-sided. It is normally an act of collaboration in which the partners are constantly assuming and relinquishing the roles of speaker and listener. But even if we assume, for the moment, a unilateral scheme of communication, it would still be wrong to suppose that the speaker is the sole repository of all attitudes towards person or theme, while the listener is an untempered innocent, a sort of razed personality waiting for new construction. The listener, silent though he may be, still has an attitude to the speaker and his theme. We have hitherto chosen to ignore this possibility, or else have assumed that the attitudes of speaker and listener are substantially the same, that they are in sympathy, or ' see eye to eye '. This may not by any means be the case. The speaker may be involved in his theme much more profoundly than the listener. He may feel for the listener a personal enthusiasm which the latter does not reciprocate; or he may project into language an attitude towards himself implying a personal image much at variance with what the listener sees. In such cases, when parties are unequally involved, it is the task of the active party, the speaker (asuming that he is aware of the disparity) to persuade the listener to accept and share his own attitudes. If communication is unilateral, the burden of this task falls entirely on the speaker; but if it is bilateral, if the listener is permitted to respond verbally and so take his turn as a speaker, then the partners may talk their way towards a concord of attitudes.

In ordered exchanges, only one person can speak at a time, so that the S of our primary diagram may pass as an accurate symbol; our L on the other hand, may not, since language may be addressed to a single listener or it may be addressed to several – indeed, to several hundred or several thousand, depending on the type of social situation in which language is used. (It is assumed, of course, that the ' listeners ' in all instances are people for whom the discourse has some relevance, and not merely ' overhearers ', bystanders to a transaction.) The listener may be an individual whose role is completely passive, never commuting with that of speaker; though this is on the whole unlikely, implying as it does that the speaker has some especial social or personal power over his one-man audience. If the listener in due course assumes the role of speaker, we have the state of affairs which we are to know by the name of *interlocution*. It may happen, however, that the ' listener ' is collective, a group of listeners, who by chance and casual opportunity take turns in becoming speakers and in developing the common theme; this is really no more than a more complex form of interlocution – dialogue rather than duologue – but the fact there are several partners in discussion rather than two alone may very well have an effect on the language they use. A further possibility is that there are several listeners, a group, a gathering, a crowd, listening more or less passively to one speaker. This is one of the ritual situations for which our culture makes provision, and we may simply call this form of communication by the name of *address*.

We thus propose two main types of discourse, in each of which certain proprieties of language are assumed, or are socially required. The conventions of the language of address are somewhat different from those of the language of interlocution – we may compare, for example, a speaker's approach to his audience at the beginning of a lecture or sermon, and the same speaker's approach to an informal group at the beginning of a discussion. (This comparison is often easily made, when a lecture to a fairly small audience is followed by questions and discussion.) Within the two domains, however, further differentiations are possible. When interlocution is bilateral, a two-person exchange, its forms, as we have noted, may differ somewhat from those ventured in exchanges among several persons. Similarly, the kind of address which is simply an admonition of one person by another will almost certainly have a linguistic character different from the sort of address which is directed at a small group of known persons, which in its turn will differ from an address calculated to reach large numbers of people unknown to the speaker. There are, in short, different audiences and they are approached in different ways.

The approach to communication, the conventions used to maintain it, and the manner of its cessation, are features which also have to be taken into account. Neither interlocution nor address is so obvious or natural an activity as to allow us to proceed without some allusion to our awareness of entering into a personal relationship, of perhaps intruding on another life in a way that demands justification, or even a placatory gesture. Speech is a kind of intimacy, and one that we do not venture upon without some preliminary touchings and gesturings which proclaim an identity and establish an intent. The character and length of the approach depend partly on cultural convention (in Arab countries, for example, it is difficult to embark upon business discussions without going through a ritual of polite exchanges which seems over-elaborate to a Westerner), partly on the type of situation being enacted, and partly on the existing personal relationship of the parties involved; our approach-formulae, in fact, are conditioned by the selfsame powers that condition the general play of our attitudes in a situation. Obviously, the approach to conversation with an old friend is shorter and less ceremonious in language than the approach to an acquaintance with whom one is on a more formal footing. A late-night phone-call to the old friend might begin with the words *Sorry to bother you* . . . , whereas the formal acquaintance would have to be placated with something rather more elaborate, e.g. *I must apologise for disturbing you at this time of night* . . . People who have known each other for a long time will occasionally embark on a conversation without going through any preliminaries, sometimes resuming conversations that have been broken off hours or possibly days previously; but as a rule even close acquaintances feel the necessity of repeating some few ritual formulae (perhaps some observations on the weather or the government) as an indication that contact has been made, is acceptable and can lead on to the exchange of opinions or the transaction of business. Even in a shoulder-rubbing, commercial society like ours, we prefer an approach to be made if possible with a certain style and breadth of timing. The approach to an address might be quite peremptory (*Now listen* . . .) but it is surprising how often the address is begun after an almost oriental elaboration of approach. At a political meeting, for example, or a meeting of a learned society, the speaker is not allowed to begin his address, which opens with some appropriate formula (*Ladies and Gentlemen, I received your invitation to come here to-night with a mixture of trepidation and delight, delight because, etc. etc. etc., trepidation because I am only too keenly aware, etc. etc. etc.*), without first being ' introduced ' by another speaker, better known to the audience, whose introduction is also couched in ritualised approach formulae (*Ladies and Gentlemen, tonight I have the honour of discharging an unusually pleasant duty, namely, etc. etc.*). This stately mummery can be observed at any lecture or club meeting, being paraded with skill and relish by down-to-earth men who would perhaps laugh at the Turk for the circumstantial courtesy of his approaches to business.

Once engaged in communication with our fellows, we are forced to exercise a certain skill in maintaining contact until the transaction is finished. This may seem self-evident, but the fact is that we can speak to other people without really communicating with them; or, to put it in terms of a useful distinction, we can go through the gestures of *communication,* without achieving *communion.* The *communion,* the feeling between interlocutors, or between addressor and addressees, that they are united in purpose and mood, is a necessity of any useful discourse. Anyone who regularly has the task of lecturing or public speaking will have experienced, at some time, the distressing sensation of ' losing ' his audience, of watching the glaze of inattention gradually spread over the polite faces before him. To recover communion under such circumstances is an almost impossible task. Interlocutors may likewise ' lose ' each other, or may feel, as current idiom has it, that they are ' not getting through '. The sensations accompanying this loss of contact go beyond regret or frustration at the failure to transmit a message; there is also the oppressive, dismaying sense of having failed personally, and thus of being isolated and rejected. It is presumably for this reason that our discourse is punctuated by phrases alluding directly to, and appealing for, a community of understanding; phrases like *you know what I mean don't you?, do you see?, I know I needn't tell you . . ., you understand, if you take my meaning, do you follow me?, we can take it . . . ,* etc. The appeal to a community of spirit may appear in quite simple linguistic forms. Lecturers and writers (the writer of this book being a manifest example!) will often use the pronoun *we* inclusively, presuming on the reader's willingness to be a partner in discourse.

The manner of relinquishing discourse can also present problems. To get up and go, to shut up and pack up, requires considerable self-confidence. Some gesture of disengagement is normally required. Even among close friends this gesture will appear in some rudimentary form, perhaps as the single word *Well . . .*; and even a routine-bread-and-butter-lecturer will round off his weekly stint with some seasoned old formula, such as *There, I think, we must leave it . . ., or Next week we shall . . . .* At the close of formal conversations, or exchanges between strangers, the formulae of disengagement are more ceremonious, e.g. *I'm so glad to have met you, It's been nice talking to you . . . , Thank you for a most interesting meeting, and I hope we shall meet again some time, May I express a hope that this will have been the first of many meetings,* etc. The set-piece lecture is brought to a close more elaborately than its routine counterpart. The peroration of a public address is something more than a summing-up of the content of the address; it is an artistic, stylised, way of releasing the audience from its voluntary captivity in discourse. The process is continued and concluded after the end of the lecture with the chairman's vote of thanks, which, like his introduction, may be full of quasi-ritualistic formulae: *It only remains for me to thank . . . , This has been an occasion of unusual interest . . . , And now we must release Mr X*, etc.

Communication thus involves cultural and psychological factors which as a rule go unrepresented in models and outlines. The interplay of attitudes, the whole view of one important aspect of communication as an attempt to create an attitudinal harmony, cannot be put into a diagram. It is difficult, too, to show diagrammatically the consequences in language of the adoption of the different types of discourse we have called, broadly, ' interlocution ' and ' address '; and virtually impossible to demonstrate the effect on communication of a sense of social and psychological proprieties at different stages of discourse. Models, as we have observed, generalise; and by being simple for convenience can become inconveniently simple. And here it must be remarked that many models and diagrams of communication allow us to make what is indeed an astonishingly simple assumption, namely that language is necessarily used for *conveying* something; for carrying the assortments and blends of fact and feeling to an expectant consumer. The image is somehow deeply imprinted among our thought-patterns. When we think of communication we envisage a sender packaging, for immediate despatch to a receiver, an assertion consisting of a subject followed by a verb followed by an object. Now while a traffic of information, etc. may be the general substance of communication, it is by no means true to say that it is the substance of every act of communication. Some conversations begin (after due allowance for the approach-phase) with statements, e.g. *The committee will meet on Friday, I saw Jobson yesterday, I liked your essay.* But they might very well begin with questions: *When does the committee meet?, Have you seen Jobson?, Did you like my essay?* It is an obvious point (but the obvious is easy to overlook) that in having recourse to language, we seek to elicit information, as well as to convey it. It is a corollary of the same point, that we can offer information on our own initiative, or we can give it by way of response. Our responses to the other people's conversational initiatives are of great importance in creating a collaborative act of communication; they may function not only as replies or acknowledgements, but also as conductors, directing the conversation towards its next point of development. This aspect of language is to be considered at some length in the chapter called *The Language Game*.

Another occasion for recourse to language has nothing to do with information, given or received. We often use language to direct the actions of other people, to our own immediate advantage, or to more or less altruistic ends. When we say, for example, *Fetch me the scissors,* or *You ought to clean your teeth after every meal,* or *Love thy neighbour,* or even *Honesty is the best policy,* we are not informing, we are controlling or regulating; in some instances by personal (perhaps even enforceable) command, in others by way of recommendations which have some general cultural sanction. All in all, our T-for-Theme symbolises more, in the way of the actual operation of language, than can be readily covered by the term ' information '.

Furthermore, it is merely good-natured to assume that language is always used with positive intent, that we always *want* to convey information, to achieve communion. Language can also be used negatively to withhold information and frustrate communion. There are more ways of doing this than simply by being rude or evasive in one's responses. It is possible to initiate discourse with the aim of *not* communicating, or of going through the gestures of communication so elaborately and with so many involutions as to frustrate communion. The language of political masquerade, or of bureaucracy, provides us with daily examples of this. Such negative or masquerading language may even be identifiable by its phraseology; there is an old joke to the effect that when a man says *The truth is* . . . he is about to tell a lie, and we may suppose, in the same spirit, that when a politician or bureaucrat says *Let me be open with you about this* or *Let me be quite frank,* he is bent on the dissimulatory concealment of facts he judges it inconvenient for us to know. At the ordinary social level, there are plenty of day-by-day occasions when we are met with, or are responsible for, equivocations, excuses, things said for saying's sake, all of which might be thought to belong to this bleak domain of communicative non-communion. There is even something of language-as-concealment in the tropes and figures of literary art, though there it might be said more fairly that the artist's purpose is to make communion fuller by drawing attention to subtleties or difficulties in the means of communication.

The ' means of communication ' – the *media,* to use the currently fashionable word – are of considerable importance in shaping the forms and effects of language. In the previous chapter we have already devoted some attention to sound and writing; these, of course, are the basic media and the special communicative effects and devices of other media are largely derived from these. We assume as a matter of normal circumstances that when language occurs as sound, speaker and listener are in each other's presence. Physical presence is important, for it permits the incorporation with language of certain extra- or para-linguistic elements, such as gesture and facial expression. The opportunity of using these can rescue the speaker from the difficulty of finding words to express more or less subtle shades of meaning, or constructions to indicate precise relationships. Indeed, it is not unlikely that in face-to-face communication we rely more than we know on the effectiveness of gesture, not merely as an auxiliary to our exchanges, but as part of the clue-giving apparatus of language. Directive gestures such as pointing or mimicking an action, and affective gestures, such as pulling a face or the clenching of a fist, provide the listener with situational references which often anticipate his reception of the actual words used by the speaker. These directive and affective gestures can, of course, be transferred into the domain of language proper, through its phonic concomitants of accent and pitch; we can say, for example, *not* NEXT *week, but the week* AFTER, where the pattern of accentuation does the work of a gesturing finger, or *I'll give you perhaps*! where the appropriate intonation would suggest the wry face of a humorous threat.* The existence of a power or phonic gesture, as part of the normal resources of spoken language means that there are some situations, first and foremost the telephone conversation, in which the interlocutors are not in each other's physical presence, and yet can with some success transmit and interpret the effects of physical gesture.

When writing is our medium, we immediately forego the advantages of physical and phonic gesture, and are often forced to re-arrange our method of communication so that the elements of meaning which we would have conveyed through a shrug of the shoulders, an accentuation, an intonation-pattern, can be expressed in some other way. Of course there are phonic commonplaces, stock patterns recurring frequently with reference to conventional responses, which need no

* The utterance *I'll give you perhaps*! looks odd in print and out of context. I had in mind some such exchange as the following:
   Mother: Jacky, will you go and wash now?
   Jacky: Perhaps.
   Mother: Perhaps?! You young rascal—I'll give you perhaps!

particular marks of interpretation in writing. For example, if we were to meet in print the sentence *I expected to be surprised, but I didn't expect anything as surprising as this,* we would probably have no great doubts as to the pattern of stress and intonation which the writer intended to project. On the other hand, there are plenty of utterances which cannot be set down in writing without some indication of the vocal or physical gesture which is a determinant of their meaning. Even the most skilful novelist may be forced, on occasion, to furnish his dialogue with adverbial tags which will guide the reader in interpreting the mood and relationships of the characters. Thus, the remark *I'll give you one for Christmas* may have to occur in written report as ' *I'll give you one for Christmas* ', *he said with a little sneering laugh,* or ' *I'll give you one for Christmas* ', *she said, her face brightening.* Another trick of the fiction-writer is to spike his reported utterances with lexical items roughly indicative of the speaker's attitude, e.g. ' *I'll give you one for Christmas* ', *he snarled/ laughed/cooed/bellowed/exploded/hissed/beamed/gurgled/snapped,* etc. One of the factors contributing to the growth of our lexicon may well be that the written code has to absorb and transmute the power of physical and phonic gesture, one means of transmutation being the lexical item, which enables us to differentiate between a smirk, a smile, and a sneer, or between a cry of happiness and a crow of triumph.

When Mr Everyman writes a letter, he is often puzzled by the problem of how to word it, a problem which includes the task of making lexical choices reflective of a mood and a sense of personal relationship which could be physically or phonically established in face-to-face exchange. He knows that there is a difference between (say) *I would appreciate your cooperation* and *I would welcome your cooperation;* and although he may not be consciously aware of it, he is at least instinctively aware that this difference is something more than a difference in degrees of feeling on the writer's part, that it also embraces the writer-reader relationship and the properties of bearing and formality specific to that relationship. He is aware, too, that the gestures and tones appropriate to a relationship may also be reflected in an artful choice of grammatical form. Thus, there is a personal and attitudinal distinction – a distinction bearing on the formality of a relationship – between *I would appreciate your cooperation* and *Your cooperation would be appreciated;* or between *It is to be hoped* and *We hope;* or between *Should you agree, I would be glad to help* and *If you agree, I will be glad to help;* or between *In view of the fact that your letter was late in coming* and *Because your letter came late,* etc. Through appropriate choices in lexis and grammar (stylistic choices which carry with them the reminder of unchosen alternatives) some of the deficiencies resulting from the loss of direct (physical) and indirect (vocal) gesture, may be repaired; furthermore, writing has a range of punctuational devices, albeit limited and inadequate, which enable it to parallel some of the effects of speech.

We should take notice, however, that writing as a medium is not always used with the aim of echoing speech, or of providing ingenious solutions to problems arising from the absence of phonic resources. There are social and cultural situations which demand of language that it shall provide a permanent, accurate, logically-arranged record of an argument, a contract, a series of events. In such cases, writing is the prior medium; a legal contract, a detailed narrative, a carefully qualified piece of close reasoning, demand recourse to elaborate symbolic structures which are only effective because they can be kept before the eye, so that their interrelationship can always be established or re-established by glancing back and forth along the lines of print.

Speech is used both for interlocution and for address; writing serves one of these purposes only, since even a letter from one good friend to another must be thought of as a species of address. Communication between interlocutors is a joint endeavour; they build their understanding, as it were, by taking it in turns to add a word or turn of phrase that will contribute something to the meaning they are together piecing out. If I enter into conversation with a friend on some subject of our common election – music, or football, say, or the latest political events – then I do not bear sole responsibility for making the conversation an interesting one, one that reveals something new and striking about the subject. My partner is equally responsible with me for the fruitfulness of our exchanges, and will show his responsibility by taking up and elaborating my suggestions, by helping me out when I am unable to find the right word or phrase, by correcting my exaggerations or inexactitudes, by making me see what I might have ignored. This means that in conversation, while I must certainly relish the pleasure of propounding the *mot juste,* I do not feel it to be especially incumbent on me to produce the exact word, the precise construction. My partner's readiness of mind may offset my inadequacies, as, indeed, my occasional quickness must compensate for his slowness. In any case, we do not insist on exactitude of vocabulary, logical order of presentation, impeccable syntax, etc., as a condition of good conversation; since the partners to a conversation are speaking impromptu, we regard a smooth turn of phrase as a lucky brilliance, to be applauded though not expected. On the other hand, if my observations take the form of a lecture, a public speech, or even an off-the-cuff harangue from one man to another, then I am solely responsible for the direction of my discourse, and everything I say must be as exact and complete as is necessary for the purpose of conveying my meaning. In this respect, spoken address resembles writing, for there, too, the initiator of discourse bears responsibility for its completeness and adequacy. Indeed spoken address is often not really a matter of true speech, but rather of writing speechified; the lecture or sermon that is written or read aloud is hardly to be considered a pure example of the spoken word, though its written artifice may be conveyed through the dynamics of speech. However, the deliverer of a lecture may at any point break into ' true speech ' as he observes the responses registered in the faces (perhaps occasionally in the voices) of his audience. This opportunity is denied to the composer of a written address. The man who writes a set of instructions has to make very sure that his directions are unmistakable and unambiguous, since the reader cannot make use of questions to resolve any doubts that might arise; and when we write letters to our friends, we have to remember that although we are engaged in a sort of interlocution, it is not the type of exchange that will permit us to correct a wrong impression instantly. It is a common experience that letters give rise to misunderstandings which have to be corrected by personal confrontations. In writing, the addressor must anticipate and provide for all possible responses of the addressee; in speech he can deal with them as they arise, directing and re-directing as he goes along.

The electronic media which we now use a great deal in interpersonal and mass communication impose upon language conditions which are either modifications or blends of the characteristics of speech and of writing. What these conditions may be we can see more clearly if we consider three present-day commonplaces; the telephone, radio, and television. The telephone is a means of interlocution, but one which requires that we shall forgo the advantages of significant gesture and facial expression which we have in physical confrontation. Since we thus lack an important range of cues, we have to be careful to enunciate clearly. In a 'phone conversation, it would be fairly easy to confuse *I think he's sweet* and *I think he's weak,* or *Bring a map* and

Bring a mat, or *They're coming at five-thirty* and *They're coming at nine-thirty* – especially if, in the general context of the conversation, either alternative were possible. Furthermore, in telephone conversations, the dynamics of our speech must fulfil the role that in face-to-face conversation would be assumed, at least in part, by physical gesture. We may find ourselves giving to enumerative or contrastive expressions, e.g. *In the first place . . . in the second place, This one . . . that one,* rather more emphasis than we would use in face-to-face conversation, partly to compensate for the loss of finger-and-hand communication, and partly to ensure that our listener has registered the construction – a circumstance which we might gather from his smile, or affirmative nod, if we were actually in his presence. Furthermore, we have to make very sure that remarks of the kind generally known as ' personal ', e.g. *You're a lazy devil, That wasn't very clever of you, Well, you'd better think again about that, hadn't you?,* which might give offence if not interpreted in the proper spirit, are accompanied by the phonic equivalent of a smile or placatory gesture, to guide the listener in his interpretation. It is even possible that in talking to strangers on the telephone (especially strangers in a professionally or socially superior position), we might consciously strive to produce an attractively modulated voice, remembering that in such situations the voice is the only index to the personality. The telephone permits the interlocutors to remain out of each other's sight, and so robs them of the clue-giving resources normally present in gesture, facial expression, physical appearance, etc.; these resources have to be re-created as pure speech.*

The radio shares with the telephone this most important characteristic that speaker and hearer are remote from, and unseen by, each other. But of course the resemblance ends there. The telephone is primarily an instrument for interlocution, whilst the radio is used for various purposes of information-giving, entertainment, etc., which can be brought together under the general heading of ' address '. Furthermore, telephone communication takes place between one speaker and one listener (whose roles, of course, commute), while the whole point of radio – as expressed in the metaphor of ' broadcasting ' – is

---

* Readers of Stella Gibbons', *Cold Comfort Farm* may recall an episode in which the heroine, Flora Post, uses a telephone fitted with some sort of video-screen. This, I learn, is no longer mere fiction, such 'video-phones' being already obtainable by subscribers in the USA. If and when they become general, phoning will become a mere extension of the ordinary speech-situation.

that its transmissions should reach as many hearers as possible. This mediation between a central source of transmission and a multiplicity of hearers constitutes a relationship which is perhaps peculiar to our time and culture. The ' speaker ' in this case may be an individual, or may be a group of individuals engaged in discussion, or even in the performance of a play; whatever the case may be, there is no doubt some justification for supposing that the millions of people throughout the country who listen to the radio feel themselves to be engaged in a personal relationship, not so much with actor or newsreader or lecturer, but with the radio itself, with the BBC, a sort of corporate super-Speaker. The super-Speaker's general manner towards the listening thousands needs to be finely contrived, since it must always seem to be interpersonal (as from a particular ' me ' to a private ' you ') while remaining supra-personal, or in some cases deliberately impersonal. Much depends on the kind of message to be transmitted. The newsreader attempts a delivery of the news which comes as close as possible to the demands of impersonality; his voice changes, marginally and respectfully, when he has to give news of an accident or some other unhappy event, but on the whole he contrives to withhold from his reading any indication of a personal and private involvement. The deliverer of a broadcast talk or lecture has a rather different problem. His is essentially a literary exercise (the broadcast talk being ultimately a derivative of the essay, and in some cases no more than ' writing speechified '), an exercise in which stylistic effects initially devised in the medium of writing have subsequently to be translated into the medium of sound.

The most necessary effect is that of ' interpersonality ' – the individual hearer has to feel that *he personally* is being addressed, cajoled, diverted; but interpersonality must needs be achieved through ' suprapersonality ' – the broadcaster has to achieve a manner which will serve as a common style, suitable for a wide and varied audience, and yet intimate enough to convince each and every listener in an audience of thousands that he is being addressed as an individual. The need to establish the interpersonal through the suprapersonal has moulded the conventional language of the broadcast talk, impressing upon it characteristics which are not found in other forms of address. The broadcaster attempts to make his voice ' bright ' with lively variations in tone, calculated to keep the hearer's interest awake; other speakers in other situations do much the same thing, of course, but they can do it in conjunction with explanatory physical gestures. This resource is denied to the broadcaster, whose intonations must there-fore be all the more powerful or seductive. Tempo and pause have to be carefully judged by the broadcasting lecturer, whose rate of delivery cannot be as rapid as it might be in the lecture room, but who dare not, on the other hand, read too slowly or leave pauses of too great a length, since mere pauses in speech become yawning gaps in a broadcast talk. The broadcaster, like the telephone conversational-ist, must be sure that his delivery is as clear and generally intelligible as he can make it; and it is perhaps in connection with this need that we have seen the emergence of a favoured speech-form, popularly known as BBC *English,* which is in effect a harnessing to the purposes of mass communication of the otherwise somewhat fugitive concept of *Standard English* or RP (Received Pronunciation).* Probably nothing has done more than sound-radio to make RP a genuine stan-dard, a norm of reference accepted by and intelligible to all listeners in our community. Not only is a clear and pleasant diction required of the broadcaster; he must also try to achieve the exactitudes of vocabulary and syntax that he would strive after in literary composi-tion – and for the same reason, namely that discourse is one-sided, that the audience cannot put questions or ask for explanations, that the demand for explicitness is consequently a once-for-all demand. The broadcaster may address his audience with the apparent casual-ness of one speaking privately to an individual listener; but his dis-course must be composed with the care devoted to a product designed for the enjoyment and understanding of people of all sorts and condi-tions.

Another problem with which the communicator-by-radio must con-tend, is that of supplying the listener's imagination with data which would otherwise be visually conveyed. When a play is broadcast,

---

* I use the words 'a fugitive concept', because although one may be able to postulate and describe a set of theoretical norms of pronunciation, it is not at all easy to find, outside the BBC, manifestations of these norms commonly acknowledged and deferred to in our society. When I taught in Sweden, my pupils there used to complain that during their travels in Great Britain they could find very few people who spoke the so-called Standard English which they were compelled to learn. Firth remarks that 'The BBC . . . is a "lan-guage-giver"', and in reference to Daniel Jones' claim that the pronuncia-tion of the public-school educated Southern Englishman is readily under-stood in most parts of the English speaking world, observes: 'Actually there are very few types of educated English, including polite Scots or Irish, of which the last remark could not be applied. And American film English is if anything, more universal.'—*Firth, I, 5, p. 17.*

details of setting and atmosphere have to be carried by the actual language given to the characters to speak; something can be gained by using a narrator, or by devising various sound-effects, but on the whole the burden of implying a scene and of conveying a sense of the physical actions and reactions of the characters, is borne by the actors as they speak the dialogue, or ultimately by the author who devises words for the actors to speak.

Television is the youngest, and ostensibly the most potent of the media. The speaker can be seen by his audience, and consequently his language no longer needs to be overcharged with functions which can be entrusted to gesture and facial expression. He reverts, in this respect, to the ordinary conditions of address. However, there is one obvious detail in which he is at a disadvantage, when compared with the public speaker addressing a so-called ' live ' audience. He cannot judge audience reaction from the responses which ordinarily occur during the course of an address – the smiles or frowns, nods of approval, looks of blank puzzlement, murmurs, shouts, cheers, and so forth. It is possibly for this reason, among others equally cogent, that the so-called ' studio audience ' is an important element in those television programmes in which some gauge of public reaction is desirable. The pretence of interlocution, the illusion of intimacy, are effects towards which the television medium is constantly directed. The feeling that the television set is an extension of the family is reflected over and over again in letters written to programme journals. Camera technique administers to this illusion. The speaker is often shown at close quarters, sitting in a chair, or at a desk (or he is shown at very close face-to-face range, in which case he is simply a head filling the screen) with no background that might distract the viewer's attention. In some instances he may be shown seated in an area containing chairs and other furniture arranged in a lay-out suggestive of the average living-room – a domestic illusion which establishes his pretensions to a certain *tutoiement* of manner and tone, even though he happens to be addressing a large audience of complete strangers. Visual background may be used primarily to inform the eye, but its use is not without linguistic importance; a scene of magnificent architecture, for example, or a mountain landscape, speaks for itself and reduces the requirement for rhetoric, whether in the form of epithets and superlatives, or of marked intonations and emphases. When the subject of a programme is a narrative, cast, perhaps, in the form of a play, musical and sound effects, together with skilful camera technique, can be used so much more powerfully than pure language that, once again, the demand for rhetoric – or even the demand for words – can be greatly reduced. Television is not a medium which promotes eloquence; it tends rather to postulate a sort of verbal naturalism, a cultivation of common-denominator speech, which can sometimes be set off with remarkable effect against violent or unusual visual images. And as television is without doubt the most influential of present-day mass media, it is possible that it may have the consequence of encouraging us, the viewing public, to dislike the kind of eloquence that charmed our forbears.

Indeed, the various media through which language can now be directed or processed have affected not only language itself, but also our general views of what language is and ought to be in its normal manifestations. Writing has greatly influenced our ideas of beauty in language, of eloquence, of wit, of insult. Writing has made possible the development of elaborate syntactic structures which mere considerations of memory and respiration would exclude from speech; but some of the bookish constructions with which we all become familiar in the course of our education have undoubtedly entered into our speech-repertoire, providing us with alternative effects appropriate to particular situations. It might be appropriate to a straightforward speech-situation to say, for example, *He was ill so I let him off*; but a more literary variant of the same sentiment, e.g. *In view of the fact that he was ill, I excused him* might serve to express some gradation of personal attitude not implied in the former example. Writing, moreover, has often provided a sort of laboratory or centre of manufacture, from which speech can be served. This is notably true with regard to our vocabulary. Thousands of words survive in English as creatures of the written code; but they are therefore always available for speech, whenever they may be required.

The popular media have had some considerable effect in promoting concepts of decorum in language by putting before the public models of various kinds of linguistic usage. People who perhaps would not concern themselves with literary forms such as the dialogue, the essay, the report, readily accept their equivalents in the transmuted guise of the radio discussion, the television interview, the documentary, the newscast, etc. Even the advertisements shown on the commercial channel of our television service have a socio-linguistic significance, firstly in reflecting the copywriter's ideas of how ordinary people behave and speak, and secondly in impressing upon people at large a model of supposedly ordinary behaviour and language. As we watch our television sets night after night, we enter into a common culture, one feature of which is the use of a recommended language; there is a way of quarrelling, a way of being humorous, a way of discussing politics or religion, a way of telling a story, a way of probing for information, a way of addressing friends and members of the family, etc., all these ways being exemplified by the supposed projections of ourselves flickering through their television lives. Professor Marshall McLuhan may (we trust) be wrong in prophesying the decay of the ' print culture ', but there is no doubt that with the advent of TV and the advertising media we have been presented with models of usage which as social paradigms may come to have considerable effect simply through being frequently and intensively rehearsed. *He talks like a book,* it used to be said of a certain kind of speaker whose language was marked by a pedantic faithfulness to literary models; is it not possible that models are changing, and that we may soon have occasion to say *He talks like a* TV *commercial* or *He talks like a serial character?*

All this commentary involves so much more than is represented by the simple diagram with which we began, the ' primary cell ' of Speaker-Listener-Theme. The basic reaction, however, remains in all its simplicity. An ' I ' manifests verbal behaviour towards a ' you ' on account of a ' this '; modifications and refinements of the pattern occur because ' I ' and ' you ' are products of a culture manifesting itself in certain institutions and concepts, and also because they are free individuals asserting their own volitions, either against or in concert with general social pressures. To say ' free ' individuals, however, is perhaps to beg the question of what freedom really is. Freedom is a great evocative word; but in speaking of man and society we should perhaps be realistic and resigned enough to speak simply of ' survival '. The aspirations of the individual within society may then be generally assessed as the desire to survive with advantages – with reputation, with respect, with a little honour, a little power. To this goal, it may be said without cynicism, almost the whole of our linguistic effort is directed. Our encounters in language with other individuals take on the competitive-collaborative aspect of a game, a game with rewards; our linguistic dealings with society at large resemble something more like a patiently negotiated contract. Here are two images, two hints about the relationship of language, individuality and society, which certainly invite further exploration.

3 The Language Game

There are obvious senses in which language is not a game; it is not
a marginal activity undertaken for amusement and recreation, nor
do we normally think of ourselves as winners or losers when we retire
from each day's talk. But it has strong analogies with game-playing,
analogies which become more marked when we consider what games
require, and what they demonstrate. We think of them primarily as
requiring opposition; but they also require collaboration. The opponents in a game collaborate with each other to the extent that they
furnish and acknowledge a common objective; they accept the location, the rules, the do's and don'ts of the game. When the players
oppose each other, the point of their opposition is that one of them
should reach an agreed objective, by stipulated means, before the
other is able to do so. To this end, procedures are laid down, allowing
for some latitude of choice. The amount of choice available to either of
the collaborators at any stage of the game depends on choices already
exercised by the other, and the winner of the game must be one who
at every stage makes the correct choices, or the least number of incorrect choices. Now if we call language a game – or rather, since there
is some slight difference, if we refer to ' the language game ' – it is
not because language is an amusing and pleasant exercise, or because
people sometimes use language playfully; it is because the kind of
language we use in day-to-day exchanges can be said to have characteristics similar to those we have attributed to games. It presupposes a
collaboration, even in opposition; it has procedures which allow of,
and even vary with, a pattern of choice; and it can even be said to
have ' winners and losers ' in the form of speakers who consistently
say the right thing or the wrong thing in given situations. This game-
resembling quality is most obvious in interlocutory language; in spoken
address, or writing, the analogy is less apparent.

Common usage alludes to 'the power of language', almost as though language were an apparatus which, when appropriately activated, would release energy, like a muscle or an electric cell. It is in fact worth questioning this general, folk-wise assumption that language has power. Certainly, we can point to characteristics which, if we choose, we can call its powers. It has, for instance, a declarative, or denotative, power; it enables us to distinguish between, and to demonstrate the inter-relationships of, the phenomena which make up our experience. It also has an evaluative, or expressive, power, in that it enables us to give expression to our emotions and judgements. We rarely have to call on one of these powers without bringing the other into play. Pure 'evaluation' must be extremely rare, if it exists at all, and pure 'declaration', or denotation, is a matter for special kinds of composition – the scientific account, the legal report, the cookery recipe.

In most situations, language is an infusion of the declarative and the evaluative. However, to return to the question of 'power'; if language merely enabled the speaker to denote elements in his experience and to give expression to his feelings about them, it might be more appropriate to speak of its 'facilities'. There must surely be some other characteristic of language which justifies the common phrase and makes 'power' a truly fitting term? Such a characteristic in fact becomes apparent if we consider that on the whole we do not speak for speaking's sake – to relieve a psychological pressure or to be merely passively understood. We speak as often as not to gain an end or modify a position, using whatever arts of language the situation may seem to recommend. In many situations there are objects to be moved, literally or metaphorically; we speak because we want action of some sort to proceed from our speech. Moreover, there are few situations in which we do not have some sort of personal stake; dignity is constantly at risk, tact is under scrutiny, distance must be maintained without being mistaken for indifference, authority has to be exercised without being allowed to blunder into tyranny – indeed we cannot even buy a box of matches without taking up into language the delicate balance of a personal relationship that has to be maintained to the satisfaction of both sides. In short, language is something more than an outlet for our intellectual and emotional needs; it makes things happen, it has an effect on the world about us, it is no mere facility for description or response. Thus, while it is quite right to say that language has declarative and evaluative facilities, we ought to add that these facilities are contributory to its ultimate, *regulative* power. Declaration and evaluation are qualities of language as a *manifestation* – we ask ourselves, *What did John say, and how did he say it?* But the perception of a regulative power in language demands that we should associate utterances and *consequences* – *And then what did Henry do, or say?* It is when language is most overtly regulative that we become aware of its resemblances to a game. There are countless situations in ordinary life in which a ' John ' consciously or unconsciously seeks to control a ' Henry ', not as a puppet master marshals a puppet, but rather as a dancer guides his partner, or as a player in a game anticipates and compels the manoeuvres of his opponents.

Much of the game-resembling quality of interlocution arises from the fact that the exercise of the regulative power in spoken language is a matter of rapid decisions and re-appraisals, apparently random and spontaneous like the strokes of a tennis-player or the punches of a boxer, and yet, like these, conforming to archetypal and often pre-dictable strategy. In this respect, the regulative ' moves ' of inter-locutory language differ from the regulative planning of written or spoken address. A sermon or an essay or a piece of advertising, or any other literary production intended to have a persuasive effect, manifests the proposed design of its author, a design which does not have to be reconsidered at every turn because of objections or un-wanted contributions from a partner with a mind of his own. A conversation, on the other hand, is a two-man design which cannot be wrought into a satisfactory pattern by the sort of conversationalist who is unskilled in the art of producing language adequate to the un-foreseen shifts of situation – i.e. by the sort of person who is often condemned as ' tactless ' or ' inarticulate '. Oliver Goldsmith was such a person. He constantly said the wrong thing; his acquaintances cherished anecdotes about his conversational ineptitudes. Yet of Goldsmith as a *writer*, his friend Dr Johnson was able to assert (in lapidary tribute) *nullum quod tetigit non ornavit*. We may wonder how a man who could earn such a tribute to his gifts as a writer – gifts which are in any case manifest – could have earned the reputa-tion of being so unskilful in speech. And yet there is no contradiction here. Writing is locution so well rehearsed that the phases of regulation are separated and slowed down; we can consider them separately, without being forced to flounder through them, as poor Goldsmith was forced to muddle through his talk.

These phases of regulation, through which we move in any purposeful use of language, whether spoken or written, may be described as
follows. We are aware, initially, of an *intention*, that is to say of the
will to reach a certain objective by using language. To realise this
intention, we produce a *strategy*, in the form of an appropriately
conditioned and coordinated sequence of linguistic symbols – i.e. a
piece of language manifesting choices in vocabulary, syntactic structure, intonation, stress, etc., which we hope will be commensurate
with our intention. We are subsequently enabled to judge the *adequacy*
of this strategy, either by observing the actions and responses of an
interlocutor, or by introspective assessment of its efficacy – as, when
writing, we look through a completed paragraph to see if it ' reads
well ', ' hangs together ', or ' makes its point '. If the strategy proves
adequate, we are able to feel that we have met the demands of the
situation; but if for any reason it appears to be inadequate, a
re-appraisal is forced upon us. When we are engaged in writing, we
can put our re-appraisal into effect simply by cancelling the offending
sentence or paragraph. It is otherwise with speech, however; words
slip out, and are not to be recalled. An unlucky choice of word, the
wrong tone of voice, may result in a loss of regulative power which
must be immediately recovered by some compensatory effort. *What a
small room!* exclaims the visitor, on being shown to his bedroom;
then, realising from the expression on his hostess' face that his tone
has not been altogether complimentary, hastens to add – *so cosy!*
' Cosy ' is his effort to compensate for ' small ', and so to re-
establish his intention of paying bright and acceptable tribute to his
hostess.

That the strategies of writing differ from those of speech will be
obvious to anyone who has struggled with the problem of committing
to paper a well-tempered sentence. In writing we are denied the full
play of the natural resources of language; intonation, stress, timing,
to say nothing of facial expression and gesture, are lost, and can only
re-emerge on the written page in transmuted guise, as metaphor, as a
set of carefully-balanced lexical choices, as a sentence-structure or
word-order designed to convey a certain rhythm or tone. Yet in
writing we at least have the opportunity to cancel, extend, or re-design
our strategies. The re-designing, to be sure, can be an exacting and
time-consuming business, but we are as a rule content to use our
time in this way, because we are convinced that there is an intellectual profit in this discipline, and because we have been brought up

to revere written composition as an art. We are no doubt justified in our convictions, but perhaps we might consider that mere interlocution can also have its discipline, its profit, its art. Every exercise of language may be thought of as a specialised art yielding something to the development of the personality; Bacon makes the point precisely in a well-known passage from his essay *Of Studies*:

> Reading maketh a full man; Conference a ready man; and Writing an exact man; and therefore, if a man write little, he had need have a great memory; if he confer little he had need have a present wit and if he read little he had need have much cunning to seem to know that he doth not.

Interlocution – *conference,* as Bacon calls it – indeed requires 'a present wit'. It is an opportunist's art, demanding sudden appraisals of a situation that changes as language unfolds, asking for shrewd assessments of the character of a respondent, and for rapid and co-ordinated choices, made in the light of these interpretations, from the phonic, syntactic, and lexical repertoire of the spoken language. To formulate the process so cumbrously is to make mere speech, our common heritage, seem impossibly difficult. But really efficacious speech *is* difficult even for the highly literate; we have already commented on the seeming paradox that a gifted man like Dr Goldsmith might 'write like an angel' and yet 'talk like poor Poll'.* But it was an achievement on Goldsmith's part to have raised at least one linguistic skill to such heights of performance. Not many people play the language game with any sort of brilliance, or, indeed with more than sporadic attempts to sparkle; but we are all players, willy-nilly, and whether we fumble or fizz we play under common conditions.

In speaking, we produce sequences of meaningful sound conventionally known as *utterances*. If, as analysts of language, we want to be more precise about this rather vague term 'utterance' – which, after all, means no more than 'something said' – we have to indicate a perspective or point of view which will enable us to classify utterances by relating them to some function or some place in a hierarchy of linguistic terms. For instance, if our point of view happens to be that of the phonetician, our concern might be to identify an utterance

---

* David Garrick, *Impromptu Epitaph* on Dr Goldsmith:
    Here lies Nolly Goldsmith, for shortness call'd Noll,
    Who wrote like an angel, but talk'd like poor Poll.

as a sequence of sounds marked by specific features of stress and intonation. Looking at the same utterance as grammarians we might argue about its status and function as, say, a clause or a phrase. A philosopher might have no interest in these matters, but might be solely concerned to assign the utterance to one of the categories 'meaningful' or 'unmeaningful', or even (dare one be so bold?) 'true' or 'untrue'. There are several perspectives on language and in each the 'utterance' is identified through different categories. At the moment, we are not concerned with phonetics or grammar or even philosophy; we are primarily concerned with the regulative power of language as manifested in spoken exchanges, or interlocution, and it is in this perspective that we have to label our utterances. As it happens, the labelling is simple and commonplace.

In exercising the regulative power of language we have at our disposal four basic types of utterance, four operators by means of which we try to reach acceptable conclusions or evade unacceptable contingencies. These four operative types can be named quite simply, as *statement, question, directive* (or 'command') and *response*. What matters about these categories is not so much their realisation as distinct forms, though each type can have distinct syntactic and phonic manifestations, as may appear from four possible samples: *I slept badly, Do you know that man? Shut the door, Tomorrow, all being well*. Of course these formal manifestations are important, but we are not concerned here with the relationship between certain labels and certain grammatical or phonetic possibilities. We are rather concerned with the labels as indicators of regulative strategies proceeding from distinct intentions. Thus, the sort of utterance we identify as *statement* is designed to carry information, or to express an attitude, or quite possibly to do both things at once. The type we know as *question* elicits information, or elicits information whilst also expressing an attitude, or calls for the expression of an attitude – or, again, does all these things at once. Language of the *directive* category most commonly takes the form of an overt command – *Give me that, Open it, Don't pay him* – and is intended to influence, or even compel, the behaviour of a partner in discourse.*

Finally, utterances of the type we identify as *response* function as supplementaries to some precedent furnished by the partner; they

* Of course there are forms of directive other than command. *Good children clean their teeth*, for example, is no less directive than the overt order *Go and clean your teeth, Johnny*.

return required information, they amplify a statement, they express an attitude provoked by the foregoing utterance, etc. Statement, question, and directive imply the initiation of discourse, or of a phase of discourse, by the speaker; response alone is a secondary, or complementary, category, a language-role assumed by the listener. Response is therefore the Janus-face of our foursome, the transition from passive to active in the interlocutory game; for when the listener responds, it is quite likely that what he produces will be both a response and an initiation, or at any rate a response leading to initiation:

> *Who is that man over there?*
> *— He's called Martin Jones.*

(The response is itself a *statement* which might in its turn elicit responses – *Ah yes, I thought so, Is he?, From Abergavenny?,* etc.)
or:

> *Why do you keep scratching your nose?*
> *— Do I? I didn't realise that.*

(The initial response, the conventional *Do I?* is amplified by a statement which meets the original question and opens the way to some placatory, instead of merely assertive, answer, e.g. *Yes, it's odd how one has unconscious habits,* rather than *Yes, you do.*)*
or:

> *You never say you love me*
> *— Well I do love you. Now shut up.*

(The initial response is merely an exasperated yielding of a required form of words and is immediately amplified by the true response, which is a conversation-stopping directive.)
or:

> *When is the club dance?*
> *— Next Friday, I think, Are you going?*

(The response, which returns the required information, is immediately followed by a question which initiates a new phase of discourse.)
or:

> *Pass me the scissors.*
> *— Certainly. Here they are. You'll have to stretch.*

(The conventionally polite response is followed by a 'performative'

---

* The 'placatory remark' need not necessarily follow. The response might be a sharply conclusive assertion, e.g. *Well you realise it now.* The point remains however that the utterance *I didn't realise that* leaves an open choice making it possible for the conversation to continue on friendly lines.

statement, i.e., one expressive of the action it accompanies, which in its turn is followed by a form of directive related to the unfolding of the situation – the intended recipient of the scissors has put out his hand, but cannot quite reach.)

Any pair of interlocutors is involved in this sort of game, the language game. They are enabled to play the game by virtue of the simplicity of principle which allows for great complexity of actual variants. In any context, as we see, we can expect only four basic types of utterance. Our grasp of this enables us to anticipate moves in the game, and allows us to guess at the type and intention of an utterance on the strength of minimal clues of tone, word-order, situational probability, etc. We often have the beginnings of a response at tongue-tip before a partner's initiating utterance has come to an end. We can still be surprised, or pleased, or in some way moved by the actual realisation of an utterance, for the possible variations are great; but we are rarely at fault in our recognition and anticipation of the basic strategy. This is just as well, for the ease of everyday living depends on our being right for something more than ninety per cent of the time. The odd percentage is the margin of linguistic chaos we allow to wits and cross-talk comedians.

The game has rules of a sort, though of course the word ' rules ' ought not to be too strictly interpreted. A ' rule ' in the language game is a sort of consensus of behaviour. For instance, one very important ' rule ' is seen in the assumption that an initiating form requires a contextually-related response; to which may be added the further assumption that the response will usually be conditioned or developed in some way that will indicate the respondent's willingness to continue the game. The signal that the game is closed is given either by refraining from making the required form of response, or by using one of a limited number of verbal gestures recognised as conclusive – e.g. by saying *Good-bye* or *I must be off* or *Cheerio,* before one's language-partner has the chance to resume discourse. To depart from these principles is to brand oneself as mad, unreasonable, anti-social, or merely deaf – at all events as an outcast from the community of language. We do not normally expect exchanges like this:

> *Who is that man over there?*
> *– Tomorrow, if you like.*

or this:

> *Shut the door, please.*
> *– I like bananas too.*

or this:

> *I am going to write a book on Goethe.*
> *– How's your father?*

Such responses offend against the normal rules of the game. They are permissible only under special rules which allow for the expression of humour or the declaration of hostility. Humour, in some of its manifestations, is anarchical, asserting the right of the individual to break free from the collective, cooperative habit, to rebel against the tyranny of empty statements and silly questions:

> The man in the wilderness asked me
> How many strawberries grow in the sea?
> I answered him, as I thought good,
> As many red herrings grow in the wood.*

Normally we do not answer ' as we think good '; our replies complete a presupposed pattern, and to break pattern in cross-talk or double talk is either to create humour or to give offence – humour and offence being often next neighbours. When Prince Hal parodies Hotspur's style of conversation, he makes humour out of Hotspur's offensive habit of refusing to play the language game like any well-nurtured subject:

> I am not yet of Percy's mind, the Hotspur of the North, he that kills me some six or seven dozen of Scots at a breakfast: washes his hands and says to his wife, fie upon this quiet life I want work. O my sweet Harry says she! how many hast thou killed today? Give my roan horse a drench (says he) and answers some fourteen, an hour after: a trifle, a trifle.†

As soon as we initiate conversation, we are vulnerable; for by refusing to play the game according to the conventions, a respondent in effect withdraws his fellowship from us, leaving us isolated and unsure of ourselves. In such moments the social value of language is impaired for us, and we are therefore less certain of its strength at our next encounter. A calculated insult, or a joke turning, at our expense, on the disjointed response, may deprive us of some of our confidence in the power of language to build bridges and throw out lines. It is

---

* According to the *Oxford Dictionary of Quotations*, this rhyme occurs as a manuscript addition to the Bath Municipal Library copy of the *Whole Duty of Man*.
† Shakespeare, *King Henry IV, Part 1*, II, iv, 116

perhaps because of this that we find such humour, and such offensiveness hard to bear and hard to forgive.

When we write or make speeches, we are in sole charge of the language we use, but interlocution is shared discourse. 'Discourse', like 'utterance' is an obligingly tractable term. Here it is taken to mean a sequence of utterances related to and developing some agreed topic of reference. Consecutive utterances are as a rule situationally or symbolically linked – meaning that the connection between one utterance and the next is either implicit in the situation itself or is overtly demonstrated by some element in language – a lexical allusion, a grammatical connective, etc. It is in this linkage that the pattern of discourse is to be sought, and it makes a most interesting study. In the language of address we are bound to assign considerable importance to symbolic linkage. It is in the nature of written communication that the potential responent is out of the initiator's sight, and, indeed perhaps not within his acquaintance; it therefore becomes necessary to demonstrate the coherence of a developing argument of theme by means of anaphora, conjunctions, sentence-connectors, parallel constructions. In spoken address there is a similar pressure to demonstrate the wholeness of a theme by contriving a symbolic coherence; though if the speaker confronts a familiar audience, with whom he shares sympathies and common interests, this coherence may find symbolic realisation in gesture, facial expression, tone of voice, and so forth.

It may seem that this matter of linkage is less important in the case of interlocution, which is often informal and familiar, than in the case of address. But although interlocution makes possible a different kind of linkage, based on the tacit understanding of the interlocutors, linkage is nonetheless vital, not solely as a linguistic convention supporting the coherence of discourse, but also as a social convention reflecting the contract of a personal relationship. It must be borne in mind that when we converse we not only demonstrate the coherence of our language, but also the coherence of our social system. The linkage of utterances in shared discourse can tell us something about the interlocutors' personal and social attitudes to each other, about the environment in which their discourse takes place, and about the social significance or indifference of its subject-matter. It may seem that this linkage is a random affair, various and unsystematic in its manifestations, but in fact it can be shown to depend on a few simple principles, so that we might even venture to speak of ' laws of response ' by which we are guided when we play the language game.

We have already glanced at a fundamental principle – the requirement that utterance and response shall have a common reference or
point of departure, so that Atkins says something about apples,
Baker's response will likewise have a reference, direct or oblique, to
apples. There are three ways (at least; perhaps the inventive reader
will be able to see more) by means of which this condition can be
met. Firstly a respondent can be said to rely on *situational linkage*
when his reply turns on the evident facts of the situation as projected
by the foregoing utterance, without using or echoing any part of the
language of that utterance. For example:

> *When can you come?*
> *– On Thursday, if that's all right.*

or:

> *When does the train leave?*
> *– I don't know, I'll find out.*

or:

> *Perkins gets my back up.*
> *– Try to be patient.*

or:

> *Write a report for me.*
> *– About how long?*

It is clear in such cases that the interlocutors acknowledge a common
reference which is established in the initiating remark and needs no
further definition in language. The situation itself, the particular set
of circumstances with reference to which the initiating remark is
made, is so clearly defined that interlocution can proceed without the
necessity of demonstrating by linguistic means the connection of
response to preceding utterance. At times, however, an overt demonstration of the coherence of discourse is felt to be necessary, and
responses then show a tendency to repeat, echo, or allude to, the language of foregoing utterances. This kind of pattern (we shall call
it *symbolic linkage*) might be illustrated by the following exchanges:

> *Do you think Perkins is suitable?*
> *– It depends what you mean by suitable.*
> *I mean is he a good mixer?*
> *– Oh, he's a good mixer all right. Yes, in that sense
> he's suitable.*
> *That's the sense I had in mind.*

Apart from the fact that they agree to talk about Perkins, it can hardly be said that these interlocutors have established from the outset a common situational reference. Their conversation is held together by overt linguistic allusions relating each utterance to its predecessor: *suitable – I mean – good mixer – that's the sense*. We might suppose in such cases that conversation turns on symbolic rather than situational linkages because the relationship between language and the phenomena to which it refers is ambiguous or obscure, and needs to be clarified, if necessary by a nagging insistence on defining the scope of words and phrases. It is not only in philosophical argument that we are forced to ' define our terms '. In everyday discourse, where so much may be taken for granted, regarded as self-evident, left unspoken, there are nonetheless junctures at which we *must* have recourse to explicit definition in language as a means of establishing or re-establishing common ground. This work of clarification is not, however, the only linguistic and social function of symbolic linkage. We often use it to make a point clear, but we can also use it to obfuscate a reference. It can be used non-cooperatively as well as cooperatively, and there are many instances in which it occurs as a means of expressing a social dissent, a refusal to accept the situational reference projected by a speaker.

For instance:

> *What's the time?*
> *– What's the hurry?*

or:

> *What's the time?*
> *– Time you were in bed.*

In these exchanges, the response takes up part of the form of the foregoing utterance (thereby establishing a symbolic linkage) but does not take up the intended situational reference. It can be assumed in such cases that the respondent does not wish to meet the initiator in the latter's chosen situation, but wants to go on using language in order to turn the situation to his own liking; and so makes use of forms of symbolic linkage which acknowledge a preceding utterance, but assert a different view of the situation. The playful, and mildly aggressive, nature of such linkage is apparent, even in print, where we are deprived of important clues of intonation and stress. We might illustrate this by comparing two possible ways of controlling a situation with an appropriately-turned response. The bare examples may be enough to suggest the nature of the imagined situation and the character of the interlocutors:

But my dear little doggie loves his bikkies.

– Don't be sentimental.

Here the respondent gives a direct rebuff; the linkage, it will be noticed, is the type we have called situational. But he might equally well – and indeed with greater effect – give the rebuff oblique:

But my dear little doggie loves his bikkies.

– But my dear little Aunt Fanny loves her kippers.

This is an example of symbolic linkage used with hostile intent; and, given the appropriate phonic features, i.e. the mimicry of the initiator's vocal timbre, speech tempo, and intonation-pattern, it is much more abrasive and insulting than the simple reproof 'Don't be sentimental'.

The third form of linkage is a blend of the situational and the symbolic. It is possible for the accord between interlocutors to be complete at the primary, situational, level, whilst it is also demonstrated at the symbolic level. In the following examples, responses are clearly linked to preceding utterances by overt, symbolic, means, but it is also clear that the interlocutors are not moved by antagonisms or troubled by obscurity of reference:

Have you finished with the paper?

– Yes, I've finished with it now.

or:

Perkins is a nice man.

– ISN'T he a nice man!

or:

Pass me the hammer, Noakes.

– The hammer, sir, yes, sir, one hammer coming up.

or:

Guess who they've picked for captain?

– They've picked Crunchpole. Am I right?

All too lamentably right.

– Crunchpole. Think of it.

You think of it. I daren't.

These are ostensibly examples of symbolic linkage, but they do not function in quite the same way as our earlier examples, where such linkages were apparently used to question references or to sharpen conflicts. In these examples, there is no conflict and no need for a definition of terms. In situation and symbol alike, the interlocutors are agreed, and their reiterations seem merely to confirm and assert this agreement. Since the linkage extends through the whole context of situation plus language, *contextual linkage* might be a suitable term for this third 'mixed' type. Contextual linkage is frequently a characteristic of rather formal, even stylised, interlocution – it can occur, for instance, in the so-called 'scripted' interview of radio or television; but the last example given would also suggest that, like symbolic linkage, it can be used with something approaching playfulness. In the one case, however, the playfulness would appear to be exclusive or divisive, an expression of hostility or repudiation; while in the example of contextual linkage quoted above, the playfulness of the interlocutors is clearly inclusive, a shared sprightliness depending on the fact that they are at one in their view of the situation.

There is obviously a relationship between modes of linkage and the formality or informality of interpersonal attitudes. In casual or informal discourse, especially between acquaintances in commonplace situations, there is some likelihood that linkages will be mainly situational:

> *When does the train leave?*
> *– At half-past three, I think.*

This could be the question-and-answer of fellow-passengers. An exchange between a passenger and the guard of the train might reflect greater formality of attitudes and so might very well turn on a contextual linkage:

> *When does the train leave?*
> *– The train leaves at half-past three, sir.*

Or, again, the passenger's quotation might be met by a sardonic reply from a friend and fellow-passenger, a response saying in effect, *Don't ask me, how should I know?* In such an instance a symbolic linkage might be used:

> *When does the train leave?*
> *– When will pigs fly?*

This way of saying *I don't know* is of course the strict prerogative of equal speaking to equal. We cannot suppose that our train-guard would venture such a response to a passenger's enquiry, under any but the most exacerbating circumstances. This does not mean that a social 'inferior' is never able to rebuke a 'superior' by the manner of his response. There is at least one style of covert symbolic linkage by means of which the servant-in-the-situation can effectively reproach the master:

> *Waiter, when do you tie on the feed-bags?*
> *– Dinner is served at 7.30, sir.*

The linkage here is ostensibly situational, but it is quite possible for the waiter, by gentle emphasis and appropriate intonation, to make his phrase *Dinner is served* sound like a general reproof of the guest's off-hand vulgarism *tie on the feed-bags;* and hence there is in this instance a kind of oblique symbolic linkage. It would be socially impermissible for the waiter to reply in such a way as to make the symbolic linkage overt and direct:

Waiter, when do you tie on the feed-bags?
– The – er ' feed-bags ' – will be – er ' tied on ' – at 7.30 sir.

This might be accounted impertinence, and could have grave conquences for the waiter; whereas, though the hapless guest might feel the power of an oblique criticism, he could hardly allege it in complaint.

The ' laws of response ' are thus in part concerned with contextual relationships which reflect social and interpersonal attitudes. They define the options open to a respondent when an utterance is presented to him. We have used the phrase *the language game* as a label for this pattern of options and the procedures of choice. Certain popular expressions indicate that the idea of language as a kind of game is by no means new. Interlocution is sometimes compared with such pastimes as fencing or tennis – we talk of the ' cut and thrust ' of argument, or we describe the processes of polite small-talk as ' patting the ball back '. Now a game of tennis, as we well know, involves rather more than the tame process of patting the ball back. Analysis of a typical game would show that the player has at his disposal a range of return shots appropriate to various intentions and emergencies. Similarly, analysis of the conversational game suggests that there are a number of ways of coping with, or ' returning ' a response. One is simply to make a bald reply to the initiating utterance, without attempting to carry any further the topic projected by that utterance. To do this consistently is strictly speaking a crime against interlocutory convention, a breach of the principles of fair play. The respondent is a dialogue such as the following would surely be thought ungracious, if not downright hostile:

Hello! When did you arrive?
– This morning.
Did Mary come with you?
– No.
I see. How long will you be staying?
– Three days.

Peter will be jolly pleased to see you.
– I expect so.

Here is a type of non-committal response for which the term *rejoinder* is appropriate. Usually we do not expect, or tolerate, 'rejunctive' series like the exchanges in the imaginary conversation laid out above. When we engage in interlocution with a friendly and cooperative partner, we suppose that in the pattern of responses, the situation will be symbolically extended and developed by constant additions to what has gone before; we expect continuation thus:

Hello! When did you arrive?
– This morning. Mary couldn't come, unfortunately.
Oh, pity. How long are you staying?
– Three days. I'd like to see Peter if I can find the time.
Yes, he'll be jolly pleased to see you.
– Well, you know its been two years, etc.

This continuative pattern corresponds to the image of 'patting the ball back', and indeed this is the dominant image, in most of our minds, of interlocution; set to write a piece of stage dialogue, we should probably write something in this continuative vein because this is 'cooperative' discourse as we ordinarily know it. A rejunctive dialogue suggests non-co-operation, and we should write such a dialogue only if we wanted to indicate hostility or disharmony between our characters. It is probably true to say that the layman's concept of dramatic dialogue does not extend much beyond the cooperative/continuative and isolative/rejunctive patterns of which he is readily aware as elements in his daily experience of language. Some of our contemporary dramatists, however, have shrewdly perceived that commonplace interlocution is often *recursive;* the partners keep alluding back to earlier remarks, either in puzzlement, or mere inanity, or because their discourse is a process of linguistic gesture without real communication. Recursion is often accompanied by symbolic linkage:

Where's the boot-polish?
– It's in the cupboard. I see Liverpool are playing Spurs this week.
They'll cripple 'em. Where is it?
– What do you want?
The boot-polish.
– It's in the cupboard. Cripple 'em? I should live to see the day.
What cupboard, for Pete's sake?
– I should live to see it. The kitchen cupboard, you great Herbert.

> *I mean Liverpool, mate, Liverpool.*
> *– Liverpool what? What about Liverpool?*
> *Liverpool'll cripple 'em. Cripple Spurs. Look, I can't find it.*
> *– Now what can't you find?*
> *I can't find the boot-polish.*
> *– Well why don't you try the kitchen cupboard? Look, Spurs are for the chop, mate. I'll just tell you that.*
> *What d'you mean, you'll just tell me? Haven't I just told you?*

We may feel that such interlocutions – whether they occur in real life or as ornaments of dramatic fiction – are best described in Dogberry's phrase, 'most tolerable and not to be endured'. We prefer, as a rule, to cherish the illusion that all our conversations move efficiently towards an object; we like to feel that information is safely conveyed, and that the topic may be shifted occasionally. There is accepted technique for shifting the subject or moving the conversation along a little; the term *incursion* might be used to describe the kind of response-pattern answering this technique. An incursive response is acceptable within the rules of the game only when the preceding utterance does not require an explicit rejoinder or continuation; if these are expected, they have to be made before the respondent makes his incursion into a fresh topic:

> *How's that boy of yours getting along?*
> *– Oh, he's fine, thanks. Are you coming to the dance next week?*

or:

> *Look at that fellow over there – fat isn't in it!*
> *– Yes, he must weigh all of two hundred and fifty pounds. By the way, I went to see Dr Williams last night.*

An incursion may change the subject of conversation completely and abruptly but it need not have the effect of giving offence; it may be found surprising or disconcerting (this is especially so if more than two people are engaged in conversation and the incursion is made by one who for most of the time has listened passively) but it does not have to be a crime against social usage. The game can, to be sure, be broken off insultingly – or simply not be taken on, which is as offensive as a sudden breach; and for such acts of linguistic hostility we may devise a further response-category, *dissociation*. The most effective form of dissociation is mere silence, emphasised, perhaps, by the physical action of turning away. But a pointed changing of the subject, after an appropriate interval of 'loaded' silence, is also an effective expression of hostility:

That's a lovely picture. I wouldn't have recognised your wife.
– . . . Mrs Endicott, you were telling us about your husband's work in Basutoland.

or:

I suppose you make a pile of money in your racket?
– . . . Geoffrey, pour Mrs Hackforth-Bone another sherry, there's a good chap.

Snubs of this sort work effectively in larger companies, where a convenient third party, a ' Mrs Endicott ' or a ' Geoffrey ', may serve to emphasise the swivelling of attention which most markedly excludes the preceding speaker. The perpetrator of a tactless remark can by such means be exiled from the community of language; and so effective is this exile from discourse that the victim ceases to have social identity, ' to be there '. In situations where antagonisms are awakened, the verbally skilful can often make use of a bystander's presence to create the illusion of an interlocutory partnership, a sort of micro-civilisation, from which the offender is excluded. This is not possible when the company is confined to two persons. Then, the best that the offended party can usually do by way of response is to produce a sulky rejoinder:

I didn't think you played much of a game today.
– Didn't you.

The presence of a third party would give the respondent the opportunity of making a pointed dissociation:

I didn't think you played much of a game today.
– . . . How are the children, Tom?

This is a convenient escape from the threat of insolence, a way of surviving with dignity intact. The kind of response most of us would like to make in such circumstances is something boldly continuative, with a pointed symbolic linkage – perhaps something along these lines:

I didn't think you played much of a game today.
– Perhaps I didn't play hard enough. Or perhaps you didn't think hard enough?

But such agreeable wolfishness demands a readiness which most of us can only achieve in afterthought.

The rules of the language game are not written, and the ' laws of response ' do not bind us on pain of punishment. They are principles governing the forms interlocution may take in our particular culture, with its situational types, its social procedures, its notions of respect and insult, of obligation and independence. If we offend against these cultural *mores,* penalties of a kind are exacted. We pay the penalty of being thought anti-social, or inept. We are exiled from the situation we have mismanaged, and so are no longer in a position to control it; which means that in one instance – and so, potentially, in many related instances, if we do not learn better – we have failed to apply the regulative power of language, that power which enables us to manage our affairs at the symbolic level and so to avoid the scuffles and drudgery of the mere animal. The game is serious; our survival as a species depends upon our playing it well.

4 Social Determination Versus Individual Expression

There are occasions in the life of man that wear a once-only look; but they seldom make great demands on the linguistic inventiveness of the individual. The bridegroom, the patient on the operating table, the prisoner at the bar, are not as a rule expected to display a turn for badinage or dialectic. Their roles are socially prescribed, and their parts are more or less written for them. These are, it is true, special cases involving situations that are relatively uncommon; one may, after all, go through life without being sentenced in a court of law, without undergoing an operation, or even without getting married.

However, many situations in which we find ourselves, though not so sharply defined and not so ritualistic in word and act, are nonetheless social stereotypes, commonplaces of our culture, with its composite of institutions, hierarchies, artefacts, and behaviour patterns. Our aggregated experience of the institutional and hierarchical determinants of behaviour in our society enables us to identify the stereotyped situation and, if we are involved in it, to produce the language and behaviour appropriate to our socially-prescribed role. Our words and actions may not be as rigidly laid down as the language and procedures of the marriage service, but they can certainly be said to be limited to fairly small, and exclusive, confines of choice.

We might illustrate this claim by resorting to an essay in plausible fiction, along the following lines: in a London street there is a man wearing dark clothes and a bowler hat, and carrying an umbrella. The street is full of traffic. The man stands at the edge of the pavement, raises an umbrella much as a sword might be raised in salute, and shouts to a passing vehicle, 'Taxi!' The vehicle draws in to the kerb. The driver, who wears a cloth cap and is swathed in an old but serviceable greatcoat, leans over and asks, 'Where to, then, guv?' The bowler-hatted man gives an address, which the driver repeats, nodding his head slightly and raising one hand briefly in a 'thumbs-up' signal. His passenger gets into the taxi, and they drive off. This is a commonplace situation; something like it may be observed actually taking place somewhere in the streets of London, on any day.* To understand the situation fully, we have to be versed in the details of English culture and social organisation. The encounter says something about our class-structure and the way its lines of demarcation are observed or ignored in meetings between members of different classes. The social factors at work in the situation are revealed not only by the dress of the two men and the fact that one is obviously summoned by the other in a fashion that postulates a kind of master-servant relationship. Our example is, of course, fictional, but the plausibility of the fiction might be tested by putting the case to any Londoner – or for that matter to any Englishman.

A native arbiter of this particular case would surely see in the bowler hat and the umbrella indications of a social status guaranteeing a certain style of conduct; a style which would permit the passenger to use the word 'driver' as a form of address, but not the familiarities of 'mate' or 'chum', nor yet (without due cause) the arrogance of 'fellow', or my 'good man', or 'you there', since familiarity or arrogance would alike belie the social claim made by the passenger's clothing and general bearing. The driver might likewise be expected to use certain forms of address – 'sir' for respect, 'guv' or 'squire' for sturdy man-to-man civility, but not 'boyo' or 'china' or any of the terms which belong to the repertoire of working-class companionability. Our arbiter would no doubt accept as plausible the actions of brief nod and raised thumb here ascribed to the driver; but he would certainly reject with merriment any account of the matter that made the driver bow, or touch his forehead in obeisance, and he would perhaps express some disbelief if the narrative described the passenger as summoning the taxi with an imperious crook of the forefinger, instead of the raised arm and shout. He would have seen this type of situation enacted often enough for him to be able to appraise the probabilities of word and action.

* From the correspondence columns of *The Sunday Times*, 6 Dec. 1970 and 13 Dec. 1970, I gather that I may be presenting an outmoded image of the London cabbie, and that the cloth cap and greatcoat are things of the past. Nevertheless, I think this figure of English folk-culture will be recognised.

We are all capable of making such appraisals, but in doing so – and here is the point – we take for granted a great deal of stored information about our society and culture. The matter is most adeptly formulated by J. R. Firth in his book *The Tongues of Men,* where he remarks that ' the force and cogency of most language behaviour derives from the firm grip it has on the ever-recurrent typical situations in the life of social groups and the normal social behaviour of the human animals living in these groups. Speech is the telephone network, the nervous system of our society much more than the vehicle for the lyrical outbursts of the individual soul. It is a network of bonds and obligations.'*

Firth perhaps does less than justice to the importance of individual creativeness in language, but it was necessary, when he wrote his book, to insist on a re-direction of attention from the individual producer of language to ' the ever-recurrent typical situations in the life of social groups ' and to the ' network of bonds and obligations ' manifested by language as a social act. It is still necessary to emphasise the social nature of language, but perhaps it is also possible to show how individuals may accept language's social norms and yet still manage to achieve some degree of expressive freedom. From our earliest days we are faced with the problem of reconciling the claims of selfhood with the claims of the community. It is not a case of choosing one or the other; the egocentric person is self-doomed, but the person who thinks he can sink his individuality in the collective is self-deluding. The problem is, how to ' find oneself ' (as the popular phrase has it) without neglecting one's obligations to a community. To neglect such obligations is to risk becoming an outcast, and an outcast can never ' find himself ', since he no longer has any social bearings by which to identify his position. The problem takes varied and recurrent forms, and is often resolved with the aid of language, whether by rational analysis or by some species of word-magic, the semantic engineering that can bridge chasms of difference with the charm of an acceptable phrase.† Language may thus bring individual and collective to a working compromise on many social practices. But language is itself a ' social practice ', and the individual must learn, in his language-

---

* *Firth, I, 5, p. 113.*

† For example, the dustman or garbage-collector does what he may well feel to be a humiliatingly dirty job. In some communities, the dustmen are officially known as *sanitary workers,* or something in the same style. This is not mere euphemism; it allows the lowly individual to feel something of the pride of necessary public service.

behaviour as in everything else, to make a concord between self-assertion and what the community demands of him. As a matter of social principle, there is no difference between having to ask oneself the question ' how can I express my taste in dress without embarrassing my family, scandalising the High Street, and getting myself sent home from work?', and having to ask oneself, ' how can I proclaim my individuality through language without forfeiting the convenience of being understood and socially accepted by my fellows?' In language as in other forms of behaviour we are subject to traditional codes of *done* and *not done* which we gradually acquire as our days lead us through the various enclosures of relationship that make up our life in the community.

For Western man, and perhaps for most of the world's peoples, the first of these ' enclosures ' is the form-giving, paradigmatic institution of the family. It is as infant members of a family that each of us first learns that he is not a monstrous feeding ego, surrounded by solid objects and soft comestibles. We begin, with the help of language, to differentiate the realities of our environment – we learn that cats are not squirrels, that squirrels are not rabbits, that rabbits are not rats, that tables are not stools, that pins are not needles, etc. We also begin to learn something of the conceptual world into which we are born and which will govern our thinking and our assumptions; we learn – again through language – about time parcelled out in yesterdays, todays and tomorrows, about space distributed between here and somewhere else, about the actual and the potential expressed in *is* and *might*. But what is important is that we learn that these realities and concepts are not a show put on for our benefit alone, but are shared with other people, and indeed in some respects virtually depend for their existence on this fact of sharing. Language converts us insensibly to the view that the world is not ' the ball I own ', but rather ' the orange I share '. With our early, family-born awareness of sharing the world with others, we enter into the ' network of bonds and obligations ' which language asserts and creates. In the family we learn where to look for authority, and how to respond to authority; where to look for friendship and equality and how these things are expressed in word or action. We discover the limits of self-expression and self-assertion; we recognise the occasions and the phases of relationship which permit the venturing of jokes and pleasantries, and we come to know when respect is demanded of us. We assimilate some of the notions which will govern our lives in the larger world. We learn what

politeness is, how it is expressed, when it is called for. We learn that
some kinds of questioning are in order while others are not. We learn
how to give commands, and how to express refusal. We discover that
some topics of conversation are forbidden to us, or may only be
broached with great delicacy. We observe that the linguistic forms
which pass current among our equals in the hierarchy of the family
are not quite the same forms that we might use in addressing our
superiors. The family is the training-model which prepares us for
a lifetime of talking.

When we go out into the world, our ability to deal with its vastness
and strangeness depends on our being able to find other models, other
' enclosures ', other networks of relationship, made more or less in the
familial image. Not surprisingly, we find them ready-made and waiting for us. The image of the family is impressed upon our culture.
The trade-unionist has his ' brothers ', the member of a religious order
his ' brethren '; the Roman Catholic addresses his priest as ' father ',
all Christians pray to our Father in heaven; the typesetter refers to his
shop-steward as the ' father of the chapel '; we speak of the ' sons '
and ' daughters ' of a college or school; we may call our social clubs
' fraternities ' or ' sororities '; we often award ourselves the status of
' auntie ' or ' uncle ' in our dealings with children who are not actually
related to us – our language bears frequent witness to our inclination
to treat the world around us as one great big more-or-less happy
family. It was a sound instinct that made Orwell call his dictator Big
Brother, for, all irony apart, the family is one of the most perdurably
tyrannical institutions ever devised, and would hardly be tolerated
were it not evident that its functions are protective, regulative, and on
the whole beneficent. We find images or echoes of the family organisation in our schools, in our various work-environments, in our clubs
and institutions devoted to leisure activities. These organisations may
be controlled by stricter rules, the play of individuality may be less
important than the functioning of the collective, the individual's role
may be more rigidly defined, discipline may be stricter and indulgence
rarer – but school, office, factory or club are all, like the family,
' enclosures ', and they are enclosures within which basic familial
principles operate. Within each there is a scale of seniority, a principle
of authority hierarchically manifested. There are allotted areas of
responsibility; there are modes of relationship between principals and
subordinates, or between equals; there are situations where a strict
protocol governs behaviour, and others in which it is relaxed; there

is the obligation of the leader to the led, and the duty of the led towards the leader.

The passage from the family environment to the school environment, from the school environment to the work environment, may cause each of us some mild anxiety, perhaps some actual trouble, but in fact once the entry into each new enclosure has been effected, it is not so very long before we begin to feel at home. It is the non-familial, unenclosed, situation which troubles us most, especially when we are very young and have little experience of dealings on the open market of human relationships. We are not sure how to deal with the tradesmen who call at the house, how to turn aside a shopkeeper's pleasantry, how to deal with an enquiry from a complete stranger, or indeed how to make an enquiry of someone we do not know, how to address a policeman, how to cope with old ladies, how to respond to the unfunny jokes cracked by funny old men. There is no familiar map, no recommended set of procedures, to guide us in these ' open ' exchanges, and it is only by degrees that we learn the alphabet of such situations; we learn to judge trades and professions according to the evaluation current in our society, we identify uniforms or styles of dress with positions in a social hierarchy, we learn what dues we are expected to pay to age and sex. Some of these things we may have inferred ourselves from the observed attitudes of the family, or we may actually have been taught them, at home or in school, as part of a ' proper upbringing '; but assurance comes slowly, and indeed we probably never acquire the same measure of assurance in the open situation that we can enjoy in the close community.

As mature, reasonably experienced beings, we enter upon the verbal exchanges of any situation, whether ' enclosed ' or ' open ', with certain assumptions which are directive of our behaviour. We assume, for example, that certain topics may be raised or expatiated upon in a given environment, whilst others are less likely to occur, even to the extent of being virtually prohibited. We know whether the encounter is governed by the observation of rank and status, and we can judge the extent to which our language ought to take cognisance of a hierarchical scale. We know the degree of formality of the relationship we are involved in, and we can therefore judge the admissibility of jokes, the propriety of revealing personal dispositions and attitudes. We know the extent to which the language used in the situation will be governed by social ritual. These considerations are so compelling, that if we are asked to imagine certain speakers engaged in conversation with others we can make predictions as to the type of language they will use, at least to the extent of being able to say what topics and expressions will *probably not occur*. Thus, we would no doubt accept the following exchange as a piece of verbal behaviour quite appropriate to the specified characters:

Milkman: Good morning, then, Mrs Finch. And how are you keeping?

Old Lady: Oh, my poor dear budgie passed away this morning, and I'm so upset. Well, it does upset you doesn't it?

Milkman: Oh dear, dear, dear. What a shame. Poor little fellow. This morning, you say? Well, well, never mind. Happens to us all, doesn't it. Happens to us all.

We would certainly be less ready to accept it as a slice of real-life language if the exchanges were ascribed to different characters, say a Sergeant-major and his Colonel, or a teacher and his headmaster, or even to the same old lady and her next-door neighbour, a middle-aged accountant. Sergeants and colonels do not, in their professional relationship and in the normal pursuance of their duties, discuss the death of a budgerigar; or if they do by any strange chance venture upon this unlikely topic, the language they use is likely to be rather different in style and tone from the language used by the milkman and the old lady. The same observation would apply to the other conversational partners suggested here, though the topic is more likely as a casual subject broached between a headmaster and a member of his staff, or as a matter of conversation between neighbours. Still, the fact remains that in each case the language used would be socially determined by factors of status, class, age, sex, formality, etc. These are variables over which a proficient script-writer can exercise a ready and intuitive command; if he fails to do so, indeed, his audience will reproach him for writing lifeless, or stilted, or absurd dialogue. He may sometimes, for fun or effect, flout the probabilities of the situation, creating, say a police constable who baffles his superiors with a Wildean elegance and wit, a docker who bewails, as he consumes his fourth maraschino cherry, the desperate fatigue of unloading pig-iron, or a bishop who conducts his theological discussions in the *argot* of the street-trader. But the very effectiveness of such occasional tricks of characterisation only serves to underline our point, that in the situations we have experience of in everyday life, we expect language which, allowing something for the play of individuality in vocabulary and idiom, answers the demands of propriety. We have more or less fixed ideas as to how people from various walks of life ought to talk. If, for example, I were set the task of writing a piece of dialogue in which two schoolmasters discuss the death of a budgerigar it is very likely that the result would look like this:

Assistant: Good morning, headmaster. I trust I find you well?

Headmaster: Ah, good morning, Peters. Yes, very well, thank you, though a little distrait, I'm afraid. Our budgerigar died this morning, A trivial event, of course, but one is upset, you know. One is upset.

Assistant: Of course. I'm so sorry, headmaster, Misfortunes are misfortunes, large or small.

Headmaster: It was a very small bird.

Assistant: ' Qui nunc it per iter tenebricosum illuc, unde negant redire quénquam.'

Headmaster: I don't quite –

Assistant: Catullus, headmaster. On the death of Lesbia's sparrow.

Headmaster: Ah yes. Very apt, Peters. Well, apt in some respects.

I must confess, in reference to this piece of home-baked comedy, that I have never in my life heard schoolmasters talking in quite this style, but the dialogue still seems to me to carry the warrant of social probability, or at any rate not to manifest any obvious social improbability. In much the same ignorant-knowing fashion I might forecast the probabilities of a Sergeant-major – Colonel exchange as follows:

Sergeant-major: Good-morning sir.

Colonel: Sarnt-major. Do you think you could manage not to stamp?

Sergeant-major: Sir.

Colonel: Not a good morning. Morning's a damned nuisance. Budgie died on us. Damn' bird.

Sergeant-major: Sir.

Colonel: Yes, sarnt-major, what is it? What are you after now?

Sergeant-major: With respect sir, sorry to hear about the budgie sir.

Colonel: Yes. Well. Damned disgrace. Buy a bird and it dies on you.

For all I know, there is not a colonel in the British army who uses the swear-word ' damned ', and my specimen dialogue may be ludicrous as a simulacrum of real Sergeant-major – Colonel relationships. On the other hand, I feel as certain as introspection can make me that headmasters talking to their juniors, or old ladies talking to milkmen, or accountants talking to old ladies, etc. would certainly not talk in this style whereas Colonels talking to Sergeants *might*.

The reader may object that all this dialogue-writing is well enough by way of amusement, but that inasmuch as it is not reported from the life it has no value as evidence. To which it can be replied that the important evidence is not the dialogue itself, but the implicit procedures of choosing and rejecting that go on in my mind as I attempt to compose these scraps of conversation. I have spent some time in the world, I have met old ladies, milkmen, soldiers, schoolteachers, accountants, I am conversant with the generally current attitudes towards these personages and professions, and consequently I have my own ideas as to the freedoms and limitations of their usage under various social conditions. My impressions, as realised in invented dialogues, may be quite unlike the actual language of particular old ladies or milkmen or colonels, but if they seem to a sufficient number of people to reflect convincingly the personalities, attitudes, and social relationships involved, then it may be presumed that my impressions answer to realities in the social determination of language. This is perhaps the ultimate answer to these stubborn literal folk who object to stage dialogue because ' people I know don't talk like that '. The task of a dramatist is not to make his dialogue match the language of people known by the members of his audience, but rather to make it seem commensurable with a given set of social determinants. If he shows a duchess in conversation with a chambermaid, his concern is to use language to establish credibly the distances and perspectives of the relationship, not to repeat the usage of duchesses and chambermaids he has actually known. But this is a digression, and we must return to our discussion of social determinants and individual freedoms.

It may have seemed hitherto that we are to reject or belittle the notion of individual freedom in language; that we are to assign to the individual will a role of minor importance, a mere walk-on part as compared with the great stage-possessing action of custom and social organisation. In fact, the individual has a good deal of linguistic freedom; he is certainly something more than a programmed robot producing a scheduled output in response to a given input. To understand where his freedoms lie, however, and how they are exercised, we have first to accept the fact that in his language the individual has a liaison with society which we may think of in terms of a contract. A legal contract carries with it certain benefits, while its breach invites certain penalities. The individual's unwritten and normally undefined linguistic contract also carries benefits and penalties of a sort, which we may discover by examining the ' terms ' of the contract.

Firstly we should state what benefits result from the observance of the contract. These may seem obvious; but unless we attempt to state them, we may gravely underestimate them, for in sum they are little less than life, liberty, and the pursuit of happiness. In return for his willingness to abide by ' rules ' or ' terms ' which, though unwritten, nonetheless have a contractual power, the Englishman is allowed to use the English language throughout the length and breadth of England (not to mention considerable territories elsewhere) in the prosecution of his affairs and in the control of his life. For this is at the heart of the contract, that language is the individual's principal aid in helping him to adapt himself to his surroundings, to make negotiable frontiers between himself and his fellows, to reconcile himself to his community and his fortunes.

These benefits follow upon the observance of a number of terms, some necessary and absolute, others conditional or relative. In the first place, as a necessary term, I am obliged in speaking to observe common rules of order and reference in the phonic, grammatical, and lexical make-up of the code. I do not choose my own sounds or determine their distribution; I do not invent constructions to suit the whim of the moment; and if I am wise I at least try to use words in the same way that other people use them. Of course I am perfectly free to resort to the gobbledegookery ineffaboil of scramblespeak, but if I do so I must be prepared to suffer the penalty of not being understood. I must be prepared, that is to say, for something more than the inconvenience of being merely *misunderstood;* I will not be understood at all, I will not achieve *any* meaning whatsoever within the understanding of a partner in discourse. I am naturally free to use the vocabulary of the tribe as colourfully as I choose. I may even invent words, provided that I supply clues of language or situation clear enough to explain the meaning of my invention; but if I invent too intensively and supply no clues, I will have broken the fairly generous terms of my contract, and I will not be understood. Lewis Carroll could write

> Twas brillig and the slithy toves
> Did gyre and gimble in the wabe
> All mimsy were the borogoves,
> And the mome raths outgrabe.

thereby perpetrating a piece of comic verse which any cultivated
Englishman knows and *understands* – but it is known and understood
because in his narrative Carroll himself explains its secrets, and it is
acceptable, initially, because its setting is the setting of a fantasy
world, just as Joyce's word-inventions and semantic double-takes are
language appropriate to the dream-world or the world of the psyche.*

Such liberties are less easily tolerated in the ' ordinary ' language-
guided situation. If I approach a friend working in his garden and
cry out *Lube all your doofers cully,* then neither the grammar of my
utterance nor its lexicon can be sufficiently clear for him to relate
them to a situation, and so construct a meaning. If I say *Lube all
your doofers properly,* a grammatical structure, at least, emerges; and
if I say *Prune all your doofers properly,* I leave him with the
relatively simple task of identifying the reference of *doofers.* My
formulation may still be a trifle slipshod, but at least I will have made
an effort to respect linguistic convention. Some effort is always
demanded if we are to use language intelligibly, but we accept this
effort because of what we are able to achieve by it; symbolising gets
results, so we go to the trouble of symbolising according to the common practice. Occasionally there are situations in which we feel that
words can achieve no result worth the effort of finding them; we may
prefer, in such instances, to scream, to strike, to gibber, to break
things. But if we wish to achieve the objective control of our affairs
which only symbolising can attain for us, then we must not break
that condition of our contract which demands that we use the same
linguistic symbols as everybody else in our community, and in the
same distributions and references.

Not to be understood is one form of contractual penalty. Another,
slightly different, form of penalty is to be misconstrued. This, too, is
the result of a failure to symbolise in accordance with common convention, but in the case of the misconstrued, as opposed to the unin-
telligible, utterance, the failure is not deliberate on the part of the
speaker and is not initially detected by the listener. Both parties act
in good faith. The speaker innocently supposes himself to be making
accurate use of common symbols, whilst the listener obligingly applies
the speaker's utterance to the only reference or range of references
that seem possible under the circumstances. Thus, if I allow my pronunciation of the word *soap* to approach too closely to that of *soup,*

* It is of course acceptable because underneath the lexical strangeness there
are familiarities of grammatical and phonetic structure.

I am going to get the wrong results if I go into a shop and apparently ask for a packet of *soup-powder,* when I want *soap-powder.* The fact that *soup-powder* is quite possible in the context of a grocer's shop means that my error will go undetected at the first exchange and will only become apparent when the assistant begins to ask questions about the kind of soup I want. Of course, if my request should be for *toilet soup* or *soup flakes,* or a *bar of carbolic soup* the oddity of my speech would be immediately obvious, and the assistant might well supply my wants without being at all confused, or even particularly struck by the ambiguous tendency of my pronunciation. Many misunderstandings are eliminated or precluded by the fact that we have, so to speak, two bearings on meaning, one from the context of situation, the other from the context of words. If one of these bearings should prove ill-defined or unreliable, we may be satisfied as to the accuracy of the other. However, we are not entitled to rely under all circumstances on this linguistic double-checking. Even though the language-code must sometimes betray us into ambiguities and misconstructions, we have to be able to make the general assumption that it will be adequate to our needs; and we cannot make this assumption unless we respect the structural principles of the code.

The code at all its levels is a balanced economy of oppositions, of Xs and not-Xs. The sound-system, for example, is such an economy; interference with its balance at any one point may necessitate adjusting the balance at other points, lest the whole system should fall together. If the pronunciation of *bay* begins to shift, say, in the direction of the the pronunciation of *buy,* then the pronunciation of *buy* must in its turn begin to shift, perhaps in the direction of *boy.* Make one change in the economy, and others became necessary; in some limited areas there may be a sort of general post.* Only by keeping the linguistic economy in balance can verbal ' meaning ' be maintained. It may be for this reason that phonetic change tends to be rather stubbornly, sometimes polemically, resisted; the speakers of a language may have an instinctive awareness of the fact that one change leads to many.

Of course this is a fact of grammar and lexis as well as of phonetics. I am obliged to maintain careful distinctions between grammatical constructions which imply different modes of reference –

---

* There is an example of such a ' general post ' in the history of English. It is known as the ' great vowel-shift '. *Bloomfield & Newmark, III, 26,* p. 233-34

for example, I distinguish between *I was writing a letter this morning* and *I wrote a letter this morning*. And naturally I accept and follow common practice in differentiating the references of lexical terms, so that I distinguish between a *desk* and a *table*, or even between a *desk* and a *writing-table*. These distinctions are currently important in the economy of English, but it does not follow from this that they are absolute or immutable. I am told that in the English spoken in Nigeria the distinction between *I wrote* and *I was writing* tends to be merely stylistic; and one can imagine that in some communities the distinction between *desk* and *writing-table* might be a meaningless refinement. However, the fact remains that in so-called Standard English it is necessary to maintain a distinction of pronunciation between *soap* and *soup,* to observe distinct applications of the simple and progressive verb-forms, to keep distinct the references of *table* and *desk,* and likewise in a thousand-and-one specific points to maintain the structure of distinctions on which the code has to depend if it is to operate for us, in our time, in our culture. If we fail to maintain one of these distinctions, ambiguity may result; and not so far behind ambiguity there lurks the fear of chaos, of a state in which the code will cease to work. The normative fury which possesses some defenders of ' pure ' or ' correct ' English may in many cases be attributable to such a fear.

That we should accept the symbolic ordinances, and that we should not disturb the balance of the symbolic economy, are two necessary terms of our linguistic contract with society. Other terms are conditional; to break them will not mean the collapse of communication, but under certain conditions and in certain social relationships it may be that the right to communicate will be withdrawn and only grudgingly admitted. One such conditional term is to be observed in commonly resistant attitudes towards linguistic innovation. We have already suggested a motive for this resistance that the whole balance of some portion of the symbolic code may be under threat. There are, however, other motives which have more to do with our feelings for the cohesion and tradition of our society than with the actual efficiency of language. It is natural that we should maintain and defend our social institutions with some passion, for if institutions are allowed to fall through carelessness from within or incursion from without, how can we feel sure of our identity as individuals, how can we be secure in our social roles, how can we bear the necessary conviction that our community is organised to promote the excellence towards which generations of our forefathers have struggled? How can we be satisfied, in short, that we are 'the people' and that our ways are the right ways?

Now language is also a social institution, the object and repository of much lore and tradition. It is representative of the culture and achievements of the tribe, and it must therefore be protected against the impertinent devices of the foreigner and the undisciplined native. English newspapers regularly carry letters complaining about the subversive effects on the mother tongue of slovenly usage – the so-called 'intrusive r' is a favourite target – and, worse, of malign Americanisms. A reader's letter in the *Daily Telegraph* (20.11.1967) contains the following typical outburst: 'I am disgusted to note that on BBC Radio 1 we continue to hear such peculiar Americanisms as 'a half after six' and 'twenty before seven'. What is wrong with 'half past six' and 'twenty to seven'? Moreover, why 'right now' instead of 'now' – two words instead of one with precisely the same meaning?' This letter represents quite well the strategy of protest common in such cases. Words like 'disgusted' and 'peculiar' betray the inherently emotional and irrational character of the letter-writer's objections, which, however, are opportunely huddled into the guise of a specious rationality – e.g. 'two words instead of one with precisely the same meaning'. Complaints and criticisms of this kind (a good anthology could very quickly be put together by any regular reader of the correspondence columns of our newspapers) are generally based upon ostensible grounds of logic or aesthetics, grounds to which they very rarely have much title; they have a much deeper psychological base in the individual's feeling that his security, dignity, identity, are invested in the saving of a collective face. Not all individuals have this feeling, but its expression can be powerful to the point of vindictiveness, and it is dangerous for the would-be innovator to risk too sharp a challenge to the little linguistic orthodoxies of our society. Idiom and construction change very slowly in the face of a conservatism which regards sudden and sharp innovation, however intelligible or useful, as a species of betrayal, and which also regards in this light too great a readiness to accept change from outside the culture.

To be castigated for linguistic subversiveness is the contractual penalty visited upon those who would innovate too boldly and too blatantly, or who would dare to copy the habits of an alien people. There is a related form of penalty which is worth distinguishing because it is more subtly levied. This is the penalty of suspicion; and it is laid upon the person who is too much of an individual in his use of language, even though he may respect the symbolic conventions, observe the economy, and never attempt to innovate. Poets, satirists, wits, ironists, and even plain truthful people often come under this ban. The case is frequently that the individual takes and uses some language form in a sense or application rather different from that in which it is used by the community at large. This difference of usage may simply mean that the individual is trying to be more accurate or more thoughtful than those around him; but to the community at large this may look like a form of criticism, and criticism breaks one of the terms of the unwritten contract which says that you may not, by your own language, implicitly criticise the common usage of the community. If, for instance, I use the word *aggravate* in its strict sense of ' to add to the gravity of ', ' to make worse ', I may compliment myself on the accuracy of my usage, but I need not expect admiration from my neighbour who uses the word in the very common, though unetymological, sense of ' to annoy ', ' to irritate ', ' to exacerbate '. It is not good to be thought a pedant; pedants are outsiders. Even the clown, a privileged insider, must take due care. He may challenge social usage, but he must be sure that the challenge is not made with a vivacity that might be taken for wholeheartedness. We may recall here Sir John Falstaff's remarks on the subject of the word *honour*:

> . . . honour pricks me on; yea, but how if honour prick me off when I come on? how then? Can honour set to a leg? No. Or an arm? No. Or take away the grief of a wound? No. Honour hath skill in surgery then? No. What is honour? A word. What is in that word honour? What is that honour? Air. A trim reckoning. Who hath it? He that died a Wednesday. Doth he feel it? No. Doth he hear it? No . . .*

This is a deadly exercise in general semantics, a sermon on the vanity of mistaking words for things. Falstaff takes a word, *honour* and holds it up to question, exposing its pretentions in a way completely at variance with the cultural acceptance of that word in Elizabethan times – the acceptance illustrated in this play (*Henry IV,* Part 1) by the character of Hotspur. Falstaff is allotted the role of the insider with special privileges, but suspicion mounts against him, and in the

* Shakespeare, *Henry IV. Part 1*, IV, ii, 131.

end he suffers the cruel and lonely death of the outcast. We lesser creatures may hope to be spared Falstaff's penalty when we are seemingly too critical in our use of language; but we must expect to be exiled to the bleak confines of some despised palisade, to be rejected as ' intellectuals ' ' eggheads ' or ' smart Alecs '.

Another conditional term is the expectation that we shall observe a linguistic usage appropriate to the company we keep. There are certain words and expressions we do not use in the drawing-room. On the other hand, in some companies these same words and expressions might be socially *de rigeur*, and to omit them could be to risk mockery and humiliation. To be a non-swearing man in aggressively male societies such as the barrack-room or the mess-deck may expose one to suspicion and contempt. In a sergeants' mess it might be possible to make the request *Pass the salt* in the brisk tones of military command, but at a college high table a very different intonation would have to be used, and the utterance would have to be accompanied by the signal *Please*. To deviate from this form would be to risk being considered ill-mannered, and possibly to have one's company shunned. Of course, it is not to be supposed that any of us is so devoid of individual self-regard that he surrenders himself completely to the linguistic *mores* of whatever company he happens to be in; but it is probably the case that we always accept the habits of the company, insofar as the acceptance is consistent with our self-esteem and that we certainly do what we can to avoid or suppress practices that would not meet with the full approval of the company. In this respect we may be said to have a series of special agreements which acquire or lose force as we move from one sub-cultural environment to another.

These various conditions imply such limitations on individual freedom that we may ask whether any individuality in language is truly possible, or whether in our speech we do not always respond predictably to social and conventional pressures. Now of course there is a framework of predictability because we desire it and because language could not work without it; we accept the ' conventional pressures ' because they create the working power of language. But ' predictability ' does not eliminate the element of choice. Given that certain types of utterance are predictable within a situation, and given that the individual accepts the social pressure to produce a response, it is still open to him to express his individuality by making specific choices. For example, if I am asked *How's your father?*, it

may be predicted that I will produce a response of the type *He's well*
or *He's ill*. Such a prediction on the part of the questioner does not,
however, limit me to an actual choice. I may say *Fine thanks,* or *He's
thriving* or *Blossoming,* or *He's hale and hearty,* or *Pretty spritely,*
or *A bit down in the dumps,* or *Shaky,* or *Up and down,* or *Not quite
himself,* etc., etc. – the range of actual choices is considerable. The
factor of predictability relates to the *type* of utterance produced; the
specific choice lies within the power and discretion of the individual,
and in some instances language may be so rich in specific variations
on the typological theme, that the speaker need have no sense that
his language is rigidly determined by the situation. He should of
course be aware that his actual choices make some difference to the
situation, in expressing and directing its personal and interpersonal
attitudes. If the parish priest asks me, with due solemnity, *How's
your father?* and I reply *He's remarkably spritely for his age,* I have
made a particular choice within the type *He is well,* a choice which
might be thought to be adequate and proper to the situation. On the
other hand, should I reply *Kicking around like a rambunctious old
ram,* I will have made another specific choice within the general type,
but this time a choice the adequacy and propriety of which may be
held in question. It perhaps does not reflect socially acceptable attitudes towards the parish priest or towards the subject of our conversation. Utterances of this kind are tactless, or, as one might perhaps
say, linguistically irresponsible. To be irresponsible in this way is
always open to me; it is part of my freedom in language, and indeed
there may be situations which call for the exercise of such freedom.
But I also win a kind of freedom by accepting and manifesting
responsibility; the kind of freedom that results from carefully maintaining the balance of a situation instead of breaking it down by a
deliberately anarchical choice.

That linguistic anarchy has its uses there is no doubt; and we
have ingenious advocates for it, in the guise of specially-accredited
persons enjoying a traditionally honoured privilege of living both
inside and outside the contract. Some of these inside-outsiders are
comedians, clowns. There is an element of linguistic anarchy in the
most threadbare and greybearded of jokes, e.g.

> *My wife has gone to the West Indies?*
> *– Jamaica?*
> *No, she went of her own accord.*

or:

Do you serve crabs here?
— We serve anyone, sit down.

The comedian makes a blatant assault on a phonetic distinction or deliberately assigns a word to the wrong lexical category, and far from objecting, we gladly accord him the privilege of flouting linguistic conditions which the rest of us have to observe. He enjoys the privilege because his ingenious and carefully-calculated assaults on the symbolic convention make us laugh. But they do something more than that; they remind us constantly that the convention *is* only a convention, that it is not an immutable bond of law, that it may be teased and tampered with, and that we ourselves may, if we so choose, play truant from the routine of customary speech. This same lesson may also be demonstrated for us by the genius of the poet. He, too, is the outsider on the inside, the anarchist who relies on the conventions. He may take cavalier liberties with the syntax of the language, though he never pursues liberty to the point of total disorder; he proclaims, through word-play, image, and metaphor, his right to reassess the values of the lexicon; he may even triumphantly assert his privileged status with some turn of language that directly challenges one or other of the 'terms' of our unwritten conract. Thus, when T. S. Eliot describes, at the beginning of *Prufrock,* the streets

> . . . that follow like a tedious argument
> Of insidious intent
> To lead you to an overwhelming question

his posture is not that of meek everyman accepting the common usage of his fellows, but rather that of the angel-visited pedant who proclaims — 'behold! I remind you that *insidious* is derived from *insidiae,* meaning an ambush, and lest you have forgotten the etymology, let my cunningly-placed epithet *overwhelming* restore your jaded memory'. And instead of ridiculing the pedant for his precious scruples, we are exhilarated, we have a sense of release and adventure, as though the poet's words had magically re-disposed the elements of a familiar landscape.

Clown and poet are spokesmen for the individual's rights in language. The clown demonstrates a manner of rebellion for law-abiding men; the poet 'sings in his chains, like the sea'.* From them we learn such arts and devices as enable us to play within the confines of usage;

* Dylan Thomas, *Fern Hill*: 'Time held me green and dying Though I sang in my chains like the sea.'

our slang, our catch-words, our joke-forms, though they may in the long run become as dutiful as a uniform, at least begin in comic-poetic spirit of refusal to accept without question our language and its usage. One of many values of literature is that it puts language to the question; it demonstrates the possibility of enlarging our linguistic freedom. Literature performs another important service for the individual. In the face of the crises and trials of life, the literary artist devises powerful structures of words which enable him to cope with pain, bereavement, disillusionment – or which, for that matter, enable him to give expression to joy and hope. For the rest of us these inventions can become socially valuable, as forms having a ritual power. A religious ritual has the effect of stilling our anxieties and giving expression to our aspirations. We should not, of course, expect poetry to discharge the functions of religion; but all the same, poetry may have the ritual efficacy of religion in providing formulae which enable man to reconcile himself to his predicaments. This is even true of the debased poetry – the *poesy,* to use a word ingeniously called into service by John Ciardi – of the popular song.* The music-hall audience or the dance-floor clientele who sing the maudlin words of some popular ballad, may sing with conviction because for them the words express an acceptance of the transience of man, a faith in the enduring power of love, an affirmation of the individual's dignity and worth. ' The pygmy plan ', says William Empson, ' is one note each, and the tune goes out free '.†

So it is with the poems we learn by heart, so it is with the choruses we sing. The words provided by the poet or song-writer are words

* ' How do you the reader, distinguish between your responses to a very bad portrait of dear old Aunt Jane, and a very good one of Old Skinflint, the gentleman who holds your mortgage? The question is one that splits the reading audience straight down the middle. The tenacity with which the ladies of the poetry society will hold on to Aunt Jane with a bluebird in her hair, and the persistence with which they reject all-that-is-not-bluebirds, reaches so far into the problem of a satisfactory approach to poetry . . . that it has been necessary to evolve two terms: *poetry* for that which exists as an art form, *poesy* for that which exists as the sentimental bluebird in Aunt Jane's hair.' John Ciardi (ed) *Mid-Century American Poets,* (Twayne Publishers Inc. New York, 1950), p. XIX.

† The last line and a half of a sonnet, the sestet of which runs:
  A more heartening fact about the cultures of man
  Is their appalling stubborness. The sea
  Is always calm three fathoms down. The gigantic anthropological
    circus riotously
  Holds open all its booths. The pygmy plan
  Is one note each and the tune goes out free.

written by individuals and designed to meet the crises of individuality. And, indeed, we feel them individually; ' the tune goes out free ' – we sing the chorus or recite the poem as though song and poem had been meant for us alone. But the true poem and the good song are public property. Singing the chorus is a collective act, reciting the poem is a ceremonial observance. Initially, there is nothing more assertive of individualism than the language of literary creation; ultimately there is nothing that expresses more powerfully the cohesion of a society. When language becomes an art, whether the high art of sonnets or the low art of wisecracks, the individual achieves his meed of tears and bellylaughs precisely because he understands so well the conventions by which his unconventionality is defined. Having this understanding, he has all the freedom he can expect to achieve. We are always confronted with the proposition which forms the title of this chapter – *social determination versus individual expression*. About ' social determination ' there is not much we can do – it exists. About the ' individual expression ', we can only express our hope that it might always be possible. All we can do is to try to discover the conditions under which *versus* can be transformed into *plus*.

Empson comments: ' This *free* I am afraid only sounds an offensively false use of the great emotive term, implying merely that the pygmies and the rest of us had better be " left alone ". This may be true of pygmies, but I was trying to give the word the impact of a contradiction . . .' the contradiction being between individual creativeness and organised, collective culture. William Empson *Collected Poems* (Harcourt Brace, New York, 199), pp. 86, 113.

5 Trial by Language

One of the incidental characteristics of language is that it provokes the classifying judgements and prejudices that are called forth by any other form of social behaviour, but does so, it would seem, with a peculiar immediacy and force. The 'incidental characteristic' thereby becomes a central fact of great social importance; our language puts us on trial. Furthermore, society insists almost bitterly on the upholding of trial procedures. When the Swedes carried out a fairly modest spelling reform, at the beginning of the present century or thereabouts, the translator and scholar Erland Lagerlöf expressed particular annoyance at the dropping of a phonetically otiose *d* from the spelling of the past participle. 'Why', he remarked, 'now there's no way of knowing whether one's dealing with an educated or an uneducated person.'*

Lagerlöf's mandarin attitude towards the proprieties of the written code is one which most of us would probably uphold. Such is the social and cultural preeminence of writing, such is its fundamental importance in our educational system and the structure of our institutions, that it has acquired almost a moral grandeur, an aura of virtue. We cannot feel, for instance, that the word *physiognomy* might more easily be spelt *fizzyonomy;* easy it might be, but it is also red-nosed and subversive and unwashed. Of course, we would never put it quite like that; but what we feel at heart is probably something hardly less emphatic. This general allegiance to writing makes all the more pitiful the grubby sorrows of those of us who have known and resented that other kind of linguistic trial, trial by speech. It is the fashion now to say that on the whole this is a thing of the past, that no one now judges a man by his accent. But how many northern

* Gathered from an essay by Algot Werin in the pamphlet entitled *Erland Lagerlöf, Homerosöversättaren* (Lund: C. W. K. Gleerups Förlag, 1958).

Englishmen, aspiring to honours and promotions, can say in all truth that their hearts have never quailed when public speech has confronted them with the negotiation of a *one* or a *put*? And would even the most objective and unbiased of southerners be ready to assert that no connotations of class and background accrue to pronunciations like *drawring* or *bruvver*? These things give evidence against us; try as we will to conceal that evidence, there is always the unguarded moment when concealment must fail.

But perhaps 'trial' is after all too drastic a word. We do not condemn each other to guillotine or galley for the sake of a double negative or a divergent dipthong. It is not a sentencing we are after, but a sizing-up, a probation – a trial in that sense. Such a trial takes place with every new acquaintance we make; and it is of course a matter of trial and counter-trial, so that we are both on the bench and in the dock. It can hardly be said that these arraignments-at-language are governed by the observance of rigorously impartial norms. We grow, inevitably, in the climate of prejudice, and we carry in our heads certain social stereotypes which we commonly relate to language, e.g. concepts of refinement, vulgarity, gentlemanliness, boorishness, urbanity, rusticity. It does not follow, of course, that these stereotypes and their linguistic correlates are the same for all of us, even though we may like to imagine that our individual or local preoccupations are valid throughout the land. The pronunciations, intonations, vocabulary choices, which the northern Englishman relates to his stereotype of 'snobbish' may be just those which the southerner allocates to the concept of refinement; and aspects of speech which the southerner finds 'blunt' or 'brusque' may to the northerner carry the voucher of sincerity. It is often said that a man's speech tells us a lot about him, but it would perhaps be nearer to the mark to say that it refers him to a place in our own system of prejudice. The need to 'place' people in a social scheme is important; prejudice, great or small, is perhaps an inevitable concomitant of this need. We can best neutralise it by being aware that a linguistic assessment of others is also a revelation of ourselves, possibly in none too attractive a light. A personal judgement is a camera which also photographs the cameraman.

When we make a new acquaintance, we seek, consciously or unconsciously, for evidence that will enable us to assign him to a place in the world as we see it. Some of this evidence is of course provided by our observations of his material possessions, e.g. his clothes, his house, the sort of car he drives, while some emerges from our consideration of his physical appearance, habits, and gestures. But on the whole such evidence tends to be subordinate to the prior testimony of language. The witness of language is manifold. In the first place, it helps us to answer the question ' where does he come from?' The importance of an answer to such a question is not that it should be accurate in terms of dialectology, but that it should minister to the craving for a stereotype. In England, we have an artificial norm of pronunciation, known as RP (Received Pronunciation) or *Standard English,* the apparent purpose of which is to elude stereotyping by effacing clues as to regional origin. RP (which is discussed at greater length a little later in this chapter) would seem to ignore the question ' where does he come from?' and imply, instead, the question ' is he educated?' or ' is he one of the governors and administrators in the institutions of our society?' The millions of people who do not speak RP either practise a modified Standard in solution of some personal and local social problem, or cleave to their regional dialects. These regional speech-forms are of course numerous, and provide a vast and fascinating field of study for dialectologists.

For those of us who are not dialectologists, however, the most important consideration is not dialect type so much as dialect stereotype. Our ears are crudely trained to a rough social gamut. For instance, we all have a more or less keen awareness of the social values attached to the speech variants current in our own neighbourhood. In every town and city there is a speech-form which is associated with the nob-end and a form which is associated with the yob-end, a form which anxious parents seek to keep their children from acquiring. Similarly, in every rural district or larger urban locality, there is an awareness of the speech-habits which distinguish Them and Us, proving Our superiority and Their wretchedness. Every little Athens looks down on a little Boeotia. This local pattern re-emerges in the larger scale of national stereotypes. It is fairly safe to say that the average Englishman is conscious of some varieties of English spoken beyond the actual borders of England – varieties to which he attaches stereotypes expressive of national prejudices – and also of some dialect types occurring within the confines of his own country. His consciousness of these is as a rule rather crude, and his language-map of the whole country is probably constituted by a few broad territories, for example, ' North Country ', ' West Country ', and ' London ', or ' The South '; to these it is possible that he may add one or two recognisable urban dialect areas, e.g. ' Brum ' or ' Scouse ' or ' Geordie '. These crude perceptions of dialect type are associated with more or less complex social judgements which make them stereotypes. A primary feature of the stereotype is the ranking of the dialect types against the assumed norm of Standard English, and the consequent emergence of a scale of relatively acceptable and unacceptable dialects. Obviously, the values of such a scale are relative and idiosyncratic; much depends on where the scale-maker happens to live, and what his personal or inherited prejudices happens to be. There is, however, some consensus of agreement about the broader stereotypes, as might appear if we were to consult certain forms of entertainment such as popular novels or television plays. It is worth trying to describe a few obvious stereotypes; the English reader may care to note how far the descriptions given below correspond with his own impressions.

The south-eastern dialect type and stereotype which includes Cockney and all its suburban gradations happens to coincide regionally with an area which is in effect the heartland of Standard English. This coincidence has affected the general stereotype of south-eastern popular English. Few people seem to regard the forms of English spoken in the urban areas of Kent or Essex as genuine dialects. These speech forms appear to be thought of as a kind of ' off-white ' Standard English, manifesting ' sloppy vowels ' and implying the tawdry ambitions of the social *parvenu*. The south-east, like any other area, certainly has its rural dialects and its local variations, but these are not widely known. The speech-form which above all satisfies the craving for a stereotype is Cockney; this is made to play Leporello to the Don Giovanni of RP – or perhaps it would be more appropriate to say Sam Weller to RP's Pickwick. Cockney – to which many of us would almost automatically attribute such commendations as ' cheerful ', ' irrepressible ', ' self-reliant ', etc. – has in British cultural tradition been stereotyped as the dialect of the stage corporal or the well-tempered barmaid. It is the speech of sturdy and valiant servants. Some authors, by way of elaborate jest, have created servants whose spoken Standard is more deliberately immaculate than that of their masters – for instance, P. G. Wodehouse's imperishable Jeeves, or Dorothy L. Sayers' Bunter. The whole point of these excellent creations is that they defy, and indeed reverse, the conventions of the stereotype; the servant speaks with his master's voice. In this role, Jeeves is never less than perfect, but Bunter, at one point in his career, goes mildly off Standard, and in a fit of passion (excusable, since it concerns the condition of some precious bottles of port) reveals his true accents and origins:

> Bunter controlled himself with difficulty. The cases had been left in the pantry for safety. The police were in and out of the cellar, but, by all the laws of England, a man's pantry was his own. He said in a trembling voice:
>
> 'You have not, I trust, handled any of the other bottles?'
>
> 'Only to unpack 'em and set 'em right side up,' Mrs Ruddle assured him cheerfully. ' Them cases'll come in 'andy for kindling.'
>
> ' Gawdstrewth!' cried Bunter. The mask came off him all in one piece, and nature, red in tooth and claw, leapt like a tiger from ambush.
>
> ' Gawdstrewth! Would you believe it? All his lordship's vintage port!' He lifted shaking hands to heaven. ' You lousy old nosy-parking bitch! You ignorant, interfering old bizzen! Who told you to go poking your long nose into my pantry?'
>
> ' Really, Mr Bunter!' said Mrs Ruddle.
>
> ' Go it,' said Crutchley, with relish. ' Ere's someone at the front door.'
>
> ' Op it out of here!' stormed Bunter, unheeding, ' before I take the skin off you!'
>
> ' Well, I'm sure! Ow was I to know?'
>
> ' Get out!'
>
> Mrs Ruddle retired, but with dignity.
>
> ' Such manners!'
>
> ' Put yer flat foot right into it that time, Ma,' observed Crutchley. He grinned. Mrs Ruddle turned in the doorway.
>
> ' People can do their own dirty work after this ', she remarked, witheringly, and departed.
>
> Bunter took up the violated bottle of port and cradled it mournfully in his arms.
>
> ' All the port! All the port! Two and a half dozen, all shook up to blazes! And his lordship bringing it down in the back of the car, driving as tender and careful as if it was a baby in arms.'*

Such an enormous lapse requires explanation; and subsequently we are given a glimpse into Bunter's past life, a glimpse which reveals him as the stereotypical sergeant-in-a-tail-coat:

* Dorothy L. Sayers, *Busman's Honeymoon* (London: Gollancz, 1950), pp. 204-5 and pp. 282-3.

Harriet asked to be told about Bunter.

' Well ', said the Duchess, ' he was a footman at Sir John Sander-
ton's before the War and he was in Peter's unit . . . sergeant or
something eventually . . . but they were in some – what's that
American word for a tight place? – jam isn't it – yes, some jam or
other together and took a fancy to one another . . . so Peter
promised Bunter that, if they both came out of the War alive,
Bunter should come to him . . .'

So much for the credentials of an English Leporello. (So much, too,
for Dorothy Sayers' stereotype of an upper-class Englishwoman, model
1937; the Duchess' reluctant cognisance of ' that American word '
now seems quaint and scarcely credible.)

The stereotype of northern English is on the whole unflattering.
Indeed, there is significant evidence in our literature that throughout
our cultural history the more remote dialects – remote, that is from
the south-eastern heartland of Standard – have been regarded as
rugged, barbarous and comic, fit speech for buffoons and brutes in the
cultural foothills. When Geoffrey Chaucer wished to portray a couple
of likely lads fit to be taken in by a conniving miller, he said all that
needed to be said about them by giving them a northern dialect. The
speech he assigns to them is a species of fourteenth-century stage
Yorkshire, but the stereotype rings true enough, down to the blunt
northern manner of their revenge:

> ' This lange night ther tydes me na reste;
>   But yet, nafors, al sal be for the beste,
>   For, John,' seyde he ' als evere moot I thryve,
>   If that I may, yon wenche wil I swyve.
>   Som esement has lawe yshapen us;
>   For, John, ther is a lawe that says thus,
>   That gif a man in a point be agreved,
>   That in another he sal be releved.
>   Our corn is stoln, sothly, it is na nay,
>   And we han had an il fit al this day;
>   And syn I sal have neen amendement
>   Agayn my los, I wil have esement.
>   By Goddes sale, it sal neen other bee! '*

' By Goddes sale, it sal neen other bee ' – or, as the modern

* Chaucer, *The Reeve's Tale*, ll. 255 ff.

stereotype would have it, ' Ee ba goom, ah will an' all!' The tradition
of the barbarous north is a long-standing one. It was remarked on in
the fourteenth century by Ranulph Higden, whose Latin *Polychronicon*
was translated by a West-Countryman, John of Trevisa. A particularly
noteworthy paragraph in Trevisa's translation reads:

> Al þe longage of þe Norþumbres, & specialych at ȝork, ys so
> scharp, slyttynge & frotyng, & unschape, þat we Souþeron men may
> þat longage vnneþe undurstonde. Y trowe þat þat ys bycause
> þat a buþ nyȝ to strange men and aliens þat spekeþ strangelych,
> and also bycause þat þe kynges of Engelonde woneþ alwey fer
> fram þat contray; and gef a goþ to þe norþ contray, a goþ wiþ
> grete helpe & strengthe. Þe cause why a buþ more in þe souþ
> contray þan in þe norþ may be, betre cornlond, more people, more
> noble cytes, & more profýtable hauenes.

(All the speech of the northerners, and specially at York, is so abrupt,
piercing, harsh, and outlandish, that we Southerners can scarcely
understand it. I believe this to be because they live near to strangers
and foreigners with alien speech, and because the kings of England
always stay away from that region; and if the king does go there, he
goes with a great retinue. The reasons why our kings choose to dwell
in the south rather than the north may be, better arable land, a larger
population, finer cities, and more profitable ports.)

The attitudes implied in this shrewd piece of social analysis are still
very largely current. Northern speech still presents itself to many
southerners as ' scharp, slyttyng, & frotyng, and unschape ', or at any
rate as a means of communication only for money-grubbing mill-
owners, fiercely forthright matrons, and gradely (if mildly moronic)
lads. The stereotype is so powerful that we have more or less unconscious notions of subjects proper for northern speech. Let the reader
imagine certain lecture-topics, e.g. The fluctuations of bank-rate, The
history of the cooperative movement, The design of small marine
diesel engines, Stravinsky's rhythmic originality, Pointillisme, The
technique of Augustan verse; and let him imagine the voices of a
series of potential lecturers. No doubt he could conceive of a lecture
on economics or social history or mechanics being delivered in a ripe
Bruddersford accent, but does the imagination yield so readily when
the subject is the *Le Sacré du Printemps,* or the painting of Seurat,
or the epistles of Alexander Pope? The fact that there are plenty of

---

* See R. Morris and W. W. Skeat, *Specimens of Early English* (Oxford,
1884), II, p. 242.

cultivated northerners dedicated to the study (and even the production) of music, painting, and poetry, does nothing to disturb a stereotype proceeding from that centralisation of our culture which is manifested in the very phenomenon of Standard.

West-Country speech has perhaps been slightly better placed than northern English in our cultural perspectives. It has the advantage of being thought ' nice ' and ' countryfied ', whereas northern speech is ' harsh ' and ' abrupt ', – connoting the black desolations of the Industrial Revolution with its upstart capitalists – men like the ironmaster Mr Rouncewell, in Dickens' *Bleak House,* who inspired in Sir Lester Dedlock such misgivings about the security of the old order. The south-western stereotype is far less grim. The speech of the south west suggests cricket-commentators, gardeners, rosy-cheeked farmers, benign fishermen, and other tolerant, amiable, and unhurried individuals. It is for most of us the holiday dialect, the speech-sound of the idle summer. It is wholesome and humble, the language of the contented peasantry, not of the hard-mouthed workers who give trouble up at t' mill. On the whole, the picture is flattering. However, the western speech-style is remote from the capital and the heartland of Standard, and it has not escaped ridicule as the dialect of hayseeds and slow-grinding rustic wits. When Shakespeare's Edgar wished to conceal his identity and ward off danger behind the guise of a rock-solid rustic stubborness, he chose to affect speech of the south-western type;

Oswald: Wherefore, bold peasant,
       Dar'st thou support a publish'd traitor? Hence;
       Lest that infection of his fortune take
       Like hold on thee. Let go his arm.
Edgar: Chill not let go, zur, without vurther 'casion.
Oswald: Let go, slave, or thou diest.
Edgar: Good gentleman, go your gait, and let poor volk pass.
       An chud ha' bin zwaggered out of my life, 'twould
       not ha' bin zo long as 'tis by a vortnight. Nay, come
       not near th' old man; keep our, che vor ye, or
       ise try whether your costard or my ballow be the harder.
       Chill be plain with you.
Oswald: Out, dunghill!
Edgar: Chill pick your teeth, zur. Come; no matter vor your
       foins.*

* Shakespeare, *King Lear,* IV, 6, 236ff.

The same tones of rustic implacability (and as outrageously hammed) have since been heard from scores of grease-painted landlords and stage-policemen. It is a dialect which is the staple of the otherwise wearily unfunny rustic joke:

Willum: Ja-a-an, what did'ee give yewer 'orse whan 'e wur tewk zick, loike?

Jan: Oi gave 'un turp'ntoine.

Willum: Funnee-ee. Oi gave *moine* turpn'toine, 'n 'e *do-oied.*

Jan: A-a-ar, Soo did moine!

The real point of this dear old chestnut, one suspects, is not so much the draconic and laconic nature of rustic veterinarians as simply that *turpentine* is pronounced *turp'ntoine.*

It is more than possible that a reader with experience of English speech will have accepted some of the suggestions made in these essays on stereotype as accurate and have rejected others as inaccurate. However, considerations of accuracy or inaccuracy play little part in the creation and circulation of such images. The important thing seems to be to satisfy a psychological need to place a speaker against a background, and so an inaccurate or blatantly prejudiced stereotype may be preferred to the absence of any sort of social correlate. This observation also applies to another kind of speech-evaluation, the assessment, on the evidence of language, of a person's social class. A necessary constituent in our mental image of a person is some sort of information well- or ill-founded, as to his position in the class-rankings of our society. How we derive such information from impressions of speech is a question which defies a simple answer. It is as difficult to state objectively and systematically how I, as an Englishman, assess linguistic evidence of the probable class and background of other Englishmen as it is to say just how I know what emotional and attitudinal implications reside within a particular intonation pattern. In either event I recall the scattered details of past experience and match them against the specific circumstances of an emergent context. It is thus not easy to state any general principles for what may be, after all, a highly impressionistic and subjective process.

As far as pronunciation is concerned, it is probable that I pay some attention to certain key words containing sounds which are crucial in my scheme of judgement. My personal list includes, for example, items like *fire, heard, apparent, really, there, tower,* in which the vowel of the stressed syllable seems to be subject to social (class) variation, and also words like *china, over, happy,* etc., in which my attention may be drawn to the realisation of the second, ' unstressed ' syllable. A sentence like *I heard he went off to China after the war was over, but apparently he wasn't very happy there* invites at a number of points the sort of manifestation I would stereotype as ' upper class English '. (It might also be used as a test for other varieties of English speech.) In many of my personal key-words, the upper-class tendency, as interpreted by me, is towards an open, ' relaxed ' pronunciation, as against the closer and tenser articulations of some lower class forms. In this there is undoubtedly some commingling of fact (certain observations find support in manuals of phonetics) and stereotype (I may carry in my mind some well worn image of the lounging Oxford drawler on the one hand and the stiff Brummagem squeaker on the other). That my kind of stereotype is shared by others is evident from the practice of some class-conscious novelists who try to evoke the phonetic quality of housemaid English by writing the word *really* as *reely*. (So open is the second element of the diphthong in some upper-class pronunciations of this word, that to uninitiated ears a clubmanesque *really* can sound like everybody else's *rarely*.) Novelistic orthographies like *heah, theah, ovah, pahful* also reflect a common response to the upper-class dropjaw whose cooings and sidlings once goaded D. H. Lawrence (never one for a sunny and untrammelled humour) into complaining that ' every blooming bird is an Oxford cuckoo nowadays ':

> When you hear it languishing
> and hooing and cooing and sidling through the front teeth,
>> the Oxford voice,
>>> or worse still
>> the would-be Oxford voice
> you don't even laugh any more, you can't.

> For every blooming bird is an Oxford cuckoo nowadays,
> you can't sit on the bus or in the tube
> but it breathes gently and languishingly in the back
> of your neck.*

Lawrence may have had in mind not only the relatively open position, mentioned above, of some vocalic sounds, but also the ' mincing ', closer-than-average articulation of others. The ' refayned ' pronunciations of *cheps* and *gels* (and *refayned*!) may perhaps suggest social

* D. H. Lawrence, *The Oxford Voice.*

aspirations towards upper-class status, rather than the genuine condition. This is another feature of the class-stereotype. We accept without
malice what we take to be a genuine upper-class accent, but we note
and expose to the cruellest mockery any valiant attempt to up-grade
lower-class speech. Dropped *h*'s are forgiven; *h*'s misplaced in social
striving are quite another matter. No one is kind to the social upstart,
whether he starts up in Rotherham or in imperial Rome, like Arrius,
that over-aspirated and earnestly-aspiring public servant celebrated
by Catullus:

> Chommoda dicebat, si quando commoda vellet
>   dicere, et insidias Arrius hinsidias,
> et tum mirifice sperabat se esse locutum
>   cum quantum poterat dixerat hinsidias . . .*

> ' Hequipment ', Arrius would say, meaning ' equipment ',
>   and ' hambush ' (translate ' ambush ') was his word;
> ' Hambush ' – brought out whenever he'd occasion,
>   proving, he thought, his passing grace of speech.

This poem has a vengeful sting in the tail. Arrius is packed off on a
mission to Syria, after which everybody's ears are given a rest from
the rough breathing. But orrible and hastounding news arrives:

> Ionios fluctus, postquam illuc Arrius isset
>   iam non Ionios esse, sed Hionios.

> Since Arrius passed that way, the Ionian sea,
>   no more ' Ionian ', rolled ' Hionian ' now.

The moral of Arrius and all his latter-day descendants would seem
to be that we should cleave unaffectedly to our native speech-forms.
But that is not always so easy in English society. ' You'll have to
change your accent ', I was once told, ' if you want to get on in the
world.' The lady who told me this had little title to pronounce judgement in the matter of accents, but there was no doubt in my mind
that her advice was founded on stark reality.

As certain sounds have class-associations, so the choice of certain
items of vocabulary tends to place a person on the social scale. This
is an aspect of language which has, of course been explored by
Professor A. S. C. Ross, who has coined for us the terms *U* (standing

* *Catulli Carmina*, ed. Robinson Ellis (Oxford, 1937), LXXXIV.

for ' upper-class usage ') and *non-U*. Thus *mirror* and *notepaper* are
deemed to be non-U words having U-counterparts in *looking-glass*
and *writing-paper*. The U/non-U opposition, invented simply as a
convenience of discourse, was probably taken too earnestly at the outset
and has now degenerated into a species of casually amusing game
played by families or by individuals reflecting on their own usage. If
I play the game I discover (as, I think, do most other people) that
some of my usage falls into Professor Ross's U category, while some
of it is definitely non-U. Thus I prefer the U term *table napkin* to
non-U *serviette*, but I have few qualms about using *relative* or *relation*
where U would require *kinsman*. On the whole, I am on the side of
U when its choices seem to me to manifest a simple defiance of
pretentiousness or euphemism; thus I prefer to say that people *go to
work* rather than *go out to business*, I dislike the expression *to let
someone go*, which flaunts a hypocritical courtesy at the expense of the
verbs *to dismiss* or *to sack*, and I use the word *lavatory* (which, however, is itself a euphemism) rather than the primly respectable *toilet*
or the currently fashionable *loo*. But the proprieties of context have a
wonderful influence upon one's choice of these delicate and socially
critical items of vocabulary. I might ask, of a casual pub-companion,
the whereabouts of the *gents;* if my acquaintance happened to be a
yachtsman, or a member of the navy, or any other person with a manifest interest in the sea and ships, I might declare my intention of going
to the *head;* but if I were in academic-literary company, our sharing
of a private code might be marked by my reference to the *jakes*. The
actual choice of word (and this applies of course to innumerable
other items of vocabulary) is thus determined by various factors; by
the speaker's preference for, or aversion from, euphemism, his sense
of class, his feeling for language as a means of asserting occupational
identities, etc.

Assessments of grammar, as well as judgements on pronunciation
and vocabulary, play a part in helping us to place a speaker in a
social class. A grammatical solecism carries a double condemnation;
it makes a class judgement on its perpetrator, and it brands him as
untutored. We regard such expressions as *Them books, I seen him,
She came regular, It were him what done it*, etc. as badges of ignor-
ance; the rich testimony of literary fiction bears witness to the fact
that we also regard such blatant incorrectnesses as flowers of lower-
class speech. One of the most durable of fictional jokes, arising from
a relish for popular grammar and idiom, occurs in the splendid scene

in Shaw's *Pygmalion*, when the newly made-over Eliza discusses the
domestic life of her kinsfolk, in the accents of a perfect lady, but with
the grammar and vocabulary of a Cockney flower-girl:

Mrs Eynsford Hill	I'm sure I hope it won't turn cold. There's so much influenza about. It runs right through our whole family every spring.
Liza (darkly)	My aunt died of influenza: so they said.
Mrs Eynsford Hill	(clicks her tongue sympathetically)!!!
Liza (in the same	tragic tone) But it's my belief they done the old woman in.
Mrs Higgins (puzzled) Done her in?	
Liza	Y-e-e-e-es, Lord love you! Why should she die of influenza? She come through diphtheria right enough the year before. I saw her with my own eyes. Fairly blue with it, she was. They all thought she was dead; but my father he kept ladling gin down her throat till she came to so sudden that she bit the bowl off the spoon.
Mrs Eynsford Hill	(startled) Dear me!
Liza (piling up the	indictment) What call would a woman with that strength in her have to die of influenza? What become of her straw hat that should have come to me? Somebody pinched it; and what I say is, them as pinched it done her in.
Mrs Eynsford Hill	What does doing her in mean?
Higgins (hastily)	Oh, that's the new small talk. To do a person in means to kill them.
Mrs Eynsford Hill	(to Eliza, horrified) You surely don't believe that your aunt was killed?
Liza	Do I not! Them she lived with would have killed her for a hat-pin, let alone a hat.
Mrs Eynsford Hill	But it can't have been right for your father to pour spirits down her throat like that. It might have killed her.
Liza	Not her. Gin was mother's milk to her. Besides, he'd poured so much down his own throat that he knew the good of it.
Mrs Eynsford Hill	Do you mean that he drank?
Liza	Drank! My word! Something chronic.

Mrs Eynsford Hill	How dreadful for you!
Liza	Not a bit. It never did him no harm what I could see. But then he did not keep it up regular. (Cheerfully) On the burst, as you might say, from time to time. And always more agreeable when he had a drop in. When he was out of work, my mother used to give him fourpence and tell him to go out and not come back until he'd drunk himself cheerful and loving-like. There's lots of women has to make their husbands drunk to make them fit to live with. (Now quite at her ease.) You see, it's like this. If a man has a bit of a conscience, it always takes him when he's sober; and that makes him low-spirited. A drop of booze just takes that off and makes him happy. (To Freddy, who is in convulsions of suppressed laughter.) Here! what are you sniggering at?
Freddy	The new small talk. You do it so awfully well.*

Liza's social consciousness is reflected only in her careful accuracy of pronunciation; she is innocently unaware of the problem which can bedevil even the most experienced of us in our struggles to negotiate certain grammatical obstacles. Many quirks of individual speech-style must arise in this way. For example, some English speakers are vaguely troubled by the choice of pronoun after the conjunction *than;* should one say *You have more experience than I* or *You have more experience than me?* Often, in such cases, the speaker tries to steer a nervous passage between the alternatives, and produces some such construction as *You have more experience than myself*, or else avoids the whole problem by reconstructing, e.g., *You are the more experienced of us.* We might call such shifts and outlets 'avoidance constructions' or 'avoidance idioms'. We are forced into them perhaps more frequently than we might care to acknowledge. A schoolteacher friend once told me of the difficulty he had experienced in finding a suitable correction for the form *It were him as done it.* Was he really to insist that his pupil should say *It was he who did it?* The linguistically correct form seemed socially too good to live with. But long racking of his brains produced little; all he could suggest, apart from the simple *He did it,* was a couple of 'avoidance idioms',

---

* G. B. Shaw, *Pygmalion*, III.

i.e. *He was the one who did it* and *He was the person responsible!*
Another aspect of the class-struggle in grammar is the confusion, by
the uninitiated, of diverse grammatical functions associated with ostensibly identical forms. Thus many speakers whose English would be
generally assessed as 'lower class' are troubled by the fact that the
word *which* has several grammatical functions, e.g. as a relative
pronoun (*He produced the rent, which I then pocketed*), as an inter-
rogative pronoun (*Which did you use?*) and as a demonstrative adjective (*Liverpool, in which city he was born*). Misled by this grammatical pluralism, they may produce such constructions as *He pays
the rent regular, which he's an honest man in that respect* (for *He
pays the rent regularly, in which respect he's an honest man*). Artifice
and solecism may both be the result of a social consciousness in
grammar; and none of us is so secure in his command of the mother-
tongue as to be totally invulnerable to such a consciousness.

By his speech a man may reveal his source of livelihood, and something of the history of his working life; for there is such a thing as
an occupational speech-style. Every profession, of course, has its own
technical vocabulary, slang, jargon, which is used intensively by
members of the group in internal communication, and which may
also be used defensively, to differentiate Us from Them. However,
the speech-style is not merely a matter of idiom; there is also an
occupational phonetics, in some cases manifested in a few special
pronunciations, in others involving a general style of articulation
extending to intonation and less easily definable characteristics such
as vocal timbre. Nearly any trade will yield an example or two of the
special-case pronunciation. For instance, in the Royal Navy, the word
thwart, meaning a cross-bench in a boat, is a homophone of *thought.*
(*Not the foughts you fink,* my old instructor used to say, *but the
foughts you sit on.*) Also, the word *tackle* is pronounced as though it
were spelt *taykle.* Furthermore, the man whose life has been much
involved with the tradition of ships, shipbuilding, and seagoing, may
sometimes be recognised by his pronunciation of the words *launch*
and *staunch* as *lahnch* and *stahnch.* Other occupations will yield other
examples. When the English canal system was constructed, the water-
ways devised by Brindley, Telford, Rennie, and other great engineers
were of necessity too narrow to permit the easy turning of the
70-foot commercial craft which plied up and down the country.
At convenient intervals, however, the engineers constructed wide
ponds where the boats could be turned, and these were (and are)

known as *winding-holes,* the word *winding* being pronounced to rhyme with ' rescinding '. The era of the professional boatman is virtually over, but the canals are still used by keen amateurs, among whom the ' correct ' pronunciation of *winding* serves to distinguish the old hand from the newcomer. Indeed, all occupational pronunciations have the value of shibboleths which sort out the snow-white elect from the great unwashed. Such pronunciations tend to linger in a man's speech long after he has left the occupation in question, or, conversely, to enter his speech after he has taken up an occupation as a spare-time interest. They thus provide, to the keen observer, clues as to personal identity.

However, these specific pronunciations are perhaps of less interest socially than the general occupational speech-style, which in certain cases may be the object of popular stereotype. An obvious example is the speech-style associated with clergymen. We have a vaudeville stereotype of the clerical delivery as a nasalised chanting – indeed ' canting ' – manner of speech. Occasional literary allusions suggest that the nasal delivery is an old pulpit technique, developed long before the acoustic engineering of buildings began to make a public speaker's task a little easier; Samuel Butler (of *Hudibras,* not *Erewhon*) doubtless had the nasal style in mind when he complained of Puritan preachers ' blaspheming custard through the nose '. The parson who intones his conversation as though he were singing liturgical responses is a commonplace of music-hall parody. As we all know well enough, clergymen who actually speak in this way are hard to find; but a chanting parsonical style, with its gravely measured intonations and its deliberate sympathetic mellifluousness, occurs just often enough to give the stereotype some semblance of truth. Another much-parodied profession is that of the soldier. The parade-ground bark, the staccato accents, the curtly falling intonations, the harsh timbre – all these we have heard in play after play where the plot has required that a retired colonel should figure among the *dramatis personae*. Regardless of the fact that we very seldom meet officers who talk in this way, we have created a phonetic stereotype of the soldier. There is doubtless some physical basis of truth to the supposition that clergymen and soldiers, in the actual pursuit of their callings, find it convenient to develop a certain speech-style. The clergyman is required to preach so effectively that his every word may be clearly intelligible to people seated at different parts of what may be a large auditorium having poor acoustic qualities; the soldier has to use words as stimuli – decisive and impersonal stimuli that will produce a sharp and immediate response.

We can easily see how occupational speech-styles are developed. What the stereotype encourages us to believe, however, is that the occupational style, practised in the professional community, spills over into the individual style, practised in the personal company. We may conceivably assume that the social situation of clergymen and soldiers allows this to happen, but the assumption must appear absurd if we apply it to other occupations. It is hardly likely, for example, that the railway station announcer, whose final consonants are so carefully enunciated that they release ghostly final vowels (*the train-a, now-a standing-a, at number six-a platform-a . . .*) will take this deliberately cultivated occupational speech-technique into the domain of her private life (*the kettle-a is now-a boiling-a, warm-a the pot-a . . .*). In her case the specialised enunciation is simply one of the tools of the trade. (Though indeed the acquisition of this technique may affect her general view of language and pronunciation.) It therefore does not lend itself to stereotype and consequent social judgement; a condition of the latter appears to be that we should be able to detect in a man's private speech-habits some trace of the specialised habit of his profession. There are some instances in which private and professional phonetics are apparently kept completely separate, as distinct codes. Bernard Shaw remarked, in the introduction to *Pygmalion*, that the assistants in fashionable London shops in his day were often completely bilingual; meaning that they spoke Standard English in the shop, and their own variety of dialect or modified Standard in private life. This kind of bilingualism can still be observed. More recently, popular culture has produced another variety. We have seen in Britain the emergence of popular entertainers who have grown up speaking some urban dialect, of London or Liverpool or Leeds or Birmingham or Cardiff, etc., and who have preserved their dialect in their 'ordinary' speech, but have learned to use a species of mid-Atlantic or mock-American as the occupational speech-form to be used when singing, making announcements from the stage, and so on. This entertainer speech-style, like the occupational speech-styles of the clergyman and the soldier, can be explained as a matter of professional exigency; since the modern audience is not stratified by class or regional preference or even nationality, the entertainer uses a professional dialect which is acceptable to all and identifies with none.

Dialect, class, occupation, and all the cultural factors and pressures associated with these, help to make us what we are linguistically. However, we obviously exist as persons, as well as in the role of cultural representatives, and there is consequently a point at which the typical language-behaviour of region, social class, and pursuit, etc. fades into the specific language-behaviour of the individual, who has preferences and prejudices, and who resists or accepts the bidding of linguistic fashion. As individuals we may cling to certain speech habits because they belong to our class and generation; or fanatically reject others because they disturb those settled concepts of language which are part of a settled concept of life; or cleave to others again because we feel them to be symbolic of some obsessively-pursued social or cultural ideal. The permutations of our linguistic individuality are numerous. It is possible, for instance, that a speaker of British English might use the pronunciations *goff* and *goffer* (for *golf* and *golfer*) because his speech is 'upper class', or because he belongs to an older generation, or because he feels such a pronunciation to be peculiarly correct within the special language of golf, or for all these reasons at once. It may even be that he has simply accepted a fashion current in his working- or leisure-community. There are always a few pronunciations which exhibit the vagaries of fashion. For example, until fairly recently the second (principally accented) syllable of the word *Edwardian* was made to rhyme with *ward*; in a newish, and apparently somewhat fashionable pronunciation, the syllable in question is pronounced to rhyme with *hard*. Another example from current British English is the pronunciation of the form *-volve* in words like *involve, revolve,* etc. The majority of speakers appear to pronounce the *-ol* of this element like the corresponding sequence in *doll*, but there are some who pronounce it to rhyme with the *-oul* of *soul*. A striking feature of fashions and rivalries in pronunciation is that they provoke very strong responses. Towards a given dialect we may feel a mild antipathy; towards a coterie pronunciation we may feel something more like a savage indignation.*

---

* 'Reactions still triggered-off by the sound of a vowel, the cut of a coat, the turn of a phrase . . . Once imbued with such reactions it is impossible entirely to escape them: I know that until the day I die I shall be unable to avoid *noticing* " raound " for " round ", " invoalve " for " involve " (on that one an Army officer of my acquaintance used to turn down candidates for a commission) . . .'—Diana Athill, *Instead of a Letter*, quoted in Brian Inglis. *Private Conscience and Public Morality*. (Andre Deutsch, London, 1964), p. 95.

Similarly strong, irrational, merely-human personal judgements extend to certain usages in grammar and vocabulary. For instance, there is the perennially vexatious question of choosing a suitable pronoun with which to conduct a narrative or a piece of exposition. One may be castigated for trying to hide oneself behind the impersonal pronoun *one*, or, on the other hand, *we* might be ridiculed for indulging ourselves in our plurality, whilst *you* could be thought presumptuous if you wrote in this way (you certainly don't dare to do it when you are writing academically), and *I* might seem altogether too self-assertive. In British English, *one* indulges *one's* tastes, but if *one* indulges *his* tastes, he may be censured for trafficking linguistically with the Americans. As far as personal or local variations in vocabulary are concerned, one man's *bun* may be another man's *cake*; father's *motor* may be son's *car*; Jonathan's *topcoat* or *greatcoat* may be Jack's *overcoat*; and Jennifer's *dyspepsia* may be Judy's *indigestion*. When my wife was a student she enjoyed the services of a college bedmaker who referred to all footwear as *boots*. ('*He give me a lovely pair of boots for Christmas – bedroom boots, they was*'.) There is no end to the play of idiosyncracy. It is not unknown for individuals to advocate certain usages of their own devising and to campaign for these with all the passion of hopelessly misguided crusaders. I have known schoolteachers who have fought lonely, angry battles for the restoration to full vocalic power of the unstressed syllables in words like *afterwards, huntsman,* and *actor* (*-wards* to rhyme with *cords, -man* with *span, -or* with *gore*); and more than one eccentric who, like some latterday Holofernes, or like the New Englanders of Fenimore Cooper's boyhood, had stubbornly insisted on the sound-for-letter value of spelling pronunciation.* Such campaigners exhort us, as a rule, to renounce the laziness of our slovenly speech, or to follow the logic of the letter; desperate counsels both, since the apparent slovenliness of our speech is in general a manifestation of articulatory modifications which become established patterns of usage (see the following chapter), while the 'letter', far from having any logical rights as a dictator, ought properly to be regarded as the auxiliary, if not the dependent of sound. But the cool arbitration of right reason plays little part in our linguistic judgements;

---

* For Holofernes, see Shakespeare, *Loves Labours Lost*, V, 1, 17ff. Fenimore Cooper testifies to the frequency of 'literal' pronunciations in the New England of his boyhood; see his *Notions of the Americans* (London, 1828), II, pp. 172-4.

we may find ourselves disliking someone for a pronunciation, or a word-choice, or a turn of phrase, just as we may dislike him for his hair-style or the shape of his ears.

Trial by language, we may say, is automatic and involuntary, and occurs in the first moments or hours or days of a new acquaintance. 'Where does he come from?' demands the inward lawgiver, and 'What is his class?' and 'What does he do for a living?'; ultimately the demand may be 'Is he my kind of person?' or 'Does he resemble me?' or possibly 'Can I tolerate his divergences from my norm?' The notion of divergence brings with it the corresponding notion of a standard, and this in turn bids us examine and question the criteria by which a linguistic standard may be devised. No doubt the criterion to which the assertive Adam in all of us would most energetically subscribe is that 'everyone ought to speak like me'. However, apart from some questions of morality, there is one hulkingly large practical obstacle in the way of applying such a criterion; no individual is powerful or influential enough in his own right to impose his language-habits on his fellows. We are therefore to look for the origins of a standard in some association of individuals who happen, for one reason or another, to have acquired a collective power and status.

A standard may be institutionally or regionally centred; or its growth may be associated with an institution economically and politically tied to a region; or the original regional standard may become institutional; or a standard at first associated with one institution may later be attributed to another – the kaleidoscope of motives is ever-changing. The Germans have the expression *Bühnenaussprache,* implying the association of their pronunciation standard with the language of the stage. It may seem strange to adopt the speech-habits of the acting profession as standard for the whole language, but it is really no more strange than assuming as a norm the delivery of news-readers, which is what we imply when we speak of BBC *English.* BBC English, as a popular term for the standard, has in our century come to replace 'King's English'; the centralising institutions of king and court have given ground to the new centralising institutions of the most powerful mass-communication medium. Oddly enough, we rarely, if ever, speak of 'Southern' or 'London' English with the implication of a standard which is present in a Frenchman's allusions to 'Central' or 'Parisian' French. It is often assumed, indeed, that our standard is supra-regional, and that it represents the speech of educated men, in whatever part of the country they may have been born and brought up. This view is very cogently presented by H. C. Wyld in his *A History of Modern Colloquial English*. He mentions the speech varieties which we know as regional dialects, and then goes on to observe:

By the side of these, there are numerous other types of English which are not characteristic of any special geographical area, but rather of social divisions or sections of the population. Of these the chief is the type which most well-bred people think of when they speak of ' English '. At the risk of offending certain susceptibilities this type of English must be further described and particularised. As regards its name, it may be called Good English, Well-bred English, Upper-class English, and it is sometimes, too vaguely, referred to as Standard English. For reasons which will soon appear, it is proposed here to call it *Received Standard English*. This form of speech differs from the various Regional Dialects in many ways, but most remarkably in this, that it is not confined to any locality, nor associated in any one's mind with any special geographical area; it is in origin, as we shall see, the product of social conditions, and is spoken essentially a *Class Dialect*. Received Standard is spoken within certain social boundaries, with an extraordinary degree of uniformity, all over the country. It is not any more the English of London, as is sometimes mistakenly maintained, than it is that of York, or Exeter, or Cirencester, or Oxford, or Chester, or Leicester. In each and all of these places, and in many others throughout the length and breadth of England, Received Standard is spoken among the same kind of people, and it is spoken everywhere, allowing for individual idiosyncracies, to all intents and purposes, in precisely the same way. It has been suggested that perhaps the main factor in this singular degree of uniformity is the custom of sending youths from certain social strata to the great public schools. If we were to say that Received English at the present day is *Public School English,* we should not be far wrong.*

The ' present day ' of this text, it may be noted, is the year 1919, and the author's unreservedly oligarchic attitude is perhaps not one which could be safely or appropriately adopted in the society of the 1970s. Many people, however, would agree generally with Wyld's

* H. C. Wyld, *A History of Modern Colloquial English* (Blackwell Oxford, 1920), pp. 2-3.

observations on our linguistic standard, and would accept his assertion that ' it is not confined to any locality, nor associated in anyone's
mind with a special geographical area; it is in origin . . . the product
of social conditions . . .' Actually, there are plenty of Englishmen in
whose minds Standard English is associated with a special geographical area. The northerner associates Standard with the south; the
south-westerner associates it with the south-east. It is assumed that
anyone who, in the demotic phrase, ' talks posh ' comes from London
or the Home Counties. Historically and sociologically, there is much
to support this instinctive judgement. ' Standard English ' may not be
synonymous with ' London English ', but the fact remains that the
standard was developed in and around London because king and court
were to be found there, because it was a mercantile centre whose
natural importance as a port was increased by its accessibility to the
great wool-producing areas of the east and south-east, because, consequently, it became the centre of the judiciary and commercial
institutions, because the executive class directing those institutions
resided there, and because the children of the executive were trained
at schools and universities located nearby. All these may be the
' social conditions ' to which Professor Wyld referred, but they are
social conditions with a geographic setting. Standard English is no
doubt correctly described as a ' class dialect ', but this does not mean
that it was, or is, a constructed speech-form without regional connections; its origin may be described as the consensus of usage among
prominent or influential people whose business required them to live
close to the centres of power and money – i.e. in the south-east midlands, London, and the counties round London – and who consequently developed a general usage abstracted from the common speech
of that area.

   There is a sort of myth of Standard, the components of which will
not always stand up to examination. It is, as we have suggested, not
altogether true that Standard is supra-regional in origin or in density
of representation, though of course it has spread supra-regionally –
and been regionally modified. Another tenet concerning Standard, that
it is the speech of the educated, will only hold good at the present day
under a special definition of education; five minutes of eavesdropping
in the senior common-room of any university or college might be
enough to persuade a sceptic that plenty of well-informed cultured,
intellectual men get along quite well without Standard. There is yet
a further claim which on examination turns out to be spurious; this

is that Standard is a socially and attitudinally 'neutral' speech form, not only intelligible everywhere, but also acceptable everywhere. This is a claim which might with much greater justice be made for the mid-Atlantic entertainer-dialect mentioned on an earlier page.* It may be true that Standard is everywhere intelligible, but it is certainly not true to imply that it is everywhere regarded without resentment or suspicion. To these objections there may be added the further observation that the implications of Standard seem to be exclusively phonetic; our concept of Standard is not as a rule extended to the grammar and the lexicon, though we might very well relate these to a linguistic standard. It is, for example, surely not 'standard' grammar to say, as Eliza does, *It never did him no harm what I could see,* and the principal items in the sentence *Have you flogged that old banger of yours?* are hardly standard features of our lexicon. Of course, we would reject these examples as 'not good English', thereby implying a standard of correctness in grammar and propriety in diction. It appears, however, that the canons of correctness in grammar and lexicon constitute an academic and literary standard of fairly recent date; some points of so-called 'correct' grammar were not fixed until the eighteenth century. The phonetic proprieties, on the other hand, represent something much more like a social standard, and one that has been growing since the middle ages.

It remains to ask whether any meaningful shape can be given to these scattered and variously-derived impressions of Standard, or whether the concept of Standard English is now an idle and even mischievous fiction? We may surely say that it is not a fiction, but in saying so we must distinguish between 'fiction' and 'abstraction'. There is something which we can call the linguistic standard, and this something is of real importance as a measure of our linguistic behaviour, and therefore is hardly a fiction. On the other hand, when we try to reduce the standard to a set of recommendations and prescriptions we fall into the sort of difficulty that besets us when we try to enumerate the concrete applications of any abstraction.

'Standard', we may say, is a cultural abstraction derived from the observation of what is enacted in 'communities', and, to a lesser extent, in 'companies'. (It may be useful to remind the reader of the diagram and accompanying comment in Chapter 1, p. 28.) To elucidate this, we might ask ourselves what we mean by *the English*

* Thirty years ago, J. R. Firth made just this point concerning 'American film English'. *Firth, I, 5, p. 17.*

language. We might mean, for instance, any of the language-accompanied activities described in the first paragraph of this book – somebody silently reading a letter, an announcer giving the weather forecast, a couple quarrelling, a man filling in his income-tax return, etc. But these are specific uses of English, related to different purposes, different materials, different social contexts, different personal relationships, etc., and therefore implying different concrete emphases in vocabulary, grammar, phonetic features, and all the apparatus which expounds meaning and attitude in any situation. They invite us to consider the individual language user, in all his idiosyncracies, vagaries, and peculiarities of circumstance. The abstraction *the English language* of course purports to represent the sum total of the usage of millions of individual English speakers; but it is not really by consulting and observing individuals that we learn to use the abstraction in a way that implies ' good ' and ' bad ', ' right ' and ' wrong ', ' acceptable ' and ' unacceptable '.

Abstractions are derived from the observation of types and typical characteristics rather than of specific and idiosyncratic cases. Macbeth lectured his hired thugs:

> Ay, in the catalogue ye go for men;
> As hounds, and greyhounds, mongrels, spaniels, curs,
> Shoughs, water-rugs and demi-wolves are clept
> All by the name of dogs; the valued file
> Distinguishes the swift, the slow, the subtle,
> The housekeeper, the hunter . . .*

In language, the ' valued file ' distinguishes the characteristics appropriate to the ranges of language-activity we have labelled ' community ' and ' company '. Seen at work in the contexts typified by these labels, language sometimes appears as a public servant, accessory to situations involving formal relationships, hierarchies of rank, rituals, conventions; and sometimes occurs as the mediator of more private situations, centring on informal, non-hierarchical relationships which permit the uninhibited expression of personal judgements and atttitudes. If we accept this distinction between public and private contexts, the way towards a definition of standard becomes fairly obvious. There is a broad correlation between the forms of language behaviour which we accept as ' standard ', and the type of social context here called ' public ' and predominantly associated with the

* Shakespeare, *Macbeth*, III, 1, 92ff.

social field we have labelled ' community '. For instance, if I write a letter applying for a job, I literally dot the i's and cross the t's, as well as paying other deliberate attentions to what I do, for this is a language-act in the public domain, and I am concerned with manifesting a standard of language-behaviour. This does not necessarily mean that I will be less ceremonious (though perhaps with a different emphasis) when I write to a member of my family; my behaviour in the ' company ' situation may be nonetheless ' standard ' – or it may be boldly and uncaringly off-standard. The point is that it is in the public domain of community life that we find the greatest use for an agreed set of forms and conventions which amount to the concrete expression of a standard.

It would be pleasant indeed to feel that this view of a linguistic standard as a useful public convention, civil as a road-sign, amenable as a bike, might become general among right-thinking citizens and men of good will. But alas, this is hardly likely to happen. Right-thinking citizens acquire the habit of knowing what is right in everything, language included, and will have little truck with talk of conventions and relative standards. And men of goodwill have a way of eyeing strangers warily, as if wondering whether homely security is about to be shaken by the incursion of subversive habits. Too much of us is at stake in our language. Our loyalties, prides, aspirations, self-assertions, are bound up with it; it proclaims what we are and what we expect of others. It is no wonder that we have made it an instrument of social probation. Trial by language is something we all have to live with, perhaps even live by. If we suffer from it, and many people suffer much, we have the ultimate consolation that these things change, that language is changing all the time, is changing even as we judge and offer ourselves for judgement.

6 *The Living and Dying Machine*

A language is a birthright and an inheritance, and one that is as private as a garden and as common as a carriageway. It is private in the sense that each of us realises its potential in ways that can never be the same as anyone else's; moreover, we all have to make the discovery of language, a process which we experience as a unique relationship – so that to discover, for example the meaning of a word is an event in our personal history. On the other hand, to inherit a language is to receive something old, something at once marvellously workable and comically makeshift, something already used and cast off by millions of people. Something, moreover, that has undergone such piecemeal-profound changes that it is discernibly the thing it always was, and yet is utterly different.

The growth of the mother tongue from Old English (Anglo-Saxon) times to our own can be seen as something ramshackle yet purposive; as though language were like some patched-up temperamental machine, always in a state of deficiency and repair, always shedding rust and acquiring new parts, frequently threatening to break down, always troublesome yet always usable, always *working*, always an adequate manifestation of the culture it purports to serve. It is a machine with a human drive, a product which observes the natural cyclical property of living and dying to live again in new forms. On pp. 198-205 of this book is a selection of passages reflecting the growth of English over a period of almost a thousand years from the reign of King Aethelred down to our own day (1970).* This little anthology is designed to help the reader to interpret and elaborate some of the comments made in this chapter. However, since some immediate illustration may be useful, let us here take a

* On the choice of texts, see the introductory remarks to Appendix 2, p. 198.

sentence or two from each passage (dates are given in brackets): *

1. (*1014*)   La hwæt, we witan ful georne þæt to myclan bryce
sceal mycel bot nyde, and to miclum bryne wæter
unlytel gif man þæt fyr sceal to ahte acwæncan.

2. (*1137*)   War-sæ me tilede, þe erthe ne bar nan corn, for þe
land was al fordon mid suilce dædes, and hi sæden
openlice ðat Christ slep and his halechen.

3. (*1250*)   Þo kinges hem wenten and hi seghen þo sterre þet yede
bifore hem, al-wat hi kam over þo huse war ure
louerd was, and al swo hi hedden i-fonden ure louerd,
swo hin an-urede, and him offrede hire offrendes.

4. (*1356*)   But a griffoun hath the body more gret and is more
strong than viiij lyouns, of suche lyouns as ben o this
half; and more gret and strongere than c. egles, suche
as we han amonges us.

5. (*1469*)   'Comfort thy self', sayd the kyng, 'and doo as wel
thou mayst; for in me is no truste for to truste in.
For I wyl in to the vale of auylyon, to hele me of my
greuous wounde.'

6. (*1570*)   For if a yong ientleman be demeure and still of nature,
they say, he is simple and lacketh witte; if he be
bashefulle and will soon blushe, they call him a babishe
and ill brought up thyng. . . .

7. (*1695*)   Here, give her this, and bid her trouble me no more;
a thoughtless, two-handed whore! She knows my
condition well enough, and might have overlaid the
child a fortnight ago, if she had had any forecast in
her.

8. (*1763*)   'Sir, I love the acquaintance of young people; because, in the first place, I don't like to think of

* In the case of passage 4 (Malory) and passage 8 (Samuel Johnson, according to Boswell), the dates given are those assumed to be the dates of composition, or utterance, not of publication.

myself growing old. In the next place, young
acquaintances must last longer, if they do last; and
then, Sir, young men have more virtue than old men;
they have more generous sentiments in every respect.'

9. (*1865*) So they went up to the Mock Turtle, who looked up
at them with large eyes full to tears, but said nothing.
' This here young lady ', said the Gryphon, ' she wants
for to know your history, she do.'

10. (*1970*) The 3-second burn at 13.53 BST, although it was only
3.1 feet per second, was relatively long because of the
weight of the spacecraft.
' O.K., that's it ', Captain Lovell said.
' Yes, it looks like we had a minus point two bias at
470, we're burning ', Mr Haise radiod.
' Copy that, Fred ', Mr Joe Kerwin, the capsule
communicator replied.

Our first response to this series may possibly be to note that, after
all, there are continuities, hereditary marks, distinctive features on a
changing face. Even Bishop Wulfstan's English (passage no. 1) is not
utterly obscure, for an untrained observer would surely not require
much training to recognise the purport of *waeter* and *fyr*. Our further
reaction may be to see these passages as approaching, in more or less
overlapping phases of intelligibility, the condition of present-day English. Unless we happen to have studied Old English, we may make
very little of passage no. 1. Numbers 2–4 are obviously archaic, and
may not be wholly intelligible; nevertheless we can piece out much
more of a meaning from them than we can from the first passage.
Numbers 5–7 do not offer any profound technical difficulties, and we
follow them readily enough; however, we can hardly help noting that
hele me of my greuous wounde is not quite modern idiom, and that
what Ascham (*1570*) means by *simple, witte,* and *bashefulle* or what
Congreve (1695) means by *overlaid* and *forecast* may not coincide
with any present-day use of these words. Passages 8–10, however, will
no doubt seem to relate to our own domain of language and culture.
We understand what they say, i.e. we are fully acquainted with their
code; and we can relate what they say to the features of a living
culture, i.e. we understand their *environment,* so that we can easily

construct the requisite links and equations between language and such
matters as moral evaluations, concepts of humour, and technological
phenomena.

The more we browse through such a collection, the more we must
become aware of distinct features of change, as when we remark
orthographic (and by implication phonetic) similarities and contrasts,
extensions or changes in the meaning of words, the development, or
recession into archaism, of grammatical forms and syntactic structures.
The historian of language is driven by an almost passionate conviction of the value of such details; he will spare no pains, no treadmill
labours of collecting and collating, to re-create precisely the linguistic
experience of the past. And this is not altogether the extraordinary
self-forgetfulness of the antiquarian. History is useful. It is good to
know where you have been, for the knowledge can help you to see
where you are going. Furthermore, words, trivial things in themselves,
mere scraps of symbolism, puffs of air, paper-spoilers, can be extra-
ordinarily effective as the residuaries and mileposts of individual and
common experience. In the *bryne* and *burn* of our first and last
passages, for example (they are forms of the same word), we can read
something of the history of articulation in English and something of
the development of man's technological abilities. If we compare the
fourth passage with the ninth, it appears that Mandeville's *griffoun*
turns up with a difference as Carroll's *Gryphon*. The main difference
is that Mandeville's audience would seriously accept the possible existence of griffouns (or griffins or griffons or gryphons), whereas Carroll's
readership must know better. This elementary difference profoundly
affects the value of the word griffoun/Gryphon in the two passages;
to put it simply, it is a serious word in the one case and a comic word
in the other. Beneath this ' comic word ', however, there is a quite
serious and interesting fact; the lapse of a myth, the fading of a belief
or the possibility of a belief. The two instances of the word may thus
be said to document phases in our racial experience, or way of looking
at the world.

Linguistic history involves individuals, and it involves the community; it is made by men talking in the associations of their business
and leisure, and it is confirmed in the collective tradition of a culture.
Some feature of individual usage, whether consciously devised or
implicit in the workings of human psychology and physiology, is
transmitted to the ' companies ' of the individual's common acquaintance; and is adopted by the community; and so is taken up into the

culture as a feature of general language-behaviour, to be referred back, with extensions and advantages, through companies and communities, to further generations of individuals. A word – let us say the word *kodak*, for the example presents itself most usefully – is invented by an individual, used in the community of camera manufacture, taken up by the public, established as a synonym for ' camera ', and so enters into the common stock of English words and becomes susceptible to the kind of grammatical variation and semantic extension that may affect any comparable item in the general vocabulary.* An idiom – let us choose the expression *a flash in the pan* – is first current in the military community, where it has a precise technical meaning, is used by individuals in the community both in a technical and in a transferred, metaphorical, sense, is picked up, as a metaphor, in ' companies ' outside the military sphere, passes into other communities, becomes culturally established, and survives as a useful piece of the general lexicon long after the science of weaponry has discarded the flintlock and the priming charge. All events in language, all its lively and mutable constituents, are liable to run this ceaseless gamut, out-and-in-and-out.

The changes which we observe in language are the result of operations which it is convenient, if artificial, to regard as (a) *internal*, or having to do with the structure of the language code as managed by the human being, with all his physiological and psychological qualifications and constraints; and (b) *external*, or proceeding from changes in the material environment, in the climate of belief, in intellectual position, and so on. To anyone who is predisposed to see language in a social and cultural perspective, the external causes of linguistic change must be particularly interesting. Among the cultural and institutional factors which most obviously affect language, we may list (not necessarily in order of importance) the physical intrusion of foreign cultures, as when one people annexes, or in some way comes to share, another's territory; the intellectual and social dominance of a foreign culture, not inevitably as the concomitant of physical conquest; the material growth of a culture as the result of new discoveries in artefacts, techniques, avenues of trade, etc.; the normative consciousness which attempts to regulate and prescribe all forms of behaviour, including linguistic behaviour; the ethnically and historically determined cast of mind, or ' national character ', which directs

* The word *kodak* was invented by George Eastman, head of the firm of Eastman Kodak.

people's beliefs, emotions, habits of thought, through certain channels towards certain ends; the pursuits and practices of work and leisure, as related to institutions, geography and climate; the allocation of a significant cultural status to certain types of person, e.g. priests, soldiers, women, children; the importance attached to inheritance, property, money, and possessions in general; and all the hierarchies of personal relationship, whether formal, as in community life, or informal, as in private life.

Some of these topics are given prominent treatment in textbooks of linguistic history; for example, one would hardly expect to find a history of the English language that did not pay considerable attention to the linguistic consequences of the Danish settlements, the Norman Conquest, and the Renaissance interest in the classical cultures. Other matters which are potentially of great importance receive at best a shadowy treatment. It would be a real service, if, for instance, some-one were able to demonstrate the effects on English sentence-construction (and that of other western languages) of the European tradition of science and logic. Such a demonstration might have much to tell us, not only about the symbolic conventions of science, but also, by comparison and inference, about the symbolic conventions of poetry; not only about institutions and official grammar, but also, by implication, about the subversive, ' psychological ' grammar which so often emerges in common speech.

However, the linguist is not to be blamed if he feels that such matters lie strictly within the competence of another kind of historian, the social historian or the historian of ideas. The orthodox way of looking at linguistic change is to try to understand it as part of the internal processes of the code. This philosophy has to be adapted to cases. There are obviously some kinds of internal change which have relatively little to do with the facts or happenings of the environment, and there are others which require, so to speak, some environmental reaction. For instance, the fact that English, having borrowed the French words *message* and *messager,* then introduced into the latter a ' non-etymological *n* ', to give us the form *messenger,* is a peculiarity which can be explained in articulatory terms, i.e. with reference to probable movements of the speech-organs; such an explanation requires only that we look at the physical make-up of the individual and does not ask us to look further, into institutions or wider environmental factors. But to explain the fact that the form *caught* is now normal and *catched* is bad grammar, whereas in the eighteenth century the latter was at least acceptable (Dr Johnson used it),* demands something more than a demonstration of individual physiology or psychology. We explain it in terms of usage; which is to say, we suppose that a sufficiently large number of individuals so influenced each other, or were so influenced by institutional and authoritative example, that they set the practice of saying *caught*. This explains an internal change with predominant reference to the mediating power of companies and communities. Then again, the difference between the 'good' meaning, at the present day, of the word *enthusiasm*, and the pejorative associations it had in the eighteenth century (when it meant something like 'inspirational religiousness') may be related to shifts in the view of character, personality, and *morale*, shifts so pervasive and general that we connect them with the culture at large rather than with individuals or groups. These examples may suggest that of the three isolable types of change, phonetic, grammatical, and lexical, the first is the most 'internal', in the sense of being amenable to explanation in terms of what individuals do, while the others are more or less external, requiring some reference to the communal spread of usage. This is only roughly the case. There are numerous examples of change which can be interpreted in different perspectives, individual, communal, and cultural; and of course it is merely artificial to isolate three departments of language as distinct areas of change, when no doubt the phonetic, grammatical, and lexical moments of linguistic change are interfaced and interactive in ways which linguistic science has indicated but not yet fully plotted. Nevertheless, it is a convenient procedure to consider first phonetic, then grammatical, then lexical change, and it is of some interpretative value to associate these three types with a progressive widening of social scope.

Some changes in the phonetic constituency of a language are apparently independent of any organic cause. For instance, we are able to infer that in pre-Conquest times the word we know as *tide* was pronounced something like 'teed' (/tiːd/), while in Elizabethan English its sound had shifted in the direction of something rather like 'tayed' (/təid/).† This is an instance of what has sometimes been called 'isolative' phonetic change. The term is deceptive, inasmuch

---

* E.g. *I never catched Mallet in a Scotch accent*—to Boswell, in 1772.
† A form of the International Phonetic Alphabet, as applied to the interpretation and transcription of British RP (Received Pronunciation) is appended on p. 194.

as it implies the 'just happening' of a random and unmotivated occurrence. Such isolative changes do have an organic cause, though it is not readily perceived, being a matter of a collectively-adopted drift of articulation, a sort of infective change resulting from the vulnerability or instability of some speech-habits. The articulatory character of English is notoriously so relaxed that vowel sounds in particular become unstable and develop the glides, or tailing-away movements of the tongue, which turn them into diphthongs. This instability is not random and occasional, but is a general characteristic, so that there is a collective tendency towards change on this basis. In the changing pronunciation of the word *tide* in Old and Middle English, Elizabethan English, and Modern English, we can observe a progressive lowering or opening (i.e. as regards tongue-position or mouth-aperture) of the onset of the vocalic sound, and consequently the development of an articulatory glide between the low onset and the high close. Furthermore, the articulatory habit that is responsible for one change will also produce contingent changes, so that one isolative change implies another, and beyond that another, in a series, or 'shift', of the kind best exemplified in English by the so-called 'great vowel shift'.

In other cases, changes occur which we can explain as the obvious and discernible consequence of having to manage a sequence of articulations; the changes not only happen, but we can see how they were made to happen. In Old English, for instance, there was a word *braemel,* which in modern English occurs in the form *bramble.* Our spelling shows a *b* which corresponds to an element in the pronunciation of the word, an element not present in the original form. The intrusion of this element is not difficult to understand. What it amounts to, roughly put, is this. The consonant *m* is formed by holding the two lips together and discharging a stream of air (the carrier of the 'sound') through the nose. The consonant *l* is produced by setting the tip of the tongue against the hard ridge of gum just behind the upper front teeth, and allowing the air to escape through the mouth, round the side of the tongue. The significant articulatory difference is that one of these sounds is nasally released, whilst the other is orally released. This presents a speaker producing the sequence *m–l* with the problem of switching rapidly from one kind of release to the other. The spelling of Old English *braemel* suggests recourse to a brief 'murmur-vowel' as a transition between the two sounds, whereas our *bramble* points to a rather different process. If the lips are put together to form the consonant *m*, and then are held together and only separated after the speaker has switched from a nasal to an oral channelling of the breath, then a sound of the *b* type is produced. The intrusive *b* thus occurs as a result of the difficulty of synchronising breath-release and shifts of organic position in moving from one articulation to the next; the same phenomenon is seen in words like *thimble, humble, tumble, shambles,* etc.

Changes of this other, non-isolative kind, have sometimes been called ' combinative ', because they evidently result from a combination of articulatory factors which we can easily identify. Combinative changes are numerous, and may be broadly classified according to the type of articulatory problem involved. We have just considered the case of an intrusive consonant, produced as a bridge, or *glide,* between neighbouring articulations. It is possible for vowel-sounds to be intruded for the same purpose. Some speakers, for instance, have difficulty with words like *film, umbrella,* and *athlete,* pronouncing them ' fillum ', ' umberella ' and ' athelete '. We may regard these as more or less amusing idiosyncracies, but in fact they illustrate a very ancient phenomenon in language, for which the Sanskrit grammarians had the name *svarabhakti.* There are intrusive, or svarabhakti, vowels in our words *sparrow* and *blossom,* but these forms have long since become standard and we are unaware of the intrusion. Other combinative changes have resulted from the attempt to negotiate an awkward sequence by modifying one or other of a pair of successive articulations, so as to make it in some way resemble its fellow, or even to coalesce with it. The technical name for this is *assimiliation.* Of the various kinds of assimilation we may perhaps mention one which involves a change in the place of articulation to accommodate the transition to a following sound. Thus, our word *impossibility* is derived, presumably through French, from the Latin *impossibilitas,* which is constructed from an original prefix *in-*followed by the root and suffix-*possibilitas.* The spelling suggests that in Latin itself the original *inp* became *imp,* *n* changing to a ' bilabial ' *m* in anticipation of the following consonant *p,* also a bilabial.* A careful observer may notice a similar process at work in modern English, in the pronunciation of words like *unbearable, input,* as ' umbearable ', ' imput '. Our consonant *n,* described as a ' voiced alveolar nasal ' consonant appears to be particularly susceptible to assimilative changes.

* For the technical terminology of phonetics, which I have tried as far as possible to avoid, see *Gimson, V, 93.*

Normally it is made with a tongue position like that of *l*, or *d*, that is to say with the tongue-tip against the upper teeth-ridge, or *alveolum*. If, however, we consider what happens when we pronounce the word *non-combatant* without particular concern for precise articulation, it may appear that the second *n* in *non* is not an ' alveolar ' but a ' velar ', i.e. is made with the back of the tongue against the soft palate, in anticipation of the following *c* (/k/). And if we pronounce the word *tenth*, it will then appear that instead of holding the tongue-tip against the alveolum, we allow it to touch the rear surfaces of the upper teeth, in the same place of articulation as the following *th* (/θ/).

Another kind of assimilation affects the voicing of successive sounds. For example, if we produce the words *five* and *pence* in isolation, it will certainly appear that the *v* of *five* is voiced (made with closed vocal cords) whereas the *p* of *pence* is voiceless (made with open vocal cords). If, however, we pronounce the compound *fivepence,* the chances are that we may hear ourselves producing something that sounds like ' fifepence '; the final consonant of *five* in such a case has been de-voiced in anticipation of the following voiceless sound. The converse has taken place in our word *husband.* The final *s* of Old English *hus,* like the *s* of modern *house,* was voiceless; in the compound, however, before a voiced *b,* the sound became voiced. The workings of assimilation in bringing about organic changes, voicings and devoicings, and even the loss of sounds, are too various and complex to be illustrated here. This must also be said of the phenomenon of *dissimilation,* which represents quite another way of trying to deal with awkwardly juxtaposed articulations. Such juxtapositions may be awkward precisely because the sounds in sequence resemble each other too closely; as we know from tongue-twisters, the management of a series of organically similar sounds can be difficult. In resolution of this difficulty, the speech organs may tend to take up markedly contrastive or dissociative positions as they move through a sequence. In this connection, the phonetic structure of our word *heaven* is interesting. In Gothic the word for ' heaven ' is *himins,* the notable feature of this word being the fairly close association of *m* and *n*. The Old High German form *himil* (whence modern German *Himmel*) indicates that the sequence *m–n* was found awkward, and that it became convenient to separate the articulation of the two consonants, moving the second of the pair, *n,* to a place of formation a little farther away from that of *m*. Our Old English form *heofon* (whence *heaven*) dissimilates the awkward pair in the other direction; the second consonant, the *n*, is retained, but the articulation of the first is shifted, and becomes ʄ (/v/).

We can frequently observe interesting parallels between combinative changes which have taken place in the past and are now established in our language, and mutations currently notable in popular speech. It is sometimes suggested that our word *chimney* is traceable to some such phrase in Low Latin as *camera caminata* meaning 'a heated room', 'a room with a stove'. The participial adjective *caminata* lived on in French in the form *cheminée*, which gave us our *chimney*. However, just as speakers in primitive Germanic communities could not cope with the sequence m–n in words like *himins* and produced dissimilated forms like *himil*, so among present-day speakers of English there are those who dissimilate the *mn* of *chimney* and produce the form *chimley*. And just as our mediaeval ancestors intruded a consonantal glide between the *m-l* of *braemel*, *þymol*, etc., giving *bramble*, *thimble*, so there are modern speakers who introduce the same glide-consonant into the dissimilated form *chimley*, pronouncing it *chimbley*. This example is worth making because the reader may possibly look on forms like *chimley* and *chimbley* as 'vulgar', 'incorrect', 'slovenly', and so forth. Indeed, such judgements may be admissible in the social contexts of our own time; but the processes of phonetic accommodation which produce today's vulgarisms are no different from those which were at work yesterday and a thousand years ago, and have produced forms now accepted as current and respectable.

An important condition of many, if not all, of these combinative changes, is that they are related to speech-tempo and to the location of strong and weak accents in the flow of speech. Being by nature self-deceptive and self-protective, each of us likes to imagine that his speech-habits are never less than precise, his delivery nothing if not formal and measured. If this were so, it is possible that phonetic change might be reduced to the merest glacial budging of articulations over the centuries. But it is not so; we naturally speak at varying tempi, with different gradations of formality, in different contexts, and on the whole those contexts predominate in which informal and fairly rapid speech is customary. In such speech, strong accentuation is reserved for the lexically important syllables, and the less important items are weakly accented. The result of this is to change the vocalic quality and quantity of such syllables. This is seen most clearly in the case of the little grammatical words such as *and, at, to, from, so, for, the, do, am, you, that,* etc., which have a so-called 'strong' form in which the vowel is given its full quality (/ænd/, /æt/, /tuː/, /frəm/, etc.) and a 'weak' form, usual in colloquy, in which the vowel is much reduced (/ənd/, /ət/, /tə/, /frəm/, etc.). The establishment of the unaccented form is sometimes reflected in our orthography, e.g. *I'm, he's, don't, how d'y'do,* etc. The weakening or reduction of vowel quality through accent shift is a very important aspect of phonetic change and variation. It is thanks to this that we have, for example, a difference of vowel in the preterite *sang* and in the past participle *sung;* the vowel in the latter is a qualitatively reduced form established in primitive Germanic times before English had come into being and resultant upon the shift of accent from the stem of the word to an inflection of which we have now lost all trace. If this example seems a little arcane, the reader may consider the fate of the vowels in *photograph* when we form the derivative *photography;* shift of accent is accompanied by a manifest shift in quality. In some cases, accentual conditions may be responsible for the weakening and complete loss of a vowel or syllable. We see this in the phenomenon called *syncope,* which is observable in current colloquial pronunciations of words like *general, police, balloon, Saturday, history, honourable, family* (as 'genral', 'plice', 'bloon', 'Satday', etc.), where the reduction is favoured by accent conditions working in conjunction with certain amenable consonant sequences. We may reject these pronunciations as vulgar, but as and if we do so we must agree to ignore the fact that syncope is also well-established in standard usage in words like *evening, chimney, curtsey, halfpenny, Worcester,* etc.

If we try to relate phonetic change to its social context, it may appear that different types of change, in particular the types here distinguished as 'isolative' and 'combinative', are amenable to different kinds of social interpretation. Isolative changes, for instance, may be explained as the drift of habit from generation to generation. In any given family, the speech-habits of the children are likely to be marginally different from those of the parents, different because of small physiological modifications and because models of speech are provided by coevals as well as elders. Each family may be regarded as a small speech-community with its own peculiarities of speech, but the central tendencies towards change in the small community will be those of other families in the larger speech-community. Thus the continual shift in the basis of articulation which has produced our present-day English diphthongs and which is still producing effects in our speech, may be explained as a matter of inherited articulatory habit, confirmed and transmitted by each generation. In considering the spread of changes of the combinative type, however, we must consider the social forces which might promote or resist such change. For instance, there is currently a strong social inhibition of the so-called ' intrusive *r* ' in phrases like *law and order* (' law-r-and-order '). This is a modification of the combinative type which is unlikely to establish itself in the face of strong social resistance. The printed word has a strong conservative and inhibitive effect on pronunciation, but on the other hand there are promotive forces which are almost as strong. One of these is the rivalry of the generations (for the revolution of the young is as important, socially, as their dependence), and the role of the peer-group (schoolmates, ' the gang ', fellow-students, etc.) as a form-giver and norm-giver challenging the precepts and prescriptions of the family elders. One can imagine the confrontation of a mediaeval grandfather who used the ' correct ' pronunciation *emti*, with his grandson who had picked up the nasty habit of saying *empti*. Grandson, we may conjecture, would say *empti* not merely to tease grandsire, but also because Perkyn and Jankyn and Dickon said it, too. Other factors which may either promote or inhibit change are the consciousness of social class, the desire for a pronunciation which indicates conformity with a certain set of values, or the acceptance of some person or class of persons as a model of speech.

As for changes in grammatical form, some of these are clearly connected with phonetic changes. To take an obvious and major example: Old English was a language which worked through the systematic use of inflections (i.e. word-endings) carrying various grammatical functions. The inflections of the verb expressed concepts of person (' I ', ' you ', ' he ', etc.), number (' one ' - ' more than one ') tense (place in a time-scheme) mood (directives, options, possibilities), etc. The inflections of the noun and adjective expressed, number and gender, and also the concept of case, i.e. of the allocation of a word to a grammatical and semantic role as subject, object, indirect object, ' possessor ', ' instrument ', etc. This old English nominal case system was already undergoing a mild erosion before the Norman Conquest, but after 1066, with the administrative and cultural dominance of French, reductive tendencies which we presume to have been already manifest in the accent-patterns of the colloquial language were

accelerated, and the demolition of the case system was quite soon
achieved. We may describe all this as, initially, a phonetic modification accelerated by cultural conditions; the phonetic modification,
however, had far-reaching grammatical consequences, in that the
prepositional phrase took over the role of the inflected noun, and
word-order became an important determiner of grammatical function
in the English sentence.

A more trivial example, a mere matter of idiom, is to be seen in
the fate of the forms *had rather* (now generally out of use, or confined to bookish usage), and *had better* (still in general circulation,
and, indeed, the established idiom). The *had* of these expressions is
a false reconstruction of the original *would*. The weakly-accented
forms of the two auxiliaries are phonetically identical, so that *I would*
and *I had* both reduce to *I'd;* on re-expansion so to speak, the *'d* of
' would ' is confounded with the *'d* of ' had '. There is evidence that
this false reconstruction took place quite early in the history of
modern English; *I had as lief the town-crier spoke my lines,* says
Prince Hamlet – not, ' I would as lief . . .'* The authoritarians of the
eighteenth century objected both to *had rather* and *had better,* but
the fate of the twin constructions is a comment on the irrelevance of
many attempts at the prescriptive control of language. On the whole,
we have reverted from *I had rather* to the ' correct ' *I would rather,*
but *had better* holds the field as ' good grammar ' and unrivalled
idiom.

Some grammatical changes resemble certain types of phonetic
change in that they are ostensibly ' isolative ', i.e. developments of
grammatical convention for which we cannot easily find an explanation. Like the isolative changes in the phonetic convention, they may
appear to be unmotivated. For instance, a marked characteristic of
present-day English is the use of progressive or continuous tense-forms
side by side, with the simple forms; e.g. *was working* together with
worked, had been writing together with *had written,* and so on. These
continuous forms are such an eminent feature of the grammar of the
modern English verb that textbooks written for foreign learners of
English devote many pages to this topic, and English people themselves, when they reflect on their own language, puzzle a good deal
over the idiomatic uses of the progressive forms. The progressive
forms have not always had this status in English. They occurred very
sparsely in mediaeval and Renaissance English, and are essentially a

* Shakespeare, *Hamlet*, III, ii, 1.

post-seventeenth-century phenomenon. As it is not at all easy to say how they came to enter so thoroughly into our grammatical convention, it is tempting to shrug them off with the kind of explanation that amounts to little more than the assertion that they 'just happened'. But there is little that 'just happens' in language, and if we can do nothing else we can at least hazard guesses as to their origin and remarkable invasion of the English verb-system.

Such guesses, however, may appeal to a number of different factors. We may attempt psychological interpretations; we may speculate on the covert changes of idiom and grammar in the unrecorded colloquial language, as opposed to the overt shifts reflected in available texts; and ultimately we may turn to the available texts, to try to show that the genesis of a new grammatical type was implied in the resources of the language itself. In the case of the progressive constructions, we might argue, for example, that their origin is to be sought in the uses of the present participle as an attributive adjective *(The smiling lady)*, as a species of predicative adjective or complement *(The lady stood smiling)*, and as a verbal noun, originally marked by a preposition which first weakened phonetically and then disappeared *(The king went on hunting, The king went a-hunting, The king went hunting)*. From *The smiling lady* or *The lady stood smiling* it is not such a far step to *The lady was smiling*, and it requires no great imagination to suppose that the latter might readily come to be accepted as an equivalent of *The lady smiled*. Similarly, *The king went hunting* invites the construction of *went* as an auxiliary rather than a main verb, and so opens the way for the introduction of other auxiliaries, e.g. *have, be, will: The king has been hunting, The king is hunting, The king will be hunting.**

Explanations such as these appeal in part to the psychology of the language-user, and in doing so suggest that speakers may be more or less unconsciously affected by the patterning of forms having a contingent similarity to those which are in process of changing or emerging. Indeed, the workings of *analogy,* as the phenomenon is called, are a most important factor in linguistic change. The formation of linguistic analogies is one of the more remarkable features of

* This is merely a guess at the psychology of a rather complicated development in the history of English. For a full treatment of the *-ing* form in English and the background to the progressive verb-forms, see F. Th. Visser, *An Historical Syntax of the English Language*, Leiden, E. J. Brill, 1966, Vol. II, Cap. 9, and O. Jespersen *A Modern English Grammar on Historical Principles* (London: Allen & Unwin, 1932), Part IV, Cap. XII.

the speech of children. Often the child's analogies are correct; that is to say, he correctly deduces the shape of an unknown form or construction from the pattern of one already known. Sometimes, however, they are noticeably incorrect. For instance, children often form 'strong' verbs like *run* on the analogy of the numerically preponderant 'weak' verbs like *walk*, so that they say 'run-runned' instead of 'run-ran'. If we look back into the history of English, we can see that this particular type of false analogy has had a profound effect on the statistical balance in our language of the two main types of verbal conjugation. The once quite numerous strong types have now been considerably reduced in number, partly, it is true, through semantic loss (e.g. the replacement of Old English words by others of French or Latin origin), but also through the re-modelling of many strong verbs on the analogy of the weak conjugation. Thus, we now say *laughed, chewed, climbed, helped,* and not *lough, chaw, clomb, holp*.

Analogy might be interpreted as an effect of the speech-psychology of the individual, licensed or censored by the community. We inhibit the childish analogy 'run-runned' largely, it may be supposed, because a written standard is now powerfully established. Under other circumstances, in a less centralised culture, one can imagine its emergence as a local or dialect form which would then share in the fate of that dialect in the power-struggle between speech-variants. We may suppose, by way of further speculation, that analogies occur because the individual tries to reduce the problems of a complex system by reducing the number of rules that have to be applied in speech. Why, the unspoken question runs, should I burden my brain with the task of deciding when to apply one kind of conjugational process (e.g. in the case of *run*) or when to put into operation another (e.g. in the case of *walk*)? It is perhaps not unexpected that the individual should try to smooth out, or, to use the philologist's word, 'level', the complexities of the system. We find evidence of this levelling everywhere in the history of the grammatical forms of English. For instance, the Old English word for 'day', *daeg,* had a plural *dagas*. If the Old English forms had developed regularly into modern English, we should now speak of *one day* and *two daws*. However, the forms of the plural were re-modelled, or 'levelled', at quite an early date, under those of the singular. Another instance of the levelling of plural forms under the singular pattern is to be seen in the development of the past tense of strong verbs. The Old English verb ' to ride ', *ridan,* had the preterite singular *ràd* (with a long vowel), the preterite plural *ridon* (short vowel) and the past participle *riden* (short vowel). The Old English preterite singular and past participle have developed regularly into *rode, ridden,* but if the preterite plural form had survived we should not have to distinguish between *I rode* and *we rid.* The levelling process has spared us this complication. A levelling of the forms of the preterite and the past participle has also taken place in a number of instances – for example in the verb to *swing,* which has the preterite *swung,* instead of the historically ' regular ' *swang,* as a levelling from the past participle. Another such verb is the verb to *break.* The form of the preterite in our conjugation *break-broke-broken,* is derived from the past participle but in older texts we may observe an archaic and historically justifiable preterite *brake.* Occasionally the past participle has been re-modelled on the form of the preterite. An interesting case here is the verb *to strike.* Had the historical process been regular and undisturbed, we should now probably have *strike-stroke-stricken.* What has happened is that the preterite has not undergone the usual process of levelling under the long vowel of the original preterite singular, but has developed a form with a reduced vowel, *struck.* This form has been extended to the past participle, so that we say, for example, *He was struck by lightning,* whilst the older participial form is preserved as a fixed item in certain collocations – e.g. *fever-stricken, a stricken look, stricken with remorse, well-stricken in years,* etc.

Akin to the processes of analogy and levelling is that of *blending,* which occurs when two originally distinct patterns are confounded in such a way that neither is completely eradicated. A blend is thus a sort of grammatical ' portmanteau '. Dialectologists can sometimes point to the existence of blend-forms in areas which constitute boundaries or frontiers between dialect types. Thus in the West Riding of Yorkshire, the pronominal form *misen* (' myself ') occurs, whilst in the confronting area of Lancashire *misel* is found; betwixt and between there is a kind of linguistic no-man's-land where the blend *miseln* is to be observed.* But we do not have to appeal to present-day dialects for illustrations of grammatical blends. A number are well established in the standard language. The pronoun *she,* for example,

---

* Information gathered from a lecture given by Mr Stanley Ellis, of the University of Leeds, to the Linguistic Society of the University of Nottingham.

is possibly a blend form, of Old English *seo,* the nominative singular feminine of the definite article, and *heo,* the Old English word for ' she '. The history of this form, however, remains somewhat obscure. A clearer case is seen in the plural form *children.* This blends two Old English plural formations, i.e. the original ending in *-ru,* which would have given *childer* (now a dialect form), and an ending in *-an* which characterised certain nouns of which the only clear survival is our *oxen.* Another instance of a blend occurs in the conjungation of the verb to *slay.* This verb belonged to a class in Old English which would have produced a modern series *slay-slow-slain;* the form of the preterite, however, was affected by verbs like *blow, grow, know,* which belonged to a different class. Our paradigm *slay-slew-slain* is thus a blend of two strong verb types.

It has been suggested that grammatical change can best be interpreted in terms of the community of speech rather than in terms of the psychology and physiology of the individual. If this is indeed so, it might then appear that the examples of grammatical change so far given challenge this principle, since phenomena like analogy and levelling are amenable to psychological rather than social explanations. We must consider, however, that the border between individual psychology and communal tendency is of necessity ill-defined; and also that there is nothing that passes into the communal domain that does so without meeting resistance and censorship. All linguistic change tends to be communally suspect as ' corruption ' or ' innovation '; so much so, that any modification would probably be rejected were it not for the fact that changes in their onset are covert, devious, departing from accepted norms by margins too trivial to be observed. Furthermore, there are times when ' accepted norms ' are not available. Writing, for instance, tends to create a set of grammatical norms; if letters and literacy are not a general characteristic of a culture, or if for some reason the literate tradition is interrupted, the likelihood of accelerated grammatical change is increased. Institutions provide us with another kind of norm. At first sight, it may seem extravagant to claim that our concepts of public behaviour and of personal relationships in various contexts can have an effect on our grammatical system, but the case is not difficult to make.

If, for instance, we read the plays of Shakespeare with any sort of attention to language, it must strike us that, whereas we use one pronoun of address *you,* Shakespeare uses *thou, thee, ye* and *you.* Furthermore, while in many interesting cases Shakespeare makes a strict and dramatically relevant distinction between the familiar *thou/ thee* and the polite *ye/you,* and also between the plural subject pronoun *ye* and the object pronoun *you,* it is not difficult to find scenes in which, without the motivation of dramatic context or social convention, his characters use the pronouns in free alternation. Thus, in Henry IV part 1, Act II, Scene iv, ll. 127ff, in dialogue involving mainly Falstaff and Prince Henry, together with some bystanding characters, *ye, you* and *thou* alternate, without apparent change of personal attitude, as singular subject pronouns of address, whilst *ye, you,* and *thee* appear as object pronouns; *you* and *ye* are further used as plural subject pronouns, and also as plural object pronouns. That Shakespeare in his plays should sometimes use these pronominal forms with a clear awareness of their traditional social and systematic functions, and at other times jumble them in apparent indifference, suggests a state of transition and indistinction, not first and foremost in linguistic structure, but in cultural structure. The transition, might be thought in the first instance to affect the social paradigm of leader and follower in its various specific forms; master and servant, man and wife, lover and mistress, father and child, etc. How the traditional form of such relationships might come to be changed can only be a matter of speculation; but we might guess, for instance, that a change in religious belief, or in political structure, or in the distribution of wealth or in the laws of property and inheritance, or a combination of these and other factors might help to change the inner content of outwardly persistent relationships. In the second place, and as a sort of corollary, the transition might be from a view of social connections which permits the co-presence of intimate and formal relationships, towards a way of looking at human dealings which acknowledges the plural and official face only as decent and proper, and requires that intimacy be kept within doors. Of course it is by no means impossible for a speaker of Present-Day English to find a way of saying 'thou', or 'you-and-you-only', and to make it quite clear to a room full of bystanders that he is saying these things to one person; but since the time of our Renaissance, our culture and institutions have developed concepts of public behaviour, required conduct, 'good form', 'taste', etc., and have rejected or not overtly recognised the possible co-existence of private relationships and public dealings which might have seemed natural, say, to a Tudor nobleman in his household and estate. The move towards what might be called 'the public standard' of address is incidentally documented in our literature. In Jane Austen's

books, for instance, husbands and wives address each other with cere-
monies of *Mrs* and *Mr,* even in intimate *tête-à-tête* conversations.
One of the finest illustrations, however, is that superb speech in Congreve's *The Way of the World,* in which Millamant exclaims:

> . . . good Mirabell, don't let us be familiar or fond, nor kiss before
> folks, like my Lady Fadler and Sir Francis; nor go to Hyde-park
> together the first Sunday in a new chariot to provoke eyes and
> whispers, and then never to be seen there again; as if we were
> proud of one another the first week, and ashamed of one another
> ever after. Let us never visit together, not go to a play together;
> but let us be very strange and well-bred; let us be as strange as if
> we had been married a great while; and as well-bred as if we were
> not married at all.

Here Millamant raises a cultural standard, an elegant proclamation of
' the done thing ', which defies the intimacies of *thou* and *thee.*

It is obvious that contact with other cultures can have appreciable
consequences in changing or expanding the vocabulary of a language
– we have ample evidence for this in our stock of French words
introduced into English in the centuries following the Norman
Conquest, or in the host of Latin words imported by classicising Tudor
scholars. What is perhaps less apparent is that such contacts also
affect the forms of grammar, in some instances so grossly that we are
able to point out particular features as *Latinisms, Gallicisms, Ger-
manisms,* etc. When, for instance, we meet in the Wyclifite Bible versions such constructions as . . . *A man in unclene spirit ran out of a
biryel, to hym goynge out of the boot,* or *And Jhesus, gon out
thennis, wente in-to his owne cuntree,* it is clear that *to hym goynge
out of* and *gon out thennis* are not native English, but imitations of a
Latin model. These particular Latinisms may strike us as odd simply
because we do not meet them in modern English; but we meet, and
use, participial constructions which are not unlike these and which
represent an adaptation of English to the Latin idiomatic model, e.g.
*His task completed, he turned for home, All else failing, try cod-liver
oil, John having been elected, we can now expect some action, Saying
which, she left the room,* etc. Another instance of Latinism in English
appears in the schoolday rule whimsically expressed in the form ' a
preposition is a bad word to end a sentence with '. In native English
syntax, prepositions can easily and naturally occupy the sentence-final
position. The ' rule ' is really an observation of the literary style of

classical Latin. Slavish adherence to it can produce stilted and tor-
tuous phrasing of the kind Sir Winston Churchill was objecting to
when he rejected a pompously-written memorandum as an example
of bad English, ' up with which I will not put '.

As to Gallicisms, they abound with us and we are barely conscious
of them, for after the Conquest much of our syntax was eased into a
French pattern. This is hardly what we mean by a ' Gallicism ' now;
but all the same it is worth reminding ourselves of the early and
considerable French influence on our syntax. In the fourth of the
examples of English-through-the-ages with which this chapter begins,
there occurs the construction *And al swo hi hedden i-fonden ure
louerd,* ' and when they had found Our Lord '. This word-order
probably reflects the French influence; as a rule, old English depen-
dent-clause syntax would have required *And al swo hi hedden ure
louerd i-fonden,* ' and when they had Our Lord found '. The Gallicis-
ing influence is also seen in one or two important details of our
phrase-structure – for example, in the development of what is sometimes called the ' of '-genitive. In Old English we find *Carl Francna
cyning,* ' Charles, the Franks' king '; in modern English we say
Charles, King of the Franks. In the centuries following the Conquest
the case-inflections of the noun, including the genitive plural seen in
Franc-na, were eroded or levelled. A general type of genitive singular,
the so-called s-genitive, remained, but even so it proved more convenient in many instances to express the genitive relationship by
means of an *of*-phrase modelled on the French *de* plus nominal phrase,
e.g. to say *the back of my head* rather than *my head's back,* or *the
bottom* of *my heart* rather than *my heart's bottom* (!). In some
instances, the Germanic and the Gallic phrase-structures have provided us with stylistic alternatives, i.e. *the journey's end* and *the end
of the journey;* whilst in others the Germanic structure has been
accommodated to the formation of a new kind of compound, so that
against *the top of the roof, the sleeve of my coat, the noise of jets* we
have *the rooftop, my coat-sleeve, the jet noise,* etc.

The most powerful arbiter and modifier of our grammar, comprehending the inventive power of individuals, the effects of cultural
contact, and all other such influences, is, however, the medium of writing. Writing functions in part as an inhibitive, prescriptive, rule-giving
medium, the ultimate linguistic authority. ' What you can write ' is
a matter of higher moment than ' what you can say '. However,
writing works exhibitively as well as inhibitively. A piece of writing

need not be in its entirety a manifestation of rules; it can be a work-shop, a laboratory, the scene of experiment, improvisation, innovation. Such experiment does not have to be outrageously bold; it may simply take the form of trying to use basic structural rules and devices to produce sentences of some length and complexity, sentences which convey with complete lucidity some possibly quite involved set of relationships. This may lead (and indeed has led) to the evolution of a writing habit, the procedures of which are rather different from those of colloquial habit, but which eventually have a modifying effect on colloquy. Opening today's *Times* (30 April, 1970), I find this sentence in the second leader:

> For Americans the combinations of an apparently unstoppable rise in prices with a sharp downturn of production and company profits has produced a loss of confidence by investors – led by institutional investors – as well as rising unemployment.

This displays fairly well the characteristic of writing as an array of structures which can be visually assimilated and related; that inter-polated clause, for instance, is acceptable in a long written sentence but would be an intolerable burden on a listener's attention if it were produced in speech. In fact, if the pattern of reference underlying this sentence had to be related to colloquy the grammatical structures would be somewhat differently organised, to produce results rather like the following:

> The American investors are losing confidence. Especially the institutional investors. It's the combination of two things. There's the rise in prices, and there's the drop in production and profits. They don't seem to be able to stop the prices going up. On top of that, there's rising unemployment.

This represents an extreme of colloquial structure, which, however, we might modify thus:

> The American investors, first and foremost the institutional investors, are losing confidence. It's the combination of a rise in prices, which they don't seem to be able to stop, and a fall in production and profits. In addition, there's rising unemployment.

This is still rather more like the language of colloquy than the original sentence from *The Times,* but it is a bookish sort of colloquy, the impression of bookishness arising from devices like the amplifying *which*-clause in the second sentence, or the extended subject in the first sentence, a type of construction which we associate primarily with writing rather than with speech. The transference of language-read into the domain of language-spoken creates a particular style of colloquy which is appropriate to certain social contexts – e.g. a club, a board-room, a university common-room. Through exercise in these institutional contexts, the more useful and recurrent devices of written language enter into the domain of speech. It is very largely in this way that the concepts of ' correctness ' and ' standard ' in English grammar have been established and propagated during the last two and a half centuries.

For the layman, and perhaps for the scholar too, the most interesting, complex, and richly-documented aspect of the history of our language is the unfolding tale of its words and meanings. It may be that this aspect of language is most attractive because here code and environment demonstrably meet, here the externals of our cultural experience can be immediately traced in the innovations and changing applications of our symbolism. If we were to investigate these matters thoroughly, we would have to take into account a number of factors which make the study of semantics rather more complex and uncertain than the study of phonetics or grammar. We would have to establish, for instance, the means by which lexical items are constructed or acquired in English, and the means of generating or acquiring new items; we would have to consider how changes in the material being of the culture necessitated the invention or importation of new words and the rejection or modified use of old ones; how some symbols have come to acquire new, or somewhat changed, referents; how the meanings of some words have been extended, whilst those of others have been restricted; how the habitual use of words in certain situations or verbal contexts has contributed to the modification of their meaning – and so on.

To attempt this here would be too ambitious, but it is possible to take some of these factors into consideration if we consider the lexicon from a single point of view, i.e. as an economy, in which every symbol has a value which justifies its continuance in use. The principles of the economy may be summarised as follows:

1. No word is otiose. Every item in the living lexicon has an especial point or range of reference, declarative or evaluative, not covered by any other lexical item, even by those regarded as synonymous or closely related in meaning. Every word is uniquely meaningful in some particular context – and is hence indispensable. If a word

lacks this uniqueness it must drop out of the vocabulary – unless a special role is created for it. The shifts, expansions, and contractions of reference which we can observe in the histories of some words are the result of this, the first principle of the economy. For example, Old English had a word *ealdormann*, meaning, primarily, a man of noble rank, a chieftain. When, after the Conquest, the Normans imposed their own hierarchy on the English, the native rank-words, with a few exceptions such as *king, queen,* and *earl* (a Scandinavian word) were lost, and others like *prince, duke, count,* etc. took their place. The word *ealdormann*, or *aldormann*, however, has survived into modern times as *alderman*, but has survived only because a specific, and some-what reduced reference, has been available for it.

2. The adequacy of our symbolism may be challenged by altera-tions in our culture. These call for the modification of existing patterns of reference and the introduction of new lexical items; but the creation of new elements in the vocabulary may have an effect on the culture itself. The borrowing, adaptation, or creation of new words and expressions may have the paradoxical consequence of bringing into sharp definition cultural realities hitherto not very clearly appre-hended. In this way, *words* can perform the apparent wonder of bring-ing *things* into being. A pertinent example offers itself in the case of the word *teenager*. One wonders quite how the social vocabulary of English managed to deal with the concept in the absence of this useful word. Certainly the *thing* was felt to exist long before the *word* arrived. The old shepherd in Shakespeare's *Winter's Tale* felt the teenage impact all too shrewdly:

> I would there were no age between sixteen and three-and-twenty,
> or that youth would sleep out the rest; for there is nothing
> in the between but getting wenches with child, wronging the
> ancientry, stealing, fighting.*

However, in spite of this dismally accurate piece of social reportage it must be objected that *youth* does not have quite the same reference as modern *teenager*. Having the word has helped us to define not only an age-group, but a set of social problems which we feel to be peculiar to that group, and also a complex of social *mores* which we acknow-ledge when we talk about *teenage fashions, teenage music, teenage holidays,* etc. In sum, the situation is that Shakespeare had the word

* Shakespeare, *The Winter's Tale*, III, ii, 57ff.

youth; we have the words *youth and teenager*, the later having different overtones and referring to something specific in our social organisation. It does not, however, merely *point* the reference; the symbol has helped in some measure to *create* the reference.

3. Every language develops means by which the symbolic economy may be expanded, In English, for instance, we can derive new lexical items by means of prefixes and suffixes, or by creating compound words. Or again, we may borrow words from other languages; indeed it has been by this means above all others that our vocabulary has expanded over the centuries. But the vocabulary may also be increased by making existing items semantically polyvalent; so that the word *form*, say, is in effect a different item in *Roger came top of the form in maths, Tottenham are at the top of their form just now, The patients sat on a form in the waiting room, A familiar form appeared in the doorway, I had to fill in a form*, etc. The case here is not that the vocabulary is increased, but that the value of an item is increased. The polyvalency of items is also the result of creations in metaphor and slang; we extend the value of *round* metaphorically in phrases like *paper round, round of golf, round of drinks, round of applause*, or we give an evaluative, non-sensational meaning to *dim* and *bright* when we say *that fellow's dim* or *John has some bright ideas*. Some metaphors are fixed in long established idioms, e.g. *sailing close to the wind, riding for a fall, fishing for compliments, shooting wide of the mark*, etc. These phrases are subject to the same histories of gain and loss and shift of meaning as single word-items, and a language accumulates a stock of idioms which have a great deal to tell about successive phases in its cultural history, but which stay alive as meaningful and useful items long after the material impetus from which they originated is spent – witness *a flash in the pan* and *lock, stock and barrel*.

The lexicon may be expanded in these various ways, and the expansion may take place irrespective of expansion or change in cultural substance; but the economy is always subject to the principles outlined above, and though we may derive, compound, borrow, or coin words at will, the mere resourcefulness of our language and of our own wits is no guarantee that these inventions will have any great lease of life. The reason why slang words so quickly die out and give place to new ones is that they are an inflation in the lexical economy; there is no cultural substance to justify them, apart from the need for secrecy in small groups and societies, or the individual craving for self-assertion – neither of them strong guarantees of value. Occasionally a piece of slang supplies a gradation in the coinage, and so survives. The word *flog*, for instance, was in the seventeenth century a piece of underworld *argot*, but it became standard presumably because it supplied a reference or shade of reference in the set which includes *whip, beat, thrash, flay*, etc. Another survival is the word *mob*, a piece of eighteenth-century smart-talk (being an abbreviation of *mobile vulgus*, 'unstable crowd') which annoyed Dean Swift; the failure of whose great authority to excise this and other innovations is a proof of Samuel Johnson's assertion that 'to enchain syllables, and to lash the wind, are equally the undertakings of pride, unwilling to measure its desires by its strength'.*

Every item brought into the lexicon in answer to these principles has a derivational and semantic history, and thereby a relationship to other symbols in the lexical stock, which is naturally of great interest to the etymologist and semasiologist. The ramifications of this history are complex indeed, but we can suggest a few main lines of development. In the first place, an etymological study of English would reveal the existence of many cognates, i.e. words springing from the same origin. Thus we have a set of cognates in our words *dish, disc*, and *desk*, and we see how from a common root three distinct meanings have been produced, meanings which in their turn may be further differentiated and extended in new contexts; so that *disc* in one instance may mean a gramophone record and in another may refer to the piece of paper which the British motorist displays in the windscreen of his car as evidence that he has paid his vehicle registration tax. From one root a multiplicity of meanings may thus flower. Another interesting feature of our English lexicon is that its admixture of etymological strains has yielded a number of words which are of different origin but which are structural parallels and are allied in meaning. We have examples of this in *overseer* as against *supervisor*, or *contradict* as compared with *gainsay*, or – perhaps less obviously – *heedful* as against *obedient*.† And then again, there are items which, like these, are structurally parallel, but which do not share a field of reference; for example, *subscribe* and *underwrite*, or *remorse* and *backbiting*.

In some instances, items once structurally and semantically parallel branch into different references and become semantically remote. We

---

* From the preface to his *Dictionary*.
† The root element—*edi*—is a reduced form of *audi(re)*, 'hear', 'heed'.

see this in the history of our words *devour* and *fret*. They are of different provenance, but are structurally parallel (*de-vorare*, Goth. *fra-etan*),* and both originally had roughly the same ' objective ' or ' declarative ' meaning; *fret*, however, has shifted to an especial 'subjective ' or ' evaluative' reference, thereby justifying its continued existence as a lexical item, in accordance with the first of our principles of the symbolic economy. Another, somewhat rare, type of word-history is illustrated by the word *focus* as compared with *hearth* and *fireplace*. The two latter co-exist because they do not make exactly the same reference. Their joint coverage, however, is sufficient to preclude the necessity of any other word; so that when the Latin word *focus*, which originally meant 'hearth ' or ' fireplace ', was brought into English, it was reborn with a new meaning. Of its original significance there is no trace in present-day English common usage, so that it is perfectly possible for us to speak of the fireplace as being the focal point in a room without being aware that we are thereby declaring it to be the place for a fire.

Derivations and histories are of importance to the student of language; for the layman, they may certainly be interesting, but they do not figure as realities in his linguistic experience. For him, the items of the lexicon need never be put to the etymological question or sent to the semantic laboratory. He does not experience his vocabulary in this analytical way. His concern is, quite properly, to have names for things. And not only for things; for themes, for situations, – since what we seek to acquire in our daily barter with language is not a collection of separate word-and-thing specimens, but rather sets of terms which are related to each other in their mediation of important areas of experience, or in their manifestation of our social institutions. If, for example, we move in the world of commerce, we need a set of words answering to the theme of commercial life, a set which would include, among many others, *capital, insurance, investment, underwrite, finance,* and *broker*. Each of these words has a history which relates it to other words and things, but such histories are presumably of very little importance to a company director. What matters to him, linguistically, is the coherence of a set of terms which will enable him to discuss his affairs and do his job. The connection of *finance,* for example, with the adjective *final* or the noun *fine,* is an aspect of its separate name-and-thing history which is irrelevant to his needs. His only concern is with the importance of this name, this symbol, as an element

* i.e. ' to eat ' (*vorare, etan*) ' away ' (*de, fra*).

combining with other elements to mediate the experience of business life.

And this, finally, is how we experience not only the words, but also the grammatical constructions and the sounds of language. The machine is there to be used, in all its intricate robustness and simple vulnerability. Needing the vehicle, we use it, seldom asking how it works, seldom caring even how well it works. And it lives and dies with us, this machine of language, lurching into our change, grumbling through our decline; and living again as testily and triumphantly as ever, with the generations which follow us. But that is something else that need hardly concern us committee-men of the common tongue. Only philologists and poets, the mechanics and magicians of language, need give much thought to that.

Long, long ago, in the land of Example, there was a young fellow called Hokum, who was good for nothing in particular. All the other Exemplars (for so the members of the tribe were called) had some socially-useful office to perform. Blessum the Priest, for instance, had a remarkable talent for rain-making, and was regarded as an indispensable adjunct to burials and weddings. Foggum the Lawyer was a good man to call in when the knives were out over the possession of a wife or a lucky-coloured horse. The tribal doctor, Dosum, was valued for his comforting presence at the deathbeds of those stricken by a hostile flint or the sweating plague. As for Cookum, Catchum, Thumpum, Growum, Makeum and Mendum and all the other members of the Exemplary race, each and every one had a place and a value – all, that is, except Hokum. Hokum had very little use that anyone could see, and so to keep him out of harm's way and justify his measure of rice from the communal pot, they put him to teaching the boys and girls.

In this task, Hokum had a free hand, for the Exemplars were convinced that nothing worth doing could be taught or untaught, and therefore regarded the education of their children primarily as a matter of inculcating the appropriate tribal attitudes towards the gods, the chieftains and elders, foreigners, women, war, sickness, death, and such-like. Provided that Hokum fulfilled his obligations in this respect, people were willing to leave him alone, although there were those who grumbled about the time he devoted to unscheduled activities such as sitting and thinking. Hokum found, by trial and error, that the tribal moralities could be conveyed to the young by various means, each in its proper place as efficacious as the other. The ultimate in demonstration was the hard end of a knuckle-bone, but Hokum, during his periods of sitting and thinking, found himself increasingly moved to doubt the validity of this teaching method. As a forward-looking instructor, he felt convinced that the future lay less with actions than with words, and he began to devote more and more time to the study of the verbal technique. Parents who noted in their offspring an increase in cheerfulness and a decrease in facial contusions, were inclined to be querulous and critical. 'They don't learn anything nowadays', they would complain, 'they only play'. But Hokum, undeterred, went on to develop theories of precept, of argument, and of fable. He loved the latter best of all. When he devised fables by which to teach his pupils about the nature and the justice of the gods, he would feel a relish of heart and mind, as though he were cooking some good stew, and when some specially piquant flavour of language tickled his imagination, he would feel a delightful shiveriness about his neck and shoulders, and a tightening in his throat, and even a pricking of tears in his eyes, such as the sharpest of Cookum's sauces could not have produced. But what was best of all was the response of his audience. When he first abandoned lashing in favour of locution, they hardly took any notice of him. 'He can't keep discipline', one parent would then tell another; 'in my day, it would have been three hours spread-eagled over an ant's nest if you so much as scratched yourself – and it's done me no harm, that I can see.' Gradually, though, the youngsters began to be aware that Hokum's addresses to them had a peculiar appeal, and presently his classes began to listen, at first attentive, then spellbound, and in the end with a kind of happy hunger. It even happened that the adults of the tribe, on their way to and from their so necessary tasks, would loiter for a moment or two on the fringes of Hokum's study-circle – and they, too, would be caught in the charm of saying.

The Exemplars began to be aware that Hokum was a citizen of value, for he had developed a new skill. On all matters verbal, they deferred to him and consulted him. Blessum discovered that in the composition of liturgies Hokum was a veritable magician. Foggum found him just the chap for making an argument both tricky and un-intelligible; Dosum used Hokum's words to console the bereaved and prepare the next patient for his fate. Even people like Catchum and Thumpum had something to learn, for Hokum lent Catchum good consoling oaths to use when the quarry eluded his nets, and taught Thumpum how to fortify himself with boasts before advancing upon a resolute foe. The only person who was less than happy with the evolution of Hokum's skills was Watchum, the tribal censor. 'Words are getting above themselves ', he remarked, somewhat obscurely. ' Words are taking over from things. No good will come of it – you mark my words.' But a Hokum-orientated populace could not understand what Watchum was getting at, and laughingly dismissed him as a sour old conservative. In the meantime, Hokum had made the interesting discovery that words have the power to move masses, and in order to facilitate his experiments in this line, had founded the tribe's first political party, in conjunction with an agitator and malcontent called Pokum. They called their party the Hocus-Pocus party, HP for short. Hokum was not greatly interested in the philosophy and aims of HP, for he had come to believe that style was everything and content nothing in particular. He left policy to Pokum and concentrated on devising potent forms of words calculated to move the populace, drunk or sober, towards a glad acceptance of the party's aims. That Pokum's political philosophy was in some measure insane, in some measure vindictive, and in a great measure downright nasty, bothered him much less than the problem of contriving a thing-dissociated rhetoric that would convince an audience of the completely logical, patriotic, and humane necessity of forbidding mixed dancing and decapitating the over-forties. So strikingly did he solve this and other problems that the land was torn with rioting and civil disquiet, for which Hokum energetically disclaimed responsibility, remarking that it was one thing to say *bash* and another to go and do it.

There were, however, those thoughtful souls who considered the HP to be a danger to the community, and who felt that the Hocus element was particularly dangerous, as being necessary to the Pocus. In the civic interest, therefore, a band of resolute men waylaid Hokum one night as he was wandering somewhat gormlessly through the forest, meditating an oration on pensions for parricides. Very wisely, they allowed no time for discourse, but promptly despatched him, braying him to death with jawbones, in the grand old style, before returning discreetly to their families, warm with a sense of duty done and calamity averted. Hokum's body was accorded a state funeral, at which Blessum the Priest presided with great dignity, and where Chief Tellum held a valedictory oration of such sweetness and power that many who heard it, including Hokum's assassins, were moved to tears. They realised then that Hokum was indestructible, for round them they saw his pupils and his works, for better or worse; and if they had had the skill to say it, they might have echoed the saying of one of Hokum's sage and serious latterday apostles :

Time, that is intolerant
Of the brave and innocent,
And indifferent, in a week,
To a beautiful physique,

Worships language, and forgives
Everyone by whom it lives . . .*

But they did not have such skill, for while all may feel the power of Hokum, few can wield it; and that, we may say in conclusion of the fable, was Hokum's revenge on his enemies.

If we were to guess at the content of Chief Tellum's funeral oration, we might suppose him to have said that Hokum added three human graces to the divine ordinance of language. The first of these, we may call *ritual*. Ritual is essentially what distinguishes the high art from the low cunning of language, the distinction being otherwise hardly tenable. By ' ritual ' is meant the formalisation of some element in human experience, so that in its symbolic presence it may seem incorruptible or desirable or bearable. We have language-rituals to enable us to cope with the terrors of death, to convince ourselves of the immutability of love and beauty, to honour the assumptions of the tribe, to fortify ourselves against the apparent wilfulness of fortune, to justify the ways of God to man. Out of such ritualising, out of a need to burn fiery shapes and festive lights against the chaotic dark, the world's great literature has grown. A second ' grace ' of language may be called *purpose*, meaning a crafty and forethinking purpose as distinct from the more or less casual purpose of informal usage. Language may be used for the purpose of expounding an argument, a theory, the tenets of a branch of knowledge; or, again, it may be used for the purpose of persuading an audience to share a belief, accept certain assertions, undertake certain courses of action. ' Purpose ' like ' ritual ' is bound up with human experience, but as a general distinction we may say that while ' ritualising ' language relates to man in his universal predicaments, which he must face as an individual, 'purposive ' language has to do with the experience of men in institutions and social communities, e.g. churches, schools, political parties, clubs, etc. Ritualising and purposive language may co-exist within a situation, and even coincide. In a lawcourt, for instance, there

* W. H. Auden, *In Memory of W. B. Yeats, Collected Shorter Poems* (Faber & Faber, London, 1950), p. 66.

is much formulaic ritual, designed to emphasise the authority and continuity of the law, and there is also a good deal of purposive, 'cunning' language in the addresses of prosecuting and defence counsel. Again, there are certain kinds of philosophic writing, for example the dialogues of Plato, which are ostensibly purposive, but which in some places enter into the solemnities of ritual. Nobody, surely, could read the *Phaedo* and feel that he had merely followed a demonstration of a rational basis for a faith in immortality; he must feel also that he had attended one of the greater rituals in which man has outspoken death.

But the third, and greatest, heirloom of Hokum is the principle of *pleasure*. We may use language without pleasure, and often do; much as we may eat without pleasure, take exercise as a matter of routine, work without joy. But where art is, where craft is, where self-awareness and self-criticism are, where pains are taken for perfection's sake, there also is pleasure. There is a pleasure of receiving in language, a pleasure consisting not only of a willingness to be practised upon, but also of a keener pleasure in detecting the secrets of practice. There is also the greater, much-desired, infinitely-painful pleasure of creating. So great is this pleasure, that in our artistry we may belie the themes of our art, creating elegies in a kind of triumphal exhilaration, writing of unknown impossible loves with a splendidly contrived mournfulness. And it is pleasure which mitigates the drudge and trudge of 'purposive' language. Writing the foolish fable of Hokum with which this chapter begins was to me a gaiety, a treat, full of trivial secretive delights of allusiveness and stylistic contrivance, which I am quite content to share with myself alone. Such treats encourage us to redeem our ordinary mismanagement of language; we wake, temporarily, from the ghastly automatic slumber of long lectures and plodding pages.

Now we may take note that any text, any piece of crafty language, may be produced for the sake of pleasure alone. For instance, I am quite often requested, by my family, to produce limericks on a given first line, usually embodying a final word which will tax my ingenuity as a rhymester, or else containing a proposition that will be difficult to bend into the limerick's customary models of narrative syntax. Since these requests are often made during trips in the family car, I have furnished myself with ready-made limericks and part-limericks, manifesting rhymes for the names of local cities and towns – e.g. *There was a young lover of Leicester / Whose lass was a fervent proteicester,* or *A mother of seven in Mansfield / Slaved over her stove till her hanspield'.* Of several stored examples on the rhyme-theme of ' Nottingham ', one runs:

> There was an old poet of Nottingham
> Who ruined his verses by blottingham;
>   They would founder and sink
>   In a broad sea of ink
> Till his readers had trouble in spottingham.

The pleasures offered me in the composition of such squibs are those of overcoming, at a very crude level and working under funny-face rules, the sort of problems which beset men engaged on works of somewhat higher literary endeavour. There is problem of rhyme, a problem of metrication, and a problem of syntax or formulaic narrative development. These problems are interrelated in ways which defy brief statement, even though the limerick form is so simple. It involves only two rhymes, two metrical types, and only, as a rule, two narrative phases – a theme and first statement in the first two lines and a development plus conclusion in the remaining three. Furthermore, the composer's rhymes may be as ludicrous, the contents of his stanza as absurd, as he pleases, so long as the whole has an acceptable syntactic shape. Yet even so the permutations and constraints upon poetic practice are numerous. In the matter of rhyme, for instance, the problem is not merely to find rhyme-words, but to cope with the effects of spacing. The rhyming word in the second of the two short lines follows quickly upon its model. The rhyming word at the end of the last line, on the other hand, comes at some distance from its fellows in lines one and two, and is the ultimate projection of the syntactic development begun with the first of the two short lines. The rhyming words are thus deeply involved in the syntax and phrasing of the limerick. They are also bound up with its rhythms; it is often the case that when the ' long line ' rhymes are feminine, those of the short lines are masculine, and vice versa. It is of course the last line of the limerick which presents the stiffest challenge, because by the time it is reached the composer is not only committed to a rhyme but also, probably, to a limited set of syntactic choices. Edward Lear, however, avoided this problem in the ' classical ' form of the limerick by making the last line a repetition of the first.

To avoid the foolishness of earnestly discussing the technicalities of limerick composition, let us simply say that the limerick offers technical problems of mild difficulty, which are pleasurably amenable to ingenious and often bizarre solutions. The limerick as a form is associated with the gaining and giving of pleasure to the virtual exclusion of any other motive, spiritual or practical. However, it would be possible for me to write:

> A creedless believer in Nottingham
> Unravelled his problems by knottingham,
> > Though he did it with style
> > And a harrowing smile,
> That troubled believer in Nottingham,

and for this to be understood as a serious thought in a jingling guise. a merry-melancholy masquerade. A reader choosing such an interpretation might do so on the basis of observations consciously or unconsciously made – e.g. on the use of homophony, ambiguity, paradox, lexical oppositions, the 'classical' limerick form, etc. By seeking to test his intuitions against the evident pattern of such devices, the critic might conclude that this is no limerick-for-pleasure, but a composition in a minor key, a limerick-for-ritual, devised by the composer as a talisman against his puzzlements. Quite a different conclusion would be invited by the following text:

> Remember, you gardeners of Nottingham,
> Take care of your seedlings when pottingham,
> > Using measures discreet
> > Of topsoil and peat
> And water to rear, without rottingham.

No ritual here, but all precept and purpose; the language is a directive dance, an application of the pleasure principle to utilitarian ends. Thus we may compose (and interpret other people's compositions) in a spirit of ritual, of social purpose, or of pure pleasure, or in some admixture of these.

Another way of putting this – although it is perhaps to be avoided because of the evaluative measure it falsely implies – is that there are 'higher' and 'lower', or 'art' and 'craft' uses of language, in either of which pleasure is an informing principle, sustaining the composer and appealing to his audience. The identification of 'higher' or 'lower', however, is applicable not so much to language itself, or even to its content, as to the attitudes and intentions of the language-user.

If we write to Mr Bloggs the grocer a letter of condolence on the

death of a member of his family, we may approach the task as though
entering upon a purificatory ritual, an enactment of words which will
do more than convey sympathy, more than demonstrate the social conventions of our culture, more, even, than to assert our common
humanity – which will, ultimately, avert the menacing shades and
placate the kindly ones with an offering of the appropriate form.
The result is an essay in the ' higher ' language. If, on the other hand,
we write to Mr Bloggs as a neighbour protesting against the un-
hygienic proclivities of his bull mastiff, we may come to the work as
people bent on producing a result and scoring a personal triumph
without actually abandoning the conventions of politeness. The consequence now is an excursion into the delights of the ' lower ' language. But here we see how inappropriate, really, are the implications
of ' higher ' and ' lower '. Properly done, a missive to Bloggs gently
deploring the sad incontinence of his domestic livestock might require
enormous skill; and it is also a kind of ritual, for it provides a surrogate aggression, a thousand times preferable to violence against man
or beast, and better, on the whole, than an uncraftsmanlike *Keep
your blasted hound off my lawn*. In these instances, moreover, the
ritual, or ' higher ', and social, or ' lower ' essays in the skill of language are both made in the same form, the form of the letter, and
would draw on the same general range of technical resources, e.g.
euphony, rhythm, metaphor, precise word-choices, sentence-length
and balance, paragraphing, etc. However, it often happens that our
consciousness of ' higher ' and ' lower ' language-use is reflected in a
tendency to regard certain forms as appropriate to certain purposes. We
think, perhaps, of the sonnet as a literary form exquisitely calculated
to enable us to cope with the intolerable burdens of love and death,
whilst we are less likely to accept it as a suitable vehicle for a commercial eulogy of Dr Scholl's bunion pads. Conversely, we probably
regard the ballad-quatrain as suitable for an advertiser's jingle or for
a pop lyric, but not for a poetic meditation on the darkness of the
human soul.

These are conventional assumptions, of course. There is no reason
at all why an advertisement should not be packaged in octaves and
sestets (I fancy it has been done), or why serious poetry should not be
poignantly couched in the jingling of popular balladry (this has certainly been done). The fact is, though, that using a sonnet for a
commercial seems like harnessing a racehorse to a milk-float, whilst
using a pop quatrain for high poetry might be thought to be a little

like putting to sea in a bathtub; and it is not so much that the enterprise is unsound, as that Pegasus becomes a Dobbin, and the great ocean shrinks to a gravel-pit. The expressions 'good form' and 'bad form' here take on new dimensions of meaning. To use a limerick as a vehicle for religious meditation, for example, is to risk 'bad form' in this literary sense. As for technique, while it is true that we go to a common storehouse, whatever our literary purposes, it must be obvious that we use the technical resources of our language in different distributions and densities, so to speak, in accordance with our feeling of the appropriateness of language to purpose. Sentence-rhythm and sentence-length would probably be important considerations governing the style of both letters to Mr Bloggs suggested above, but the rhythms of condolence would certainly be differently managed from the rhythms of aggression. In writing a letter of sympathy, we might want to avoid a dandified, symmetrical, smoothly antithetical sentence-structure, whereas such an effect could be deliberately sought after, as a species of civil insolence, in a letter of complaint. Or, again, in complaining we might well have recourse to strategies of irony and insinuation that would be obviously inappropriate to a letter of sympathetic intent. Skilled language – art-language, if we like to call it that – can exist in many techniques, for various purposes, grand or mean. A common factor is that nearly all manifestations of art-language belong *ab initio* to the category of *address* rather than that of *interlocution;* and therefore demand, as a condition of successful effect, that the steps of their construction, the phases of their cohesion, shall be carefully devised, even though they may not always be made blatantly apparent. The stitching and scaffolding are part of the pleasure of art-language; the cunning maker designs his making so that some of the seams and rivets may be satisfyingly apparent, while others are no less satisfyingly hidden.

This means that in the skilled practice of language there is much conscious choosing and reflection. But there is also much instinctive assessing, much unconscious casting about, much rumouring from the common thoroughfare, much whispering from the man within. When language is used as an art-form, the normal model of communication is complicated by the introduction of a second order of message-making or encoding. That is to say, instead of this:

Sender . . . Encoding . . . CODE . . . Decoding . . . Receiver

we have something like this:

Encoding 2 . . . CODE 2 . . . Decoding 2
Sender ⟨   ⟩ Receiver
Encoding 1 . . . CODE 1 . . . Decoding 1

The normal processes of code-making are highlighted by the rein-
forcements and contrasts of a concomitant process which is in part
conceived and perceived as a background, in part felt as a power
which subsumes, selects, directs, and reorganises the resources of
common language. The processes of this second code are in some
measure overt and isolable, as devices in the repertoire of the literary
technician; and in some measure covert and implicit, either in the
primary code or in the shared situational and cultural experience of
sender and receiver. The overt, second-code processes may be
developed as specialised technical systems, but they are ultimately
derived from and dependent on the resources of the primary code.
The ingenuities of literary technique are governed by the structure
of the common tongue. A good example of this appears in the phenomenon we know as metre. Metre is a second-code device with a long
history of technical development; a book on English metres would
be weighty and complicated. Yet metre is an essentially simple concept, requiring merely that language should be accommodated to
isochronic patterns, to time-measures of equal length or value, rather
like the bars in music. The complexities of metre, as they appear to
us, are really complexities of varied rhythmical patterns in ordinary
spoken language. First-code language is not consistently isochronic –
we keep lengthening or shortening the bars and altering their accent-
patterns, changing the time-signature, as a musician might say. But
first-code language does have well-marked rhythms at the level of the
phrase – e.g. *a piece of cheese, two little boys, poor cold Fred, a
regrettable misunderstanding, God save the queen, people in glass
houses,* etc. These adventitious speech-rhythms invite the organisation,
the ' barring ', of metre, which provides the time-standard enabling
us to match phrases against each other. For example, if I run my eye
over the list of phrases I have just set down at random, I can see
certain possibilities of metrical association, e.g.

'God save the queen!' cried poor cold Fred

or

Two little boys with a piece of cheese

or

A regrettable misunderstanding
Of people in glass houses.

The metrication is achieved in these cases by picking out phrases of approximately equal value and accommodating them to a time-scheme, this being done by introducing ' filler ' words, i.e. *cried, with, of.* One of the pleasures and problems of versifying is that of finding strong metrical fillers, words which not only perform the desired function of adjusting bar-values, but also carry some more or less powerful contributory charge of meaning; as opposed to weak fillers, such as tame conjunctions or hackneyed adjectives. However, the point about the examples just devised is that in all cases the metre, or time-scheme, was suggested by the rhythm of the underlying phrases; I did not begin with some abstract metrical concept and try to impose this on language – although this is sometimes done by way of experiment and *tour-de-force,* as when poets try to impose classical verse-measures upon English, or attempt to wrench English to the framework of some eccentric musical scheme such as five-four time. As a rule, the rhythms of language are allowed to suggest the regularities of metre. Once the regularities have been promoted, how-ever, the composer feels them as a binding law, the reader as a pattern of expectations. It is here that metrication becomes difficult and exquisitely pleasurable, and here that genius and talent are marked off from mere hack-work, for in good verse the phrase-rhythms are constantly shifting and swaying, perhaps with some air of the natural artlessness of common speech, and yet never missing the metrical beat, never less than formal in their grace. Some of our pleasure in reading poetry arises from our eavesdropping on the lover's quarrel of rhythm with metre.

There are poets in whose work this dialogue, sometimes fretful, sometimes cajoling, sometimes downright strident, is a matter of central importance. It is hardly possible to read a stanza of Yeats, for example, without becoming aware of it:

> I pace upon the battlements and stare
> On the foundations of a house, or where
> Tree, like a sooty finger, starts from the earth;
> And send imagination forth
> Under the day's declining beam, and call
> Images and memories
> From ruin or from ancient trees,
> For I would ask a question of them all.

This is from his magnificent poem *The Tower,* a poem which is a model of the most precise assessment of the metrical potential of English phrase-rhythms; Yeats knows exactly how far he can take the colloquial manner without rambling into colloquial formlessness, without losing the solemnity of a measured and purposeful tread. The sense of ' barring ' is always present, the implication of regular accent is always there, yet the accents of speech-rhythm and the accents of metre do not always coincide, nor is the distribution of unstressed syllables quite what a ' regular ' metrist might consider proper. (Note, for example, how the second line begins with a little stumble of un-stressed syllables, *on the,* which is presently repeated in *of a;* and how the third line begins with a strong accent contrived by dropping an expected indefinite article; and how these apparently casual occur-rences affect the pace of the verse, finely suggesting a sporadic, fitful stirring of body and mind.) At other points in the poem, Yeats calls rhythm into open conflict with metre, e.g.:

> As I would question all, come all who can;
> Come old, necessitous, half-mounted man;
> And bring beauty's blind rambling celebrant;

If this is read aloud, the third line will almost certainly give difficulty at the first attempt. The first two lines establish a metrical expectation which the following line seems not to fulfil. It can be made to fulfil it, by paying careful attention to the distribution of strong accents. It is for the reader to decide how this distribution is to be made – and therefore to come to a decision as to the semantic interpretation of the line. What Yeats does here is something which certain poets, e.g. Donne and Hopkins, have elevated to a principle of composition; the opposition of rhythm to metre acquires a semantic value.

Rhyme, like metre, is a second-code technique, the potential of which is governed by the first code. The possibilities of rhyme in English are limited by the phonetic structure of the language, by the number and distribution of vowels and consonants, by the way syllables are built up. These are highly technical matters, and if we wish to avoid the grim trudge of theory, we had better do so by examining the possiblities and problems of rhyme in relationship to some specific cases. Let us take, for instance, the words *day, cut, switched,* and *prestige.* One of these offers no difficulties as a rhyming word; the others present different kinds of phonetic challenge. It is obviously a very easy matter to find rhymes for *day,* so easy that it would be merely wearisome to draw up a list. The reason above all others why this is an easy rhyming word is that the vowel (or rather, diphthong) is in the syllable-final position and is not followed by a consonant or a consonant-cluster. One following consonant – *date, dame, dale,* etc., would somewhat reduce the range of available rhymes, whilst a cluster – *dazed, deigned,* etc. – would reduce the possibilities still further. When the possibilities are so reduced, we are almost bound to light upon rhymes like *amazed, crazed, pained, disdained, stained* as a matter of automatic choice. The conditions of language itself direct us towards such choices, though as a rule we are unconscious of being linguistically directed and may even come to feel that there is a sort of magical necessity of association between *dazed* and *amazed* or *deigned* and *stained.*

Day is the only easy word in our list, for the remainder are all governed by the constraints of phonetic structure. *Cut* has a short vowel, and no versifier will readily allow himself to be forced into the position of having to find a short-vowel rhyme. Short vowels do not as a rule occur finally in monosyllables in English (there are exceptions to this in, for example, the reduced forms of *he, she, you*), but are followed by at least one consonant. In this case, the voiceless *t* following the short *u* presents just about the worst combination imaginable. Woe betide the poor versifier who might choose to introduce the word *cut* as one of the rhymes of a ballade! It is unlikely that the available choices would take him through three stanzas and an envoi. Consulting a rhyming dictionary (by an American author) in my possession, I find that the compiler lists the following rhymes for *cut*: 1. *ut* (?), *but, butt, phut, gut, hut, jut, scut, glut, slut, mut, mutt, smut, nut, putt, rut, strut, shut, tut, what.* 2. *abut, rebut, hagbut, catgut, woodcut, recut, uncut, haircut, clear-cut, cross-cut, besmut, peanut, chestnut, walnut, doughnut, burnut, beechnut, astrut, reshut, somewhat.* 3. *surrebut, scuttle butt, halibut, betel nut, hazelnut, butternut, coconut, occiput, Lilliput.** Of the items in this list, several are merely compounds (e.g. those in *-nut*), some are not rhymes in British English (*what, somewhat*), some are not idiomatically native to British English (*burnut, scuttle butt*), some are homophones (*but, butt*), some are not accented on the rhyming syllable and would only do for joke-rhymes or very boldly ventured light rhymes (*peanut, ha'ibut*) some are too trivial or slangy or archaic to be anything other than far-fetched rhymes (*ut, phut, tut, hagbut,* etc.). Faced with the task of

---

* *The Improved Rhyming Dictionary,* by Jane Shaw Whitfield, ed. Frances Stillman (Thames and Hudson, London, 1954).

writing something not too absurd with this word as an element in
the rhyme-scheme, I think I should feel safe only with *butt, gut, hut,
jut, glut, slut, smut, nut, rut, strut,* and *shut.* If these words suggest
any common theme or overlap of associations, it is possibly something
unpleasant. The rhyme might serve for themes of battle or bordello,
but if I were writing a love-poem I should not care to take responsibility for a word that only offers me such rhymes as *gut, slut,* and *rut.*
This constitutes a further limitation on the rhyme. With *day* you can
take up any theme; with *cut* your choices are uncomfortably restricted.

The phonetic limitations which reduce the value of *cut* as a rhyme
word are seen again in *switched.* Here the short vowel is followed by
what is for English a quite heavy final cluster of three voiceless consonants. The ingenious compiler of my rhyming dictionary offers only
the following possibilities: 1. *itched, bitched, ditched, hitched, niched,
snitched, pitched, stitched, twitched.* 2. *unhitched, enriched, restitched,
bewitched.* 3. *featherstitched* (!). It will be noted, apart from anything
else, that there is a grammatical limitation on these rhymes, which are
all preterite or past-participial forms. As for the last word in our
trial list, *prestige,* this presents a problem arising from the facts of
phonetic distribution. The sound /ʒ/ with which the word ends is
not native to English. It has developed, in word-medial positions, as a
result of combinative change, e.g. *measure* /meʒə/, *seizure* /siːʒə/,
etc.* In word-initial positions in borrowed words such as *judge, joke,
joy,* /ʒ/ has changed to /dʒ/. There remain a few words of foreign
(mostly French) origin in which the sound occurs in a final position,
e.g. *prestige, rouge, beige, garage, camouflage,* etc. These are very
few. Finding an exact rhyme for the final syllable of *prestige* is a
difficult, probably insoluble, problem. In words like *siege, liege,* etc.,
the original word-final /ʒ/ has changed to /dʒ/, thus undergoing the
same process as affects the sound in word-initial positions. It is more
than likely that this tendency will eventually overtake words like *prestige,* but at the moment the would-be rhymester's predicament is that a
sequence /iːʒ/ cannot be rhymed with anything closer than /iːdʒ/.

The technique and facility of rhyme is thus quite closely governed
by the phonetic structure of the underlying language. The phonetic
structure of English severely limits the possibility of feminine rhymes
and tends to promote hackneyed masculine rhymes of the *may-day,
moon-June* type. Our poets, of course, take an occasional rest from
rhyme and write in free or blank forms, but what is surprising, in

* The transcriptions are of common British pronunciations.

view of the difficulty and inanition of rhyme in English, is that the recessions from rhyme have not been more frequent. Instead of abandoning rhyme, however, poets have learned to cope delightfully with linguistic limitation by letting a well-worn rhyme fall on an un-accented syllable, by developing the technique of half-rhyme, and by other means which we must forbear to examine. For the poet, rhyme is meaningful, not only as a form of ornament, but also as an index to the mood of the poem, and as an organisational device marking out a framework. In these capacities it is closely associated with metre; indeed, I do not see that it is possible to describe the metre of a poem without paying some attention to its rhyme-scheme. 'Rhyme and metre', says the American poet Peter Viereck, 'are the unchanging stage on which the changing actors stumble or dance. By keeping rhyme regular, I can provide a background which, by contrast, makes more effective the utmost variety, change, and imaginative flight. When rhyme and rhythm become too irregular, there is no contrast to spotlight the goings-on of the actors on the stage.'*

Viereck's phrase 'the unchanging stage' is a useful metaphor, for it suggests regular occurrence, symmetry, design, and these are evident features of the second code. From the fluctuating conditions of phonetic distribution and phrase-rhythms, the poet constructs the regularity and design of rhyme and metre. This is not the only way in which he derives an art-material from the phonetic constituency of ordinary speech. He also subjects this constituency to what might be described as a change of density. To take an extreme (and very familiar) example:

> Glory be to God for dappled things –
>> For skies of couple-colour as a brinded cow;
>> For rose-moles all in stipple upon trout that swim;
> Fresh-firecoal chestnut-falls; finches' wings;
>> Landscape plotted and pieced – fold, fallow, and plough;
>> And all trades, their gear and tackle and trim.
>
> All things counter, original, spare, strange;
>> Whatever is fickle, freckled (who knows how?)
>> With swift, slow; sweet, sour; adazzle, dim;
> He gathers-forth whose beauty is past change:
>> Praise him.

* Peter Viereck, in *Mid-Century American Poets*, (Twayne Publishers Inc., New York, 1950), p. 19.

A dominant, indeed inescapable phonetic motif of Hopkins' *Pied Beauty* is the *l*-sound which occurs in almost every line. Some of its occurrences are perhaps merely random, but we can hardly escape the feeling that the sound has been a sort of psychological key to the vocabulary-choices, and this applies particularly to those cases in which the *l*-sound is associated with a sound of the ' plosive ' type, e.g. in the words *glory* (perhaps the phonetic and thematic key-word of the poem) *dappled, couple, stipple, plotted, tackle, fickle, freckled*. Such clusters of ' plosive ' (*p, k,* etc.) and ' lateral ' (*l*) consonants are normal in the phonetic distribution of English,* but what is abnormal or contra-normal, in the fashion of the second code, is the recurrence of several such clusters within a relatively short space, and, of course, in positions where accentuation draws attention to them. A similar observation can be made of the *r*-motif in the poem, particularly as we find it in items like *brinded, trout, trades, trim, strange,* and *praise*. In addition, the reader is bound to notice alliterating motifs in *f* and *s* and *t*, the occasional contingency of these on the *l* and *r* motifs (e.g. in *fresh, trim, slow*), and the occurrence of, as it were, minor phonetic themes, as in *adazzle* where the *zl* echoes the earlier *sl* of *slow*, or *dim,* which picks up the *d* of *adazzle*. The poem, we may say, obeys the laws of phonetic distribution, but flouts a principle of average density; one expects, as an ordinary rule of English structure, the occurrence of *p* and *k* and *g* and *s* sounds in combination with the *l*-sound, or of *t* and *b* and *p* sounds in combination with the *r*-sound, etc., but one does not expect to find so many instances within such a narrow compass and manifesting such intention of deliberate patterning. The cumulative effect of this patterning, it may be noted, is more than merely ornamental. A sort of phonetic metaphor is established; the poem presents aurally the impression of the title-word *pied*. It is worth emphasising that the densities of sound which a skilful poet contrives partly through the metrically-assisted regularities of alliteration and assonance, and partly through a free play of motifs which permeate the verse and which can emerge and recede as alliterative or accented items, are not merely ornamental. The phonetic texture so woven becomes part of the meaning of a poem. This does not mean that specific sounds or types of sound naturally suggest or symbolise particular things; it means that a poet, by working up a density of phonetic types in association with a particular theme, can persuade a reader to accept the equation of theme and phonetic motif.

* For ' plosive ', ' lateral ', etc., see the glossary of terms on p. 196.

The first code is a set of resources, given to any speaker of the language; the second code is a body of techniques by means of which patterns of selection, repetition, expectation, contrast, etc. are imposed upon or collated with the first-code material. This principle is observed in various ways in the phonetic, lexical and grammatical practice of art-language; it is one of the basic principles, perhaps the central principle, of literary style. Stylistic choices in the lexicon, for instance, derive their effectiveness from an implied contrast between the choice made and those felt to be available, or, to put it another way, between the actual individual choice and the norms of expectation established by cultural convention and linguistic usage. What pleases us about the lexical choices of a skilled writer or speaker is the quality of precision, the conviction – no doubt illusory – that this is the only and inevitable choice. A word may appear to us to be the exact word because of all the presentable candidates it is a complete outsider, and so arrives with a winning impact of surprise; or it may carry conviction because out of several possibles it seems most effective in the situational and verbal context.

One of Dr Johnson's remarks illustrates this rather well. He was being pestered, Boswell tells us, by a certain physician who claimed acquaintance with him and who felt that Johnson must have noticed him on the occasion of their meeting, if only because of the fine yellow coat he was wearing. 'Sir' said Johnson, '*had you been dipped in Pactolus I should not have noticed you.*' The extraordinary virtue of this brutally dismissive formulation is that one feels instantly the knock-down power of that exotic word *Pactolus* without necessarily having the slightest idea what it means. (*Pactolus* was a river of ancient Lydia, the sands of which were said to be the source of Croesus's gold.)

The word carries its phonetic credentials like a bludgeon and its mystery like a blunderbuss. This is one of those cases where the completely unlikely word scores the stylistic point; it would not have been one tenth as effective if Johnson had said *dipped in gold paint* or *coated with gilt*. But the word *dipped* also deserves some notice, for this is a right choice of the other kind, the best available member of a set of possibles, e.g. *coated, painted, plunged, soaked, drenched, doused. Dipped* is preferable to all these because it fights, so to speak, at the optimum weight. *Drenched* or *plunged* would have been ponderously aggressive; *coated* or *painted* too feeble and commonplace; *dipped* has just the required quantum of energy – and has the

incidental phonetic advantage that its consonantal sequence p–d
/*p–t*/ is sharply echoed in *Pactolus*.

There is a major difficulty in discussing the lexical practices of the
literary artist, in that we have no formal scale against which to assess
his stylistic choices. We have, if we will, a *metric* which enables us
to interpret rhythms, but we have no *lexic,* no similarly overt, agreed
measure, which helps us to evaluate diction. The items of our vocabulary are numerous, complex, deeply and intrinsically involved in our
intellectual and emotional life. They are a vast collection, interrelated in accordance with discernible yet fugitive principles of
patterning and association. We have seen how words may have an
external, or declarative, reference, which places them in the realm of
public discourse, or an internal, evaluative attribute which assigns
them to the domain of private judgement; or, indeed, how they may
have both characteristics simultaneously. This duality has its relevance to literary theory; the critic distinguishes between the *denotation,* or ' dictionary meaning ', of a word, and its *connotations,* or
accrued associations of feeling, cultural evaluation, remembered
experiences, various possibilities of purely personal response, etc.
Within these two modes of declarative and evaluative reference, the
items of the vocabulary are distributed in sets or families, the members
of which are sometimes numerous, sometimes few (we have described
this, in our first chapter, as ' high differentiation ' and ' low differentiation '). These sets intermingle with, and confront each other. The
word *courage,* for example, can be said to belong to the family of its
own gradations, i.e. *courage, fortitude, boldness, pluck,* and so forth,
and also to a set of words denoting the virtues, i.e. *courage, faith,
honesty, devotion,* etc.; hence it ' confronts ' the word *cowardice* and
its familiar associates. Each item of vocabulary, furthermore, may be
associated with some set phrase, or at least with some commonly
recurrent type of collocation; so that *hard,* for instance, might bring
to mind the fixed phrase *hard lines,* and also such phrases as *a hard
decision, a hard task, a hard winter,* which are not exactly fixed, but
occur with conventional frequency.

With these varying attributes, any item of vocabulary must seem
remarkably complex. How complex we may judge if we attempt a
quite superficial analysis of an apparently simple item, the word
white. The sketch on p. 168, entitled ' The World of White ', is, as
the sub-title indicates, merely a preliminary exploration. It is based,
furthermore, on one man's instrospection; a more exacting investigation

would require the charting of information from a number of sources. Indeed, the reader looking over this sketch will probably remark on a number of points where it might be extended or re-designed to bring it into accord with his own assessment of *white*. However, imperfect as it is, the diagram provides one or two points for consideration.

It is suggested that *white* has an outward aspect, or ' declarative moment ', represented by public usage of the word, and a corresponding ' evaluative moment ', involving the role of the word as an agent in the mental life of the individual. On the ' outward ' side, white denotes a colour, and this colour-name is transferred to certain familiar objects, e.g. *the white of an egg, the white of the eye*. It also occurs as an attribute in collocations, some of which are free but frequent, while others are fixed. Of the former, *white clouds* is a fair sample. Usage is not so hardened that we are *bound* to describe clouds as white; nevertheless, we frequently do. In such a collocation, *white* presents itself as a not unexpected item. It is otherwise with the fixed collocations, of which *white elephant* is a typical specimen. Here, the choice must be *white* and no other word. We cannot have a *creamy elephant*. Moreover, it is most likely that any native speaker would regard as strictly ungrammatical such a phrase as *a fairly white elephant;* one might as well talk of *a fairly mistake*. One would say, indeed, that *white elephant* is a phrasal compound, a kind of compound noun, rather than a divisible collocation consisting of an adjectival modifier followed by a noun-headword. This grammatical indivisibility is characteristic of most of the items listed under this head; moreover, it will be seen that, like *white of an egg,* etc, they represent quasi-metaphorical transfers and extensions of *white*. In such expressions as *white feather* or *white heat* we see public language giving some evidence of the workings of the ' evaluative moment '. There is an association (demonstrable in a ' matrix ' not represented in this diagram) between *white* and *weak, cowardly,* etc. There is also an association between whiteness and intensity, though no doubt this association was set up in the first instance by the observation of physical facts.

These familiar namings and collocations are further extended into ' cultural allusions ' – i.e. into phrases indicative of well-known features of literary and social experience. The list given in the diagram consists to a great extent of book-titles, a circumstance which doubtless tells more about the compiler of the list than about the object of compilation. Obviously, however, such a list is open-ended; I might, for

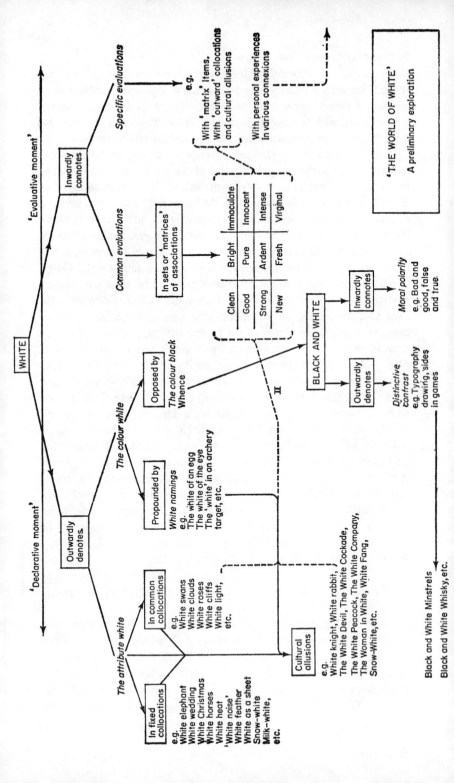

instance, have included *the white whale*, or *White Lady*, the name of a cocktail. Moreover, items listed here will probably have strong connotations that would refer them to the 'inward' side of the diagram.

In addition to being propounded by various namings and collocations, *white* is familiarly opposed to *black*, the conceptual opposition being outwardly recorded in the phrase *black and white*. The opposition, which is after all part of the meaning of *white*, thus yields a second term, *black and white*, which can in its turn be broken down into 'outward' and 'inward' elements of meaning. This is done very sketchily in our diagram, there being little space for detailed exposition. In any case, we should note that the outline suggests all sorts of junctures and points of departure into further areas of analysis. Semantic descriptions of this kind are never closed; we might go travelling on across nuance and notion until we found ourselves in some level of the lexicon remote from our point of origin, *white*.

On the 'inward' side of the diagram *white* connotes certain evaluative responses. Some of these are a matter of common psychology; in our communications we must rely to some extent on the supposition that others will react to verbal stimuli with affective responses broadly similar to our own. These common responses, it is suggested, are related in patterns, or matrices, where various connotations intermesh. One can hardly reduce to rule and line, or, indeed, to a single matrix, the complexities and shifting relationships of all the associations that go to make up the evaluative world of *white*, but a possible 'matrix', of a rather simple kind, is suggested here. *White* is seen as connoting *clean, good, strong*, and *new*, and each of these items connotes a set of its own. The resulant sets are so intimately related that the lines of the matrix may be read horizontally or vertically. Reading the lines in different directions promotes a tendency to identify different images; if I read *new, fresh, virginal*, I may think of snow or writing-paper, but if I read *immaculate, innocent, intense, virginal*, I might well think of a nun, or a marble statue. But the items of such a matrix may constantly group and re-group in new 'lines' suggestive of new images.

Apart from these common evaluations, there are specific associations in the form of highly individual and private responses to the item. Each of us will probably have a favoured reading of the 'matrix' proposed here. Each will associate the word *white* with some collocations rather than others. For me, the phrase, *white wedding* comes readily to mind; I have no idea why this should be, except that I make what I imagine to be a common association of *white* with *bridal,* an association which can be referred back to our 'matrix' pattern. Furthermore, any individual may have private experiences associated with the experience of white, and conditioning his responses to the word. We take it for granted, as a rule, that *white* has 'good' connotations; but a person who had undergone unpleasant experiences with which the sensation of whiteness happened to be associated might feel that *white* had bad, or tainted, connotations.

Such a representation as this no doubt occasions surprise that we can use the vocabulary at all, if this is indeed a superficial account of a simple specimen, let alone use it with artistic intent. Actually, the complexity and essential two-sidedness of the vocabulary is a source of power to the literary artist, whose choices must often be synthetic and instinctive rather than analytic and reasoned. Suppose, for instance, that I were to coin the phrase *a white enthusiasm.* (Be it said in parentheses that I do not thereby lay claim to the title of 'literary artist'!) What might I mean by *white* in such a context? My meaning, it may be suggested, is a composite or synthesis of a number of elements on both the 'outward side' and the 'inward side' of *white.* For example, there is a strong likelihood that the phrase has for its underlying model the common collocation *a white heat.* (It is interesting that I do not myself know whether this is so; I merely suspect it.) Furthermore, and in consonance with this, *white* here almost certainly expresses the notion of intensity. It is also not improbable that in this context I might wish to express the ideas of completeness, integrity, purity. Thus by exploiting what is publicly accepted about the word *white,* together with what may be inferred about my private experience of the word, I am able to solve a lexical problem which would otherwise be amenable only to gawky and ineffectual paraphrase. Instead of analysing, instead of talking about 'an intense, pure, all-possessing enthusiasm', I produce the powerful synthesis of the word *white.*

The synthesising instinct of the literary artist is most apparent in his use of metaphor. Metaphor is a topic which can hardly be dismissed in a paragraph, being a linguistic and cultural phenomenon of profound importance. It is a great error to suppose that the role of metaphor in language is merely to gratify our playfulness and our wish for pleasure. It is an eminent ritual device, by which we claim power over our existence and protection from the menacing darkness that presses upon our most determined enlightenment; it also has an important position in the economy of language, so that a Swedish scholar has rightly remarked that language is 'a gallery of faded metaphors'; above all, it is an important technique of definition, a technique that seeks to identify the complex qualities of experience by synthetic rather than analytic means. A metaphor illuminates one range of experience by appealing to another. This may be the only way in which a fugitive experience can be so illuminated; on the other hand, it may also be a way of making us see something quite familiar in a completely new light. Furthermore, the power of definition is made to work reciprocally. We learn about one experience by considering its kinship with another; we thereby also learn something about this other experience.

One case will perhaps stand for many in illustration of these points. In one of his poems, Louis MacNeice produces the striking phrase *the sea's tumultuous marble.** Clearly, what the poet is trying to identify here is not a simple, but a complex and even self-contradictory experience; for the sea is observed in violent movement, and yet the movement is apprehended as a stillness. The metaphor is a synthesis of this movement-in-stillness and stillness-in-movement. We may say rather prosaically that its elements are expressed in the propositions, *The waves are in violent motion, The waves are streaked with foam, The foam-streaks produce patterns like the markings on marble.* Such formulations express the primary content of the metaphor, but without the intensity that comes from selection and compression. From a range of possibilities (the ' differentiations ' of a set), the poet selects *tumultuous,* a word which, through its rhythmical energy alone, contributes to the tension and excitement of the phrase. This word is set in direct collocation with the word *marble* – a word with which, it may be noted, it is phonaesthetically bonded through the *m* and *l* sounds. This collocation sets up a striking, intensity-laden paradox, which is the centre of the metaphor; *tumtultuous* connotes violent movement (and noise), *marble* connotes an intense stillness (and silence). The paradox, it is suggested, is the result of linguistic compression alone, and is not present in the primary content of the figure, which is simply that when the waves move violently they become streaked with foam, and the foam suggests the markings on marble. In the primitive psychology of the figure there is an indirect comparison between the appearance of the sea and the appearance of

* Louis MacNeice, *Train to Dublin, Collected Poems, 1925-1948,* 3rd impression London: (Faber & Faber, 1954), pp. 83-4.

marble; in the final, linguistic, presentation, this indirect comparison
becomes a direct identification. And here the poet has made us the
happy victims of an illusion which is essential to his art. The underlying comparison between the sea and marble, or between sea-foam
and marble-markings, is, after all, an internal, private, interpretation
of phenomena. That is how one man *might* see it; there is no obvious,
objective, necessary connection. But by the time the figure is completed, we have come to accept the connection as somehow inevitable,
as though the metaphor were a revelation of external and public
experience. We feel we have learned something about the sea, something that was always there to be seen, had we but noticed it. More
than that, the revelation works reciprocally, for we also feel that we
have learned something about marble, and that having been shown
the sea's tumultuous marble we are now aware of marble's oceanic
vehemence. Long ago, incidentally, Aristotle used the term ' proportion ' in reference to metaphor, pointing out that there is a reciprocal
relationship, or proportion, between the associated elements.

Our vocabulary is thus patched with many colours. Its polyvalency,
however, is somehow controlled by the artist, the wit, the orator, and
this control must imply principles of choice. There is no *lexic,* no
overtly normative law; but it may be possible to infer determinants of
lexical choice which provide us with ghostly and subjective bearings
of the values of the words we use. What is suggested (no more than
tentatively) is that there are three interdependent principles, three
measures of verbal adequacy. One concerns the individual's desire to
inform his word-choices with affective power; one concerns, very
largely, patterns of usage and linguistic convention; and one is a matter
of the relevance of a choice to certain social contexts or to certain
themes. We may say that there are three scales, of intensity, comprehensiveness, and formality, and these scales give us subjective bearings
on what might be called the semantic contours of words and expressions. The scale of intensity measures our sense of the affective power
of a word; the scale of comprehensiveness indicates a linguistic range
from specific and limited usage at the lower end, to general applica-
bility at the upper; and the scale of formality indicates, in its mid-
range, normal social usage, with sub-formal and super-formal degrees
of usage on either side. Obviously, problems of estimation will arise,
thanks to the subjective nature of the criteria, as soon as we attempt
detailed illustration, but some simple examples should help to make
the basic case. Thus, on a scale of intensity, *intoxicated* may as a

general rule be felt to be of lower affective power than *drunk,* which in its turn is no doubt less intense than *pickled.* On a scale of comprehensiveness, *intoxicated* probably has a slightly wider range of applications than *drunk,* while *pickled* is most certainly an item of very restricted potential; one cannot be *pickled with power,* for example, or *pickled with one's own eloquence,* or *pickled by madam's perfumed beauty,* etc. On a formal scale, we would probably assign *intoxicated* to the super-formal status of special occasions and themes, and *pickled* to the sub-formal value appropriate to unbuttoned and vulgar colloquy; *drunk* would then hold the middle of the scale as an item of common formality. These speculations can be represented diagrammatically, thus:

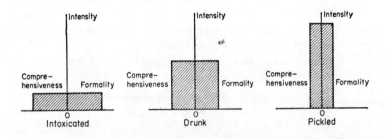

The 'semantic contours' of the three words are drawn on a frame in which the three scales run outward from a central zero point towards a maximum value. The examples conveniently represent the proposition that our vocabulary in general has areas of normality, or centrality, here represented by the square contour of *drunk,* and areas of special usage, represented by the 'peak' of *pickled* and the 'flattening' of *intoxicated.* These effects have of course been to some extent contrived by making the scale of intensity the vertical scale. The result may be to suggest the easy conclusion that there is a type of vocabulary shared by the poet, the orator, the trooper, and the schoolgirl, which in general aims at registering peaks of intensity, and another type, common to officialdom, administrators, executors, lawyers, and all pin-striped and precise men, which seeks the flat contour of the comprehensive and the formal. This is in fact too glib a distinction. Literary language, for instance, is not all peaks of intensity (if it were, poetry would be little more than a superior form of slang or swearing); the artist manages the shifting contours of a sequence of words in subtle and sophisticated ways that bespeak his awareness of values on all scales. Moreover, a peak of intensity is not the only form of stylistic culmen. Certain styles, e.g. irony, understatement, may require a high value of comprehensiveness or formality, and a deliberately low register of intensity. Thus, if I assert that *Broken glass is not fit sustenance for babies,* I choose as my peak-word (*sustenance*) an item which is almost demonstratively cool and unintense, but which would draw a long profile on the scale of formality. In fact, different stylistic intentions require different culminating scales. This can be illustrated by drawing contours with different scales in the vertical position; if the reader tries the experiment, however, he will notice that the items which produce a square contour in the first instance do so in subsequent instances. There appears to be a central vocabulary, a norm, our awareness of which makes possible the contrastive power of deviant choices. However, it is likely that we shall never have more than an intuitive grasp of the principles of lexical norm-and-variation.

The literary artist must obviously have a remarkable instinctive command of the phonetic and lexical structure of his native language. His artistry, however, is incomplete without what is perhaps the greatest endowment of all, an insight into the laws and facilities of syntax. The syntax of a language is its backbone, its architecture, a framework in which some components are rigid, invariable, fixed, whilst others are flexible and movable. To understand this, and to be able to relate his understanding to the phonetic facts of rhythm and euphony, the lexical facts of figuration and word-choice, and the situational facts of intention and strategy, puts the greatest demand on the writer's skill. The relationship between syntax and style can hardly be demonstrated without technical preliminaries of great length; so let us ingenuously beg terminological questions and propose a quite unscientific review, based on the words *order, connection, selection, replication, variation, elaboration.*

What is meant by *order* is no doubt obvious, especially if we recall that the word 'syntax' itself means an arrangement, a putting together. The units which make up the linguistic events of a piece of English, the words constructing the phrase, the phrases constructing the clause, the clauses constructing the larger sentences, occur in certain permissible sequences. In some cases order is immutable, whilst in others more than one order is possible. In the structure of the simple sentence, for instance, the ordering of subject and verb is virtually fixed, the position of a complement or a direct object is fixed

almost, but not quite, as firmly, and the location of an adverbial
adjunct may be quite free, so that one could write, for instance, *In
some cases politicians are given to exaggeration* or *Politicians are in
some cases given to exaggeration* or *Politicians are given to exaggeration in some cases,* putting the adjunct *in some cases* in one or other
of three possible positions. Its positioning could be casual, but is likely
to be determined, ultimately, by quite subtle considerations of style.
Rhythm and presentative emphasis – giving a certain idea preeminence – are two possible factors. Others might be the linkage of
sentence to sentence (adjuncts are often useful as sentence-connectors);
the evocation of a certain intonation-pattern; or even a kind of subver-
sion of the grammatical role of the movable item. For instance,
although we might call *in some cases* an adverbial adjunct in this
sentence, it ' feels ' much more like an adnominal adjunct to the word
exaggeration when it occurs in the final position, or even like a sort
of modifier to *politicians* when it occurs initially. The positioning of
such items is thus potentially a stylistic problem, the solution of which
may highlight one aspect or other of the meaning of a simple sentence.
This highlighting becomes all the more obvious when the element in
question has a normal position from which it is only rarely moved.
If, for example, I write *A hard bargain he drove* instead of *He drove
a hard bargain,* the effect of moving the object, *a hard bargain,* to a
fairly unusual position at the head of the clause is to underline it, so
to speak, to give it special emphasis. In a way, the object becomes a
species of psychological subject; there is an analogy here with the
passive conversion which we see in *A hard bargain was driven.* The
ordering of clauses in more complex sentences also offers possibilities
of highlighting by exploiting certain choices of movement. There is
thus a more than casual difference between *You shall hear how I was
rescued* and *How I was rescued you shall hear,* or between *I accepted
what he said, relying on his good faith* and *Relying on his good faith
I accepted what he said,* or *What he said I accepted, relying on his
good faith,* or, again, *What he said, relying on his good faith, I
accepted,* etc. *When she got there,* the old nursery-rhyme tells us, *the
cupboard was bare.* The reader might like to reflect on the stylistic
inferiority of *The cupboard was bare when she got there.* The order of
linguistic events is of considerable artistic importance.

Given a series of ' linguistic events ' in the form of words, phrases,
clauses, etc., we can set them together in a potentially variable order.
In doing so, we make use of certain devices of *connection* which where

necessary indicate how the events are related in semantics and in the
hierarchies of syntax. For instance, we could write *She got there, the
cupboard was bare*. In that case the only connective device is the
written comma, corresponding to the speech phenomenon of pause
and pitch-modulation. This suggests that the events of this sentence
do not manifest the syntactic relationship that grammar conventionally
labels *main* or *principal* and *subordinate* or *dependent;* and that the
semantic relationship ' this happened after that ' is implied purely by
the order of clauses. If we write *When she got there, the cupboard was
bare,* by selecting as an overt connecting device the word *when,* we
establish a hierarchy of principal and subordinate (the connector
' tags ' the subordinate clause) and also confirm and specify the
semantic time-relationship. If we write *Although she got there, the
cupboard was bare* we change the semantic relationship, and if the
statement is *She got there before the cupboard was bare,* the hierarchical relationship is changed. In brief, there are certain devices which
operate as connectors and subordinators within the compass of the sentence. Some, e.g. the simple ' comma contact ' or the coordinating
conjunction *and,* merely assist in the grouping of units of equal grammatical status, their semantic relationship being implied in the order
of occurrence; others, namely conjunctions, adverbs, relative pronouns,
e.g. *after, because, how, where, who, whose, that,* indicate both a
semantic relationship and a grammatical hierarchy. Furthermore,
similar principles govern the connection of sentence with sentence.
The connection may be indicated merely by ' full stop contact ', e.g.
She got there. The cupboard was bare. Or it may be shown by means
of a sentence-connector, e.g. *She got there. However, the cupboard
was bare* (or *The cupboard, however, was bare,* or *The cupboard was
bare, however*). Such connectors are often desirable as a means of
indicating the spanning of events when sentences grow too long to
maintain the tension of meaning: *She got there, fully expecting that
her foresight in setting aside provisions for her pet would now bear
fruit, or rather, bear a bone. For all that, the cupboard was bare.*
Sentence-connectors such as *nevertheless, therefore, however, for all
that* are a common resort in certain kinds of prose, for example the
prose of argument or exposition. They are not the only kind of device
by which we indicate the linkage of sentences. We may, for example,
show a semantic connection between sentences by means of a pronoun,
often the anaphoric *it: With her heart full of foreboding she went to
the cupboard, hoping against hope that she might still find something*

there. It was bare. Or again, a demonstrative adjective might pick up some chosen element of a preceding sentence: *She went to an indescribably filthy cupboard which stood in the corner of the room. She had never seen such filth.* (*Such* alludes back to *filthy*). Any sequence of sentences in written prose presents problems of connection. The writer has to make up his mind whether the connection of consecutive sentences needs to be overtly demonstrated, whether such demonstration will promote clarity of meaning, and whether it may have further use as a rhetorical factor serving the ends of euphony and rhythm.

In sentence and paragraph structure, the writer is offered a certain power of *selection;* our syntax makes available a number of roughly equivalent structures, grammatical synonyms, as it were, which offer us several ways of saying something. These alternatives are like lexical synonyms, however, in that they are only of roughly, not exactly, equivalent value. For example, it would be possible to couch the sentiment expressed in the sentence *It is flattering to be praised* in a number of different forms, e.g. *Being praised is flattering, It is flattering when people praise you, It is flattering when you are praised, Praise is flattering, We are flattered when praised, To be praised is to be flattered,* etc. There comes a point at which such grammatical alternants begin to modify the set of the underlying meaning; e.g. *To be praised is to be flattered* suggests *To praise is to flatter* or *Praise is flattery,* which is rather different in meaning from *It is flattering to be praised.* Nobody, in any case, would suggest that the alternatives given in our example are all of equivalent value; obviously the choice of one or other would be governed by considerations of intention, verbal context, attitude to an assumed addressee, formality or otherwise of manner, etc. However, the example does make the point that a given concept or psychological relationship may be realised in a variety of grammatical structures. If a further example is required, we might take as a theme for grammatical variations Caesar's famous, *I came, I saw, I conquered.* From this the following, at least, can be produced: *I came, saw, and conquered, I came and I saw and I conquered, I came and I saw; then I conquered, Having come and seen, I went on to conquer, When I had come I saw, and then conquered, After coming and seeing, I conquered,* etc. This ignores the possibilities offered by chopping and changing the order of presentation of the three clauses, e.g. *I conquered, having come and having seen,* or *I saw when I came, and thereupon conquered.* These variations are of course a little absurd, since it is rightly fixed in our minds the traditional rendering of *Veni, vidi, vici*, as *I came, I saw, I conquered* is the only good rendering. However, the absurd example illustrates well enough a real fact of language; that syntax offers facilities and alternatives among which we have to learn to pick and choose when we want to use language with stylistic effect.

It is a matter of common experience that in using language we may find ourselves generating and re-generating a given syntactic pattern. This tendency to replication, ostensibly an embarrassment, actually becomes a basic principle of style, and the dullest workman can hardly produce a page without committing himself to it. It is a cardinal device of the copywriter, of incantatory ritual, of certain kinds of poetry. The rigmarole of *The House That Jack Built* is an example of the replicatory principle screwed to the pitch of unreason; an instance that comes to mind from the field of ' serious ' verse is Louis Mac-Neice's *Prayer Before Birth*. Among prose-writers, Dickens uses it a good deal; the following passages occur in the first page or so of *A Christmas Carol*:

> Scrooge was his sole executor, his sole administrator, his sole assign, his sole residuary legatee, his sole friend, and sole mourner.

> No warmth could warm, no wintry weather chill him. No wind that blew was bitterer than he, no falling snow was more intent upon its purpose, no man or woman ever once in his life inquired the way to such and such a place, of Scrooge.

The magnificent opening pages of his *Bleak House* are constructed almost entirely on this principle of replication. The reader turning to those pages may also note that they make due concession to the need for *variation*. In a piece like *The House That Jack Built,* one and the same construction (' that x'd the y ') is joyously and unmercifully replicated. In more serious rhetoric we will often find the writer varying the replicated construction, inasmuch as it admits of variation, or muting its effects by introducing some other construction. The second paragraph of *Bleak House* is a nice example:

> Fog everywhere. Fog up the river, where it flows among green aits and meadows; fog down the river, where it rolls defiled among the tiers of shipping, and the waterside pollutions of a great (and dirty) city. Fog on the Essex marshes, fog on the Kentish heights.

Fog creeping into the cabooses of collier-brigs; fog lying out on the yards and hovering in the rigging of great ships; fog drooping on the gunwales of barges and small boats. Fog in the eyes and throats of ancient Greenwich pensioners, wheezing by the firesides of their wards; fog in the stem and bowl of the afternoon pipe of the wrathful skipper, down in his close cabin; fog cruelly pinching the toes and fingers of his shivering little 'prentice boy on deck. Chance people on the bridges peeping over the parapets into a nether sea of fog, with fog all around them, as if they were up in a balloon, and hanging in the misty clouds.

Among the many details which invite comment, a matter of principal note is that from the verbless sentence, *Fog everywhere,* with which the paragraph begins, Dickens develops two types which recur and blend in the replicatory series which follows. One is a verbless construction consisting of an unmarked subject (without a preceding article, etc.) followed by a prepositional phrase; e.g. *Fog up the river.* The other consists of a similarly unmarked subject, but has a nonfinite verb in the form of a present participle. This second type occurs in two variants, in one of which the participial verb is intransitive (e.g. *fog creeping into the cabooses of collier-brigs*), whilst in the other the participle has an object (e.g. *fog pinching the toes . . . of his . . . 'prentice boy*). There are thus in effect three basic variants of the replicated construction. Dickens uses these skilfully throughout the paragraph, sometimes introducing a different construction (e.g. the replicated *where*-clauses of the second sentence), and sometimes blending the types; for example, in *fog in the eyes and throats of ancient Greenwich pensioners, wheezing by the firesides of their wards,* he has a 'main' clause of the subject-plus-prepositional-phrase type, the last word of which, *pensioners* is qualified by a construction of the type participle-plus-adjunct. This variation and blending is most striking in the final sentence of the paragraph. Here, though the syntactic types are the same as before, Dickens executes a sort of grammatical 'change-step'. The obsessive subject of every other sentence, *fog,* is here shifted into the predicate, and a new subject, *chance people,* is introduced. A new grammatical subject, that is to say; the thematic subject remains the same, but this grammatical shift suggests a shift of perspective, as well as enabling the author somewhat to free himself from that insistently re-iterated word.

The replicatory principle is one way of unfolding a meaning, of piling up detail on detail, adding point to point, enforcing emphasis with further emphasis. But there is another kind of growth, seen in the burgeoning and branching, within a sentence, of qualifying and amplifying constructions. It is for this other kind of syntactic extension that the word *elaboration* is proposed. Replication and elaboration are stylistic concomitants; over and over again, in the study of carefully-shaped literary prose, we may see how replicative, parallel, constructions are amplified or qualified by elaborative expressions which may include in themselves some further replication. For instance:

> In particular, I have long felt that the prevailing tendency to regard all the marked distinctions of human nature as innate, and in the main indelible, and to ignore the irresistible proofs that by far the greater part of those differences, whether between individuals, races, or sexes, are such as not only might but naturally would be produced by circumstances is one of the chief hindrances to the rational treatment of great social questions, and one of the greatest stumbling-blocks to human improvement.

This sentence, from John Stuart Mill's *Autobiography*, is built up on a stem or basic structure which can be expressed in the words *I have long felt that this tendency is one of the chief hindrances;* fundamentally, that is to say, there is a structure of two clauses, one announcing ' I feel ', the other reporting ' what I feel '. What is felt is ' this ' tendency; and the whole stupendous weight of the sentence goes into the elaboration of ' this ', an elaboration which calls for replications and sub-elaborations in a series of steps and dependences which the reader will be able to trace for himself. To weigh this elaborative burden in terms of mere number, it may be worth pointing out that the subject of the second clause, which we can summarise as ' this tendency ' or ' a tendency ', extends to fifty-three words in the actual text. It takes a solid nineteenth-century confidence in the print-culture to produce a sentence as elaborate as that.

Random speculation on the distinction between ' replicative ' and ' elaborative ' syntax raises one or two interesting points. It is possible, for instance (though the elaborative music of *Paradise Lost* might contradict the suggestion), that verse tends to favour replicative patterns. It is also possible (this is no doubt a contingent point) that the replicative style is pre-eminent in any sort of affective, emotionally charged writing, or in rhetoric that has designs on our feelings and judgements. Certainly the style of Dickens, when he writes in poetic or portentous vein, seems to accord with this. Some examples, notably the fine passage from the beginning of *Bleak House*, have been quoted. Here, for association and comparison, is another excellent instance of emotive prose, the almost-too-beautiful closing sentences of James Joyce's story *The Dead*:

> Yes, the newspapers were right: snow was general all over Ireland. It was falling on every part of the dark central plain, on the treeless hills, falling softly upon the Bog of Allen, and, farther westward, softly falling into the dark mutinous Shannon waves. It was falling, too, upon every part of the lonely churchyard on the hill where Michael Furey lay buried. It lay thickly drifted on the crooked crosses and headstones, on the spears of the little gate, on the barren thorns. His soul swooned slowly as he heard the snow falling faintly through the universe and faintly falling, like the descent of their last end, upon all the living and dead.

These are cadences of an almost intemperate sweetness, and yet the music is simply-constructed. The first sentence of the passage as given here provides a thematic *terminus a quo*. Thereafter, the development turns on the replication of a structure consisting of verb plus adverb, and the accompanying replication of prepositional phrases. There is an almost hypnotic insistence on this material. Apart from marked alterations in the verb-adverb order, and some fluctuations of phrase-length, there is little variation or selection of alternative constructions, and little elaboration. These points appear quite clearly, if the passage is laid out thus:

It was falling	on every part of the dark central plain, on the treeless hills,	
falling softly	upon the Bog of Allen,	
		and, farther westward,
softly falling	into the dark mutinous Shannon waves.	
It was falling, too,	upon every part of the lonely churchyard on the hill	
		where Michael Furey lay buried.

It lay thickly drifted   on the crooked crosses
                              and headstones,
                          on the spears of the
                              little gate,
                          on the barren thorns.

His soul swooned slowly   as he heard the snow
        falling faintly   through the universe   and
        faintly falling,   like the descent of
                                                      their last end
                          upon all the living and
                          dead.

The verb-adverb constructions create a phonaesthetic effect, a
cadential tolling. The prepositional phrases build up an image of a
churchyard, a country, humanity, the universe. The parallel operation
of these phrases is remarkable. Thus, in sentence 1 there is a phrase
on every part of the dark central plain which is echoed in sentence 2 by
the phrase *upon every part of the lonely churchyard,* and a phrase *on
the treeless hills* which is answered by *on the hill* in the second
sentence. These parallels are more than merely ornamental, for they
bring out the contrast between, and the oneness of, the general and
the local, the whole of Ireland and one small place in Ireland. In the
third sentence this antiphon of 'all' and 'each' is heard again in
the phrases *through the universe* and *upon all the living and dead.*
The means are simple, the effects subtle. The sentence-linkage, too, is
skilful. The first sentence of the passage as quoted here provides the
key-word, *snow.* This is picked up three times by the anaphoric *it.*
Joyce allows just enough variation to make a frontier between monotone and tedium. In the third sentence, for instance, although the
anaphoric link recurs, and although the essential verb-adverb combination follows, he alters the wording of the verb-group from *was
falling, was falling softly, softly falling,* to *lay thickly drifted.* This
slight shift introduces the major innovation of the final sentence,
where the subject changes from *it,* and a new subject, *his soul,* is
introduced. However, the verb-adverb model remains, in *swooned
slowly;* and presently, the theme-word *snow* reappears in the object-
position, and from there in effect re-asserts itself as a subject governing the verb-adverb construction *falling faintly.* This is subsequently
inverted, *faintly falling,* thus echoing a similar inversion, *falling*

softly/softly falling, in the first sentence. The whole passage is arrestingly simple, and yet, within its simplicity, full of whispering subtleties.

As if it were not labour enough to acquire a command of the phonaesthetic, lexical, and syntactic resources of his mother-tongue, the artist is also required to have the technical skill to translate his conceptions into the medium of writing. However keenly we may argue the importance of the oral tradition, we are willy-nilly creatures of the print-culture, and our literary experience is gathered for the most part through the eye rather than through the ear. This imposes upon the artist the responsibility not only for making the lexical and grammatical choices which, when set on the page, will mouth a silent emphasis, but also for doing what he can with the resources of lay-out, spacing, paragraphing, and above all punctuation. Punctuation, as we know, is partly a matter of indicating clearly the intended grammatical organisation of a piece of text; but it is also important as a clue to the timing of pauses, the speed of delivery, the accenting and grouping of words and phrases, and other phonaesthetic and semantic effects. The ordinary use of punctuation in the transcription of verse, for example, is a matter which excites little attention and which is yet full of interest. Consider, for instance, the punctuation of the closing lines of Harold Monro's poem *Living* (the whole poem is a worthy exemplar of professional attention to punctuational detail):

> O cool glad pasture; living tree, tall corn,
> Great cliff, or languid sloping sand, cold sea,
> Waves; rivers curving: you, eternal flowers,
> Give me content, while I can think of you:
> Give me your living breath!
> Back to your rampart, Death.*

The punctuation here may seem random, or self-evident, or a matter of indifference, but in fact these lines are most scrupulously punctuated. Full stop, comma, colon and semi-colon have distinct values, not only as organisational devices, but also as indices to timing and phrasing. They show when, in reading aloud, we should pause fractionally, observe a longer break, or mark a clear hiatus. They also indicate, although imperfectly, something of the author's intention with regard to the intonation of the lines. In this, as in all well-transcribed poems,

---

* Harold Monro, *Living.* See *The Faber Book of Modern Verse,* ed. Michael Roberts, 2nd edn. (London: Faber & Faber, 1951), p. 134.

the punctuation has a value akin to that of the dynamic marks in music
(particularly the rest-marks), and must be respected accordingly. Compare for example, the authentically punctuated version given above,
with the following:

> O, cool, glad, pasture, living tree, tall corn,
> Great cliff, or languid sloping sand; cold sea
> Waves, rivers curving, you, eternal flowers –
> Give me content while I can think of you,
> Give me your living breath:
> Back, to your rampart, Death!

This is an impropriety, a travesty; it is to save the angry ghost
from such torments that the poet looks to the piety of the scholar.

The art and craft of words is not acquired in a moment, not in
a degree course, hardly in a lifetime of crossings-out and crumpled
pages. Those who apply themselves to the craft (and we are all
apprentices at some time, for some purpose) find it a sufficiently
exacting business, and one that enjoys but a dubious social repute.
Hokum's descendants have descended into a suspicious world, where
the trade is tricky and the custom capricious. But there are surely
consolations and glories. To write a poem, for instance – is not that
to revel in the mysterious, hackle-raising sense of answering a ghost
whose whispered riddle no other person has heard? To find the right
word, a good metaphor, a telling construction, is to feel momentarily
convinced of a magic extension of our power over experience. To
write a paragraph; to write a sentence; with a beginning, a middle,
and an end; with a rhythm; with a zest; with a meaning; is to know
that the apes are in exile in the amorphous jungle, and that the
battlements will surely hold against the ogres. Blessed are we if we
can achieve these things for ourselves. Blessed are we and many times
blessed when they are achieved for us by others, the artists, the music-
makers, the custodians of that Logos which makes the world ever
dear and morning-dandy, full of strangeness and strength and hope.

Conclusion:
Our Experience of Language

The child plays on the floor and feels under his fists the rough truth of the carpet; essays the taste of a table-leg; is offended by a lurking pin; squinnies at the motes that dance in the great shaft of light that props up the living-room window and asks constantly, 'What's that?' 'What's that?' His mother answers him, 'That is the sunshine', 'That is my good tablecloth', and 'That is something you mustn't touch, stop it, come here at once'; and so the child begins to learn the sounds, the vocabulary, the grammar, the conventions of asserting, questioning and directing that make up what tribal experience and his own piety will ever afterwards teach him to call 'the mother tongue'.

'Heaven lies about us in our infancy', said Wordsworth, who perhaps confused beatitude with mere bewilderment. Well, so much the better for our infancy. But custom also lies about us, custom, that definitive power which Wordsworth may have had in mind when he spoke of the 'shades of the prison house' which 'close about the growing boy'. Custom announces itself to us with the gift of a rattle or a spoon; its shades fall across us with the soft folds of a christening shawl. The baby lolls in his baby carriage, and the world waits on him with a customary store of cultural traditions, institutions, social organisations, hierarchies of rank, patterns of belief, all presented to him by courtesy of the mother tongue, all leaving their impress upon that tolerant medium.

In our language, as in our behaviour generally, we are compelled by the power of custom. This power is broadly beneficent, and, indeed, is necessary to the easy working of language. It provides us with clues as to social roles and expected patterns of behaviour within those roles. It guides us through the institutional complexes of our working life, it informs us in our encounters with strangers, it prescribes for us the parts we should play, at table, in the street, at work-bench or desk, this morning, tomorrow, next Saturday, in conjunction with Mabel or good old Harry or Mr Blenkinsop or Father Flanaghan or the Duke of Omnium. For much of the time we are able to communicate effortlessly, almost mindlessly, because we have mastered the relationship between language and the social conventions and coherences of our culture.

We learn to generate sentences, we learn to respond to situations; we bring a new dimension of capability to the animal's instinctive acts of self-preservation, appeal, placation, submission, warning, aggression. What we call ' custom ' in man is at all events a power higher than, and different from, the instinctive responses of the ape. The ape's learning is different from man's. The ape learns a trick, which he can repeat; man learns a trick, which he can repeat, and thereby infers the productive principle of further tricks. Apedom has no epistemology – a poor monkey can't even look the word up in a dictionary – apedom has mimesis, apedom has stimulus and response. The thickest of humans has something more than this. Nevertheless, in custom-bound language there is a good deal of the mimetic, the conventionally responsive, and this can and does stultify communication between man. The social trudge reduces our utterances to stereotypes, reduces and corrupts our symbolism till it is capable of conveying no more than a broad, lowest-common-denominator meaning. We accept language as an automatic habit, and relinquish the critical responsibility which ought at least to urge upon us the distinction between words as evaluations of a private landscape and words as declarations of an intellectual and material commonwealth. Readers of *Alice* will recall the dictatorial semantics of Humpty Dumpty:

' I don't know what you mean by " glory ",' Alice said.

Humpty Dumpty smiled contemptuously. ' Of course you don't – till I tell you. I meant " There's a nice knock-down argument for you! " '

' But " glory " doesn't mean " a nice knock-down argument," ' Alice objected.

' When I use a word,' Humpty Dumpty said in a rather scornful tone, ' it means just what I choose it to mean – neither more nor less.'

' The question is ', said Alice, ' whether you *can* make words mean different things.'

' The question is ', said Humpty Dumpty, ' which is to be master – that's all.'

On this showing, we may suppose Humpty Dumpty to have had a very confident mastery of words like *great* and *free* and *beautiful* and *right* and *proper;* we all tend to use such words with an ovoid assurance, not guessing what irreparable fall of thought and language we may be risking thereby. Another custom-caught habit is to be unthinkingly inclusive or exclusive; to say *all, every, always,* or *no, none, never,* where thoughtfulness would ask for *some, several, many, sometimes,* etc. From these two bad linguistic habits alone spring many follies and social ills: *Gipsies are never honest, All students are lazy, Everybody ought to read great poetry, Snibbo washes everything whiter, There is no cultural life in the Midlands, Americans have awful accents, The English have never learned to work efficiently, Respectable people never play billiards on Sunday, We all know what democracy means.* It is possible to contract a third bad habit in recoil from these two; the habit of qualifying and hedging and generally issuing credentials for any statement. Thus linguistic custom chivvies us on the one hand towards the comprehensive, prejudice-breeding assertions of the thoroughfare, and on the other towards the fidgety, unsinewed prevarications of the academic in his study. The just level of a truly common tongue is difficult to find.

A further, perhaps graver, consequence of the customary power of the mother tongue is that with it we inherit facilities and limitations to thought and imagination. This is not so much a matter of the environmental conditioning of language, as of its internal structure, in particular its grammar. The writings of the late Benjamin Lee Whorf have drawn attention to the fact that the linguistic system we inherit conditions our thought, our imagination, our sympathies, even our actions themselves. Whorf devoted himself to the study of an American Indian language, *Hopi,* the grammatical structure of which he contrasted with that of what he called Standard Average European (SAE). The object of this contrastive study was to demonstrate his thesis that the impress of our thought, and hence the compulsiveness of much of our behaviour derives from the ' large-scale patterning of grammatical categories, such as plurality, gender . . . tenses, voices, and other verb forms, classifications of the type of ' parts of speech ' and the matter of whether a given experience is denoted by a unit morpheme, an inflected word, or a syntactical combination '. He was able to adduce a good deal of evidence suggestive of the probability that structural differences between Hopi and SAE implied marked differences of thought-pattern. Hopi verbs, for instance, apparently facilitate the conceptualisation of such matters as inception, evolution, acceleration, increases in intensity, and so forth, which in European languages are as a rule satisfactorily expressed only in the technical language and formulae of physics and mathematics. On the other hand, the linear time-scheme which informs European tense-systems is foreign to Hopi habits of thought. Whorf is particularly interesting, and worth quoting *in extenso*, in his speculations on the psychology of the SAE tense-system:

The three-tense system of SAE verbs colours all our thinking about time. This system is amalgamated with that larger scheme of objectification of the subjective experience of duration . . . noted in other patterns. . . . This objectification enables us in imagination to 'stand time-units in a row'. Imagination of time as like a row harmonises with a system of THREE tenses; whereas a system of TWO, an earlier and a later, would seem to correspond better to the feelings of duration as it is experienced. For if we inspect consciousness we find no past, present, future, but a unity embracing complexity. EVERYTHING is in consciousness, and everything in consciousness is, and is together. There is in it a sensuous and a nonsensuous. We may call the sensuous – what we are seeing, hearing, touching – the 'present', while in the nonsensuous the vast imageworld of memory is being labelled 'the past' and another realm of belief, intuition, and uncertainty 'the future'; yet sensation, memory, foresight, all are in consciousness together – one is not 'yet to be' nor another 'once but no more'. Where real time comes in is that all this in consciousness is 'getting later', changing certain relations in an irreversible manner. In this 'latering' or 'duration', there seems to me to be a paramount contrast between the newest, latest instant at the focus of attention, and the rest – the earlier. Languages by the score get along well with two tenselike forms answering to this paramount relation of 'later' to 'earlier'. We can of course CONSTRUCT and CONTEMPLATE IN THOUGHT a system of past, present, future, in the objectified configuration of points on a line. This is what our general objectification tendency leads us to do and our tense system confirms.

In English the present tense seems the one least in harmony with the paramount temporal relation. It is as if pressed into various and not wholly congruous duties. One duty is to stand as objectified middle term between objectified past and objectified future, in narration, discussion, argument, logic, philosophy. Another is to denote inclusion in the sensuous field 'I SEE him'. Another is for nomic, i.e. customarily or generally valid, statements: 'We SEE with our eyes'. These varied uses introduce confusions of thought, of which we are for the most part unaware.*

This typifies the approach to language expounded in the essays in *Language, Thought and Reality;* a bold imaginative, yet sane, approach, which would seem to offer exciting prospects and challenges to research. At the moment, however, official linguistic scholarship is apparently preoccupied with other matters.

Thus the child on the carpet plays his way into a palisade of verbal custom. He is required, by the usages of the tribe, to observe a contract of agreed linguistic behaviour; in the rub and routine of that contractual observance, his language becomes stereotyped and stultified, and, moreover, conditions his way of seeing and thinking until he thinks it is the only way and cannot understand that others should see and think differently. But all the same, he seldom feels that language is a prison. Sometimes he is aware of chafing against the bars, he feels the fluttering of the 'fancies that break through language and escape'. But on the whole, there is so much to do; the palisade of linguistic experience is apparently so huge. There are conversations to hold, lectures and sermons to hear, books to write, situations to match with appropriate strategies. The experience of language is challenging. The media are challenging, particularly our culture's most respected and dominant medium, that of writing. But writing is a treacherous thing. It has all sorts of marvellous uses. It is a box for memory, a path for argument, a kitchen-cum-laboratory for creative experiment; and it is one of the greatest drugs ever discovered. Written composition is the opium of the people, and claims addicts of every kind, from the pitiful wretches who contribute obsessively to the correspondence columns of newspapers, to sober husbands and fathers who spend their evenings tinkering with textbooks. Common speech as a rule has its foundations in motives which are external to language; the need for information, the wish to direct a situation, the identification of objects, feelings, thoughts, the mere need to present oneself to another human being. There are, in short, common

* *Whorf*, II, 24, pp. 143-4.

social and psychological motives, of which speech is a manifestation. Language, however, can outgrow these motives, and the powers of expression which motive creates can beget an appetite for more expressiveness. The conventions of language, particularly of syntax, can be expanded, and in some measure even distorted, without apparent damage to communication; and it is merely a fact of our nature that, given an instrument, we should gradually work it to the limit of its capabilities. In this stretching of language, the written form greatly assists. Writing does not impose upon language the restrictions natural to speech, where the involutions and devolutions of syntax are limited to what speaker and listener can conveniently hold in their heads. Print makes possible the syntactic replications and elaborations discussed in the preceding chapter, for the design of a sentence is always apparent to the eye, so that it is impossible to forget how it began, or to miss the significance of a construction. This can make the written form an admirable vehicle for the literary artist, but on the other hand it can make it a dangerous subversive, undermining the directness of simple utterance, overbearing the relationship of symbol-to-thing with an elaborate relativity of symbol-to-symbol. Writing permits us to breed language out of language. Pick up any newspaper, and the first sentence to fall under the eye may present a complexity far in excess of the simple manifestations of speech. For instance, this (from *The Times*, 16 June 1970):

> The gap between the reality of the scientific and technological age in which we are living on the one hand, involving vast international combines, world markets, instantaneous world-wide communications, and intercontinental rockets with multiple megaton war heads, and on the other the unreality of the outdated national prejudices and antiquated political machinery through which we seek to run our lives, has become so great that the young are rightly disaffected and their elders are disenchanted.

Now that is a perfectly intelligible, and, one might even say, well-controlled sentence, but it is a monstrous outgrowth of the basic subject-predicate patterns of the sentence in speech, e.g. *John laughed, Most sailors drink rum, Our old vicar preached in the mornings, That little fat man was elected chairman, They made Harry secretary*, etc. In such cases we have simple manifestations of the common patterns, subject-verb, subject-verb-object, subject-verb-adverbial adjunct, subject-verb-complement, subject-verb-object-complement. The elements of structure are easily followed; the subjects, for instance, are quite simple – *John, Most sailors, Our old vicar, That little fat man, They*. The majority of grammatical subjects in colloquy, one would venture to say, are not likely to be much more elaborate than these. But in *The Times* sentence quoted above, the subject is *The gap between the reality of the scientific and technological age in which we are living on the one hand, involving vast international combines, world markets, instantaneous world-wide communications, and inter-continental rockets with multiple megaton war heads, and on the other the un-reality of the outdated national prejudices and antiquated political machinery through which we seek to run our lives*. In one way this is fun; we can see, if we have any pleasure in language, how a writer might enjoy building and balancing the semantic card-castle of such a construction. In another way, though, it is disturbing, because it hints at language, the artefact, assuming precedence over the reality it is supposed to report. We see language begetting language, implicating language, complicating language. It becomes possible for us, as language users, to sport in the linguistic maze we have created for ourselves; to be bemused and diverted by parallellisms and elaborations, to live in the facile coherences of rhetoric and neglect the awkward incoherence of reality.

It cannot be said, then, that our experience of language is in all respects elevating and edifying. It may stultify, rather than promote, our sympathies and imaginative capacities; it may present one more aspect of the tyranny of routine; it may become the dream-house or hall of mirrors where we seek to elude reality; it may even, in consequence of all this, become the most dangerous weapon of the paranoiac and the demagogue. But these are depressing judgements, and if this tale of cautions were all, we should be forced to conclude that language makes for man's damnation; whereas from time immemorial it has been considered his chief glory – ' in this above all ', said Cicero, ' do we excel the beasts '. The virtues of language, which this book has tried to demonstrate, are such that it claims its own guardians and champions. Philosophers severely demonstrate to us the unreasonableness, the danger, the wickedness even, of confounding words and things. Wits and clowns merrily fling the arbitrariness of language back into our solemn faces; ' come, laugh at this strange disguise, this bizarre mask of being '. So the experience of language becomes an intellectual challenge and a source of lively pleasure. And then the poets and literary artists come, to disturb and tease and challenge our notions of what language ought to be, to whet our appetite for life with cunning riddles and elaborate answers, to be the mythopoeic namers of true and fitting names, to furnish us with rituals by which we may learn to bear, with a little dignity, the humiliations of life, the absurdity of approaching death. Through the endeavours of the linguistically elect, the experience of language becomes strict and pleasurable and consoling.

And our experience of language is ultimately the experience of our race, of our flesh and blood, of our loves and hates, of our personal identities. My language is my entitlement to a brotherhood with history; I am able to claim Tyndale and Samuel Johnson and Thomas Hardy as my cousins and familiars in speech. In words are the lineaments of my dearest and best; my mother's turn of phrase beats blessedly in my mind. In language I make the effigies of my enmity, and create the ikons I woo and kiss. In words, in whispering, stumbling words, in the litter and ceaseless drift of words, is my pleading and searching for my own identity, the desperate commentary on my struggle to survive, the solemn colloquy and foolish cross-talk of all my days, the articulation that will go on, at the heart of all experience, till at last all burdens are laid down and I need no more words, not even amen and goodnight.

Epilogue

Loll, tired body, in your senseless bed;
Sore from your saying, look for no more to be said.
    Consider, your position is
    Finally this:
When all wise sentences have sighed and died
There are some things which survive, true and unsignified.

My brain, unhinge your talons from their prey,
    Let the fieldmouse intuition scuttle away.
    Consider that your judgement is
    Finally this:
When the hawkeye films and the hunter's lust is still,
There are hidden voices untameably piping their own sweet will.

Oh heart, exult in knowing what you know
Of the blond hillside where words can never go.
    Consider that your feeling is
    Finally this:
When phrases have set their scale on all the maps,
There is still the unpaced uncontoured meadow of perhaps.

Sleep, body, spirit, softly in the stark
Wordlessness of the comprehending dark.
    The freedom of your prison is
    Finally this:
The wings of meaning flutter between the bars.
There is hurtling light in the hollows among the stars.

Appendix 1:
Phonetic Symbols and Terminology

Throughout the text, I have done my best to avoid technicalities, but in certain contexts, notably in chapter 6, the use of conventional linguistic notations and terminologies has been forced upon me. Since the phonetic symbols and terms may be a particular source of irritation to the reader, I append the following brief notes, which may help to clarify the incidental obscurities of my text.

(a) *Symbols.* Phoneticians make use of a code of symbols known as the IPA (International Phonetic Alphabet). The working principle of this is to equate a distinctive speech-sound with a distinctive symbol. IPA symbols are used in this book to transcribe the sounds of Received British English, in accordance with the following key:

Vowels

1 / iː / as in feed		7 / ɔː / as in cord
2 / i / as in bid		8 / u / as in good
3 / e / as in pen		9 / uː / as in pool
4 / æ / as in hat		10 / ʌ / as in cup
5 / dː / as in calm		11 / ə: / as in word
6 / ɔ / as in dog		12 / ə / as in china, among

Diphthongs

1 / ei / as in day		6 / iə / as in fear
2 / ai / as in time		7 / ɛə / as in chair
3 / ɔi / as in noise		8 / ɔə / as in floor
4 / au / as in house		9 / uə / as in tour
5 / ou / as in road		

NB. In the pronunciation of many speakers, especially in the south of England, 8 and 9 are not distinguished, / ɔə / being the received sound.

Consonants and Semivowels

1 / p / as in *p*ill	13 / ʃ / as in *sh*ave
2 / b / as in *b*oat	14 / ʒ / as in mea*s*ure
3 / t / as in *t*ax	15 / tʃ / as in *ch*ew
4 / d / as in *d*o	16 / dʒ / as in *j*aw
5 / k / as in *k*ill	17 / h / as in *h*ope
6 / g / as in *g*ive	18 / m / as in *m*ow
7 / f / as in *f*at	19 / n / as in *n*ut
8 / v / as in *v*oice	20 / ŋ / as in so*ng*
9 / θ / as in *th*ick	21 / l / as in *l*ove
10 / ð / as in *th*ese	22 / r / as in *r*est
11 / s / as in *s*ign	23 / j / as in *y*oung
12 / z / as in *z*oo	24 / w / as in *w*oman

Phonetic transcriptions are conventionally shown within square brackets, e.g. /θik/, /sain/, /zu:/. The sign /:/ after a vowel indicates that the vowel is long. In transcribing words of more than one syllable, it is usual to indicate the accent-pattern of the word by placing the superscript /'/ in the transcription, before the stress-bearing syllable, thus: /ri'gret/, 'regret'. A subscript /,/ may also be used to indicate a secondary stress, e.g. /,æksi'dentl/, 'accidental'.

(b) *Terms*. Phonetic terminology relating to the articulation of speech-sounds may convey information of various kinds, but here it will be useful to distinguish three factors, namely:

      (i) the state of the vocal cords.
      (ii) the place of articulation of the sound.
      (iii) the manner of articulation of the sound.

(i) *The state of the vocal cords*

If, at the moment of articulation of a sound, the vocal cords are closed, thereby giving rise to an audible and continuous vibration, the sound is said to be *voiced*. If the cords are held apart, the resultant sound is said to be *voiceless* or *breathed*. Thus the *f* of *fat* and the *v* of *vat* are closely related sounds, but differ in that one is voiceless, the other voiced. In the flow of speech, sounds may be partially voiced, or devoiced.

(ii) *The place of articulation*

It is sometimes necessary to specify the surfaces involved in the production of a sound. The following terms, for instance, may be met in descriptions of English consonant sounds:

bilabial, i.e. pronounced with both lips. Example, *p*ill, *b*oat, *m*eet

labio-dental, i.e. pronounced with the upper teeth against the lower lip. Example, *f*at, *v*oice.

dental, i.e. pronounced with the tongue in contact with the teeth. Example, *th*in, brea*th*e.

alveolar, i.e. pronounced with the tip of the tongue in contact with the *alveolum,* the ridge of gum behind the upper front teeth. Example, *n*ight, *d*ay, *l*ive.

post-alveolar, i.e. pronounced with the tip and fore-part of the tongue somewhat behind the alveolum. Example, the usual southern English *r* as in *r*est.

palato-alveolar, i.e. pronounced with the tip and forepart of the tongue in contact with the alveolum, whilst the front half of the tongue is raised up into the 'dome' of the palate. Example, *ch*ew, *J*ew.

palatal, i.e. pronounced with the front half of the tongue in contact or proximity with the hard palate.

velar, i.e. pronounced by raising the back of the tongue against the *velum,* or soft palate. Example, *k*ill, *g*ive.

glottal, i.e. located in the glottis, the space between the vocal cords. Example, *h*ope.

(iii) *The manner of articulation*

The articulating surfaces may be used to release a sound in a number of ways. The following are to be noted:

plosive, i.e. produced by momentarily occluding the outflow of breath and then releasing it with the abrupt 'puffing' effect known as *plosion.* Examples *p*ill, *t*ax, *g*ive.

affricate, i.e. formed with an initial occlusion which is then released comparatively slowly. Examples, *ch*ew, *j*aw.

fricative, i.e. formed by restricting the escape of breath to such an extent that the outflowing air makes the hissing sound known as *friction.* Example, *f*at, *th*ick, *s*ign, presti*g*e.

nasal, i.e. formed by allowing the breath to escape through the nose instead of through the mouth. Example, *m*ow, *n*ut, so*ng.*

lateral, i.e. formed by using the tongue to block the middle of the breath-stream, but allowing an escape on one or both sides of the obstruction. Example, *l*ove.

> *frictionless continuant*, i.e. released in a manner akin to the fricative
> sounds, but pronounced with such weak breath-force that there is
> no audible sound of friction. Example, the usual English *r* in
> *rest*.

The terms described above are as a rule employed in the identification of consonants and semi-vowels. The description of the place and manner of articulation of vowels and diphthongs is more vague, though we use terms such as *close* and *open* to indicate the height of the tongue, *front, central,* and *back* to show which part of the tongue is raised higher than the rest, *rounded* to indicate a greater or lesser pursing of the lips, *nasal* to denote a release through the nose, etc.

Appendix 2:
Specimens of English, 1014-1970

The following texts are briefly quoted in chapter 6 (pp. 122-3). These lengthier examples may provide further illustration to some of the comments made there. In choosing such a series of texts I had to arbitrate between two principles. One, no doubt the more scholarly and consistent, was to pick out a series of passages manifesting a likeness of theme and treatment. The other was to choose passages reflecting the varieties of *address* and *interlocution* and expounding themes not altogether remote from each other and yet basically representative of the cultures of succeeding centuries. It will be seen that I have inclined to the second of these principles of selection. Some of the passages represent *address,* written or spoken, taking the form of sermon, narrative, or argument. Others represent *interlocution,* in the form of fictional speech and dialogue, or, in the case of the final passage, as exchanges reported from a highly-specialised real-life context. Thematic contrasts will be apparent; there are also certain thematic echoes. This is no doubt a far from perfect attempt to secure variety without surrendering the likenesses which facilitate comparison; but it seemed to me to be of greater interest, potentially, than a series of passages assignable to some common category, e.g. ' pulpit oratory ' or ' travels '.

i Understandað eac georne þæt deofol þas þeode nu fela geara dwelode to swyðe, and þæt lytle getrywða wæron mid mannum, þeah hi wel spæcan; and unrihta to fela ricsode on lande, and næs a fela manna þe smeade ymbe þa bote swa georne swa man sceolde; ac dæghwamlice man ihte yfel æfter oðrum, and unriht rærde and unlaga manege ealles to wide gynd ealle þas þeode. And we eac for ðam habba fela byrsta and bismra gebiden; and gyf we ænige bote gebidan sculan, þonne mote we þæs to Gode earnian bet þonne

we ær ðison dydon. For ðam mid miclan earnungan we geearnodon
þa yrmða þe us on sittað, and mid swyðe miclan earnungan we þa
bote motan aet Gode geræcan, gyf hit sceal heonanforð godiende
wurðan. La hwæt, we witan ful georne þaet to myclan bryce sceal
mycel bot nyde, and to miclum bryne wæter unlytel, gif man þæt
fyr sceal to ahte acwæncan.

(And be assured of this, that the devil has been tempting this nation
all too freely for many a year now, and that there has been little
faith among men, for all their fine words; and too many wrongs
have prevailed in this country, and there have never been many
people who have set their minds as fully as they should on putting
things to rights; but day by day one evil has been added to another,
and injustice has been done, and many misdeeds, all too commonly
throughout this nation. And because of that, indeed, we have
suffered many an injury and insult; and if we are to know any
redress, we must show ourselves more deserving in God's sight than
we have done up to now. For we have more than deserved the
miseries that now lie upon us, and it must be with a very great
deserving that we obtain our redress from God, if matters are hence-
forth to improve. See now, we know full well that much breaking
wants much mending, and that a great blaze will hardly be
quenched without a deal of water.)

*From a sermon preached by Wulfstan, Archbishop of York, in
the year 1014*

ii I ne can ne I ne mai tellen alle þe wunder ne alle þe pines ðat hi
diden wreccemen on þis land, and ðat lastede þa xix wintre wile
Stephne was king, and æure it was uuerse and uuerse. Hi læiden
gæildes on the tunes æure umwile, and clepeden it tenserie. Þa þe
uureccemen ne hadden nan more to gyuen, þa ræueden hi and
brendon alle the tunes, ðat wel þu myhtes faren al a dæis fare
sculest thu neure finden man in tune sittende, ne land tiled. Þa
was corn dære and flesc and cæse and butere, for nan ne wæes o þe
land. Wreccemen sturuen of hungær. Sume ieden on almes þe
waren sumwile ricemen, sume flugen ut of lande.

Wes næure gæt mare wreccehed on land, ne næure hethen men
werse ne diden þan hi diden, for ouer sithon ne forbaren hi nouther
circe ne cyrceiærd, oc namen al þe god ðat þarinne was, and
brenden sythen þe cyrce and altegædere. Ne hi ne forbaren biscopes

land ne abbotes ne preostes, ac ræueden munekes and clerekes, and æuric man other þe ouer-myhte. Gif twa men oþer iii coman ridend to an tun, al þe tunscipe flugæn for heom, wenden ðat hi wæron ræueres. Þe biscopes and leredmen heom cursede æure, oc was heom naht þarof, for hi uueron al forcursæd and forsuoren and forloren.

War-sæ me tilede, þe erthe ne bar nan corn, for þe land was al fordon mid suilce dædes, and hi sæden openlice ðat Christ slep and his halechen. Suilc and mare þanne we cunnen sæin, we þoleden xix wintre for ure sinnes.

(I lack the means and the ability to tell of all the outrages and torments they inflicted on wretched men in this land; and this went on throughout the nineteen years of Stephen's reign, getting worse and worse all the time. Over and over again they would exact tribute from the villages, calling it ' dues ', and when the poor wretches had no more to give, they would plunder and burn all the villages, so that one might very well travel for a whole day without seeing a sign of life in any settlement, or land under cultivation. Then corn was dear, and meat, and cheese, and butter, for there was none in the land. Poor fellows starved of hunger. Some, that were once rich men, went begging for alms; others fled the country.

There had never been such misery in this country, nor did the heathen Vikings ever do worse than these men, for defying all decency they would spare neither church nor churchyard, but took all the valuables they found there, and then burned church and all. They showed no respect for bishop's land, or abbot's, or priest's, but robbed monks and clerics, and each man robbed the next, if he had power enough. If two or three men came riding to a village the whole settlement would run away from them, supposing them to be robbers. The bishops and clergy laid continual curses upon them, without the slightest effect, for they were utterly accursed, and perjured, and damned.

Wherever the land was tilled, the earth bore no corn, for the land was completely ruined by such deeds; and men said openly that Christ and his saints slept. Such things, and more than we can say besides, we endured, for our sins, for nineteen winters.)

From the Old English Chronicle for the year 1137

iii Þo kinges hem wenten and hi seghen, þo sterre þet yede bi-fore
hem, al-wat hi kam over þo huse, war ure louerd was, and al swo
hi hedden i-fonden ure louerd, swo hin an-urede, and him offrede
hire offrendes, gold, and stor, and mirre. Þo nicht efter þet aperede
an ongel of heuene in here slepe ine metinge and hem seide and
het, þet hi ne solde a-yen wende be herodes, ac be an oþer weye
wende into hire londes. Lordinges and leuedis þis is si glorius
miracle, and si glorius seywinge of ure lordes beringe, þet us telþ
þet holi godespel of te day, and ye muee wel under-stonde be þo
speche of þe godspelle þat me sal to dai mor makie offrinke þan
an oþren dai, and þer-of us yeft ensample þo þrie kinges of
heþenesse, þet comen fram verrene londes ure louerd to seche, and
him makie offrinke. And be þet hi offrede gold, þet is cuuenable
yeftte to kinge, seawede þet he was sothfast king, and be þet hi
offrede stor, þet me offrede wylem be þo ialde laghe to here godes
sacrefise, seawede þet he was verray prest. And be þet hi offrede
mirre, þet is biter þing, signifieth þet hi hedde biliaue þet he was
diadlich, þet diath solde suffri for man-ken.

(The kings went on their way, and saw the star going before them,
until it came over the house where our Lord was; and as they had
found our Lord, so they hastened in and made their offerings to
him – gold, and frankincense, and myrrh. The night after that, an
angel of heaven appeared to them in a dream as they slept, and told
and commanded them that they should not return through Herod's
court, but should go back into their own countries by another way.
Gentlemen and ladies, this is the glorious miracle and the glorious
manifestation of our Lord's birth that the gospel for to-day tells
us of; and you may certainly understand from the text of the
gospel that on this day greater offerings are to be made than on
other days, according to the example given us by the three kings
of heathendom, who came from foreign lands to seek out our Lord
and make offering to him. And their offering of gold, which is an
appropriate gift for a king, showed that He was a king indeed.
And their offering of frankincense, which under the old law had
been offered in sacrifice to their gods, showed that He was in truth
a priest. And their offering of myrrh, which is a bitter thing,
signifies their belief that He was a mortal, who should suffer death
for mankind.)

From a sermon in the Kentish dialect of Middle English, c. 1250

iv In that contre ben many griffounes, more plentee than in ony other
contree. Sum men seyn, that thei han the body upward as an egle,
and benethe as a lyoun: and treuly thei seyn soth, that thei ben of
that schapp. But o griffoun hath the body more gret and is more
strong thanne viij lyouns, of suche lyouns as ben o this half; and
more gret and stronger than an c. egles, suche as we han amonges
us. For o griffoun there wil bere, fleynge to his nest, a gret hors . . .
or ij oxen yoked to-gidere, as thei gon at the plowgh. For he hath
his talouns so lounge and so large and grete upon his feet, as
though thei weren hornes of grete oxen or of bugles or of ky3n;
so that men maken cuppes of hem, to drynken of: and of hire
ribbes and of the pennes of hire wenges, men maken bowes fulle
stronge, to schote with arwes and quarelle.

> *From 'The Voiage and Travaile of Sir John Mandeville',
> 1356*

v 'Now put me in to the barge,' sayd the kyng, and so he dyd
softelye. And there receyued hym thre quenes wyth grete mornyng,
and soo they sette hem doun, and in one of their lappes kyng
Arthur layed hys heed, and than that quene sayd, 'a dere broder!
why haue ye taryed so longe from me. Alas, this wounde on your
heed hath caught ouermoche colde.' And soo than they rowed from
the londe, and syr bedwere behelde all tho ladyes goo from hym.
Than syr bedwere cryed, 'a! my lord Arthur, what shal become
of me now ye goo from me. And leue me here allone emonge myn
enemyes?' 'Comfort thy self,' sayd the kyng, 'and doo as wel as
thou mayst; for in me is no truste for to truste in. For I wyl in
to the vale of auylyon, to hele me of my greuous wounde. And yf
thou here neuer more of me, praye for my soule;' but euer the
quenes and ladyes wepte and shryched that hit was pyte to here.
And assone as syr Bedwere had loste the syght of the baarge, he
wepte and waylled and so took the foreste, and so he wente al that
nyght, and in the mornyng he was ware, betwixte two holtes hore,
of a chapel and an ermytage.

> *From 'Le Morte Darthur' by Sir Thomas Malory, 1469*

vi But yong Ientlemen ar faine commonlie to do in the Court, as
yong Archers do in the feild: that is, take soch markes as be nie
them, although they be neuer so foule to shote at. I meene, they
be driuen to kepe companie with the worste: and what force ill

companie hath to corrupt good wittes, the wisest men know best.

And not ill companie onelie, but the ill opinion also of the most part, doth moch harme, and namelie of those, which shold be wise in the trewe decyphring of the good disposition of nature, of cumlinesse in Courtlie maners, and all right doinges of men.

But error and phantasie do commonlie occupie the place of troth and iudgement. For if a yong ientleman be demeure and still of nature, they say, he is simple and lacketh witte: if he be bashefull and will soon blushe, they call him a babishe and ill brought vp thyng, when *Xenophon* doth preciselie note in *Cyrus*, that his bashfulnes in youth was the verie trewe signe of his vertue and stoutnes after: If he be innocent and ignorant of ill, they say, he is rude and hath no grace, so vngraciouslie do som gracelesse men misuse the faire and godlie word GRACE.

From ' The Scholemaster' by Roger Ascham, 1570

vii Jeremy   O sir, there's Trapland the scrivener, with two suspicious fellows like lawful pads, that would knock a man down with pocket-tipstaves; – and there's your father's steward, and the nurse with one of your children from Twitnam.

Valentine   Pox on her! Could she find no other time to fling my sins in my face? Here, give her this, and bid her trouble me no more; – a thoughtless, two-handed whore! she knows my condition well enough, and might have overlaid the child a fortnight ago, if she had had any forecast in her.

Scandal   What, is it bouncing Margery with my godson?

Jeremy   Yes, sir.

Scandal   My blessing to the boy, with this token of my love. And, d'ye hear, bid Margery put more flocks in her bed, shift twice a-week, and not work so hard, that she may not smell so vigorously. I shall take the air shortly.

From ' Love for Love' by William Congreve, 1695

viii The next night Mr. Johnson and I supped in a private room at the Turk's Head coffee-house, in the Strand. ' I encourage this house (said he;) for the mistress of it is a good civil woman, and has not much business.'

' Sir, (said he) I love the acquaintance of young people; because, in the first place, I don't like to think of myself growing old. In the next place, young acquaintances must last longest, if they do last; and then, Sir, young men have more virtue than old men;

they have more generous sentiments in every respect. I love the young dogs of this age, they have more wit and humour and knowledge of life than we had; but then the dogs are not so good scholars. Sir, in my early years I read very hard. It is a sad reflection, but a true one, that I knew almost as much at eighteen as I do now. My judgement, to be sure, was not so good; but, I had all the facts. I remember very well, when I was at Oxford, an old gentleman said to me, " Young man, ply your book diligently now, and acquire a stock of knowledge; for when years come unto you, you will find that poring upon books will be but an irksome task." '

Samuel Johnson, in 1763, reported by James Boswell

ix The Gryphon sat up and rubbed its eyes: then it watched the Queen till she was out of sight: then it chuckled. ' What fun!' said the Gryphon, half to itself, half to Alice.

' What *is* the fun?' said Alice.

' Why *she*,' said the Gryphon. ' It's all her fancy, that: they never executes nobody, you know. Come on!'

' Everybody says " come on!" here,' thought Alice, as she slowly went after it; ' I never was so ordered about in my life, never!'

They had not gone far before they saw the Mock Turtle in the distance, sitting sad and lonely on a little ledge of rock, and, as they came nearer, Alice could hear him sighing as if his heart would break. She pitied him deeply. ' What is his sorrow?' she asked the Gryphon, and the Gryphon answered, very nearly in the same words as before, ' It's all his fancy, that: he hasn't got no sorrow, you know. Come on!'

So they went up to the Mock Turtle, who looked at them with large eyes full of tears, but said nothing.

' This here young lady,' said the Gryphon, ' she wants for to know your history, she do.'

From ' Alice's Adventures in Wonderland ', by Lewis Carroll 1865

x Half-an-hour before the service module separation the astronauts completed on time their final mid-course correction burn, which slowed Apollo's descent by 2.1 miles an hour and put it as accurately as possible in the re-entry ' corridor '.

The 23-second burn, at 13.53 B.S.T., although it was only 3.1 feet per second, was relatively long because of the weight of the spacecraft.

' O.K. that's it ', Captain Lovell said.

' Yes, it looks like we had a minus point two bias at 470, we're burning ', Mr. Haise radioed.

' Copy that, Fred ', Mr. Joe Kerwin, the capsule communicator, replied.

' We've shut down,' Mr. Haise confirmed at the end of the burn.

' Roger '.

' O.K. up here. If you're happy we can manoeuvre to service module separation attitude now.'

' That's affirmative, Aquarius '.

At the time of the burns the cabin temperature had dropped further to 54°F. and the astronauts put on a second suit of underwear to keep warm. All of them reported that they had not been able to have much sleep and mission control ordered them to take Dexedrine, which they had earlier declined.

Conclusion of the ' Apollo 13 ' space flight, as reported in ' The Times ', 18 April 1970

Appendix 3: Select Bibliography

I take it that there are two kinds of bibliography; the scholarly sort, in which the researcher gives an account of his sources and references, and the promotional variety, in which the author tries to make, for the benefit of the interested reader, a display of potentially attractive and helpful material.

My bibliography is, on the whole, of this second kind. Obviously it cannot be exhaustive, or even extensive, and I am aware that in selecting such a list one may seem to be culpable of many sins, both of omission and commission. I have tried, however, to make this a coherent and informative display by organising the material in sections, and by providing a commentary to each section, explaining and annotating the choice of works. I have sometimes been at a loss to know whether a book might be more fittingly listed under one heading or another; clearly, one's choice of headings is to a great extent arbitrary, and there must be many overlaps. It will be noticed that the first two sections are the longest; here are listed a number of general works and compendia containing material relevant to the subject-headings of later sections.

Many of the books listed here are American. This is first and foremost a consequence of the status of language studies in the USA, a status which encourages the productions of so many excellent books at all levels. I am particularly glad, however, that American writings happen to be well represented in my bibliography, since this may go some way towards compensating for the inevitable bias of my book towards the forms and cultural contexts of British English. The majority of the books listed here, whether British or American, should be readily available in the library of any college or university making reasonable provision for the study of language and linguistics. Many will be available in any good municipal library.

In the notes to each section, books are referred to by author's surname, followed by the Arabic numeral against which they are listed, e.g. *Dineen, 4.* References to books in sections other than the one under immediate consideration include the Roman numeral of the relevant section, e.g. *Dineen, I, 4.*

I. *On linguistics and language in general*

There are several excellent introductions to the study of language; in some cases, however, the word ' introduction ' promises easier and briefer reading than the text in fact affords.

Some of the books listed below are introductions to language. Others, if the distinction is acceptable, are introductions to linguistic science. Among the former, *Schlauch, 12,* is a compact, easily-read, lively book, and though written some time ago is nonetheless stimulating on particular topics, e.g. social aspects of language and the language of poetic creation. *Anderson & Stageberg, 1,* and *Hogins & Yarber, 8,* are compendia covering such topics as the nature of language, the effect of language on thought, usage, regional and social varieties of English, semantics, and linguistic structure.

Students looking for an introduction to linguistics might do well to read *Crystal, 2,* a brief text defining the scope of linguistics, and *Robins, 11,* the final chapter of which may be found useful as a perspective on schools and trends of thought in modern linguistics. The British student might then go to *Chao, 3,* which seems to me to be an admirable text for the newcomer at university level, or *Lyons, 10,* perhaps a somewhat more exacting book for the beginner. American students will probably have readier access to *Dineen, 4,* or *Hall, 7;* these are also readily available in British libraries. To all these books, *Hungerford, Robertson, & Sledd, 9,* might be used as a supplementary text; it is in effect an anthology of some classic statements in modern linguistics. *Firth, 5,* is included here partly because of the intrinsic interest of the texts themselves, which are by no means outmoded, but also because J. R. Firth is virtually the founder of modern British linguistics, and demands some kind of representation.

1 Anderson, W. L. & Stageberg, N. C. (eds), *Introductory readings in language,* New York: Holt, Rinehart & Winston, 1968
2 Crystal, D., *What is linguistics?*, London: Arnold, 1968
3 Chao, Y. R., *Language and symbolic systems,* London: Cambridge U.P., 1968

4 Dineen, F. P., *An introduction to general linguistics,* New York: Holt, Rinehart & Winston, 1966

5 Firth, J. R., *The tongues of men & speech,* London: Oxford U.P., 1964
(a reprint of works published in 1937 and 1930)

6 Hall, jr., R. A., *Linguistics and your language,* 2nd ed., New York: Doubleday, 1960
(originally published under the title *Leave your language alone*)

7 Hall, jr., R. A., *Introductory linguistics,* New York: Chilton, 1964

8 Hogins, J. B. & Yarber, R. E. (eds), *Language. An introductory reader,* New York: Harper & Row, 1969

9 Hungerford, H., Robertson, J. & Sledd, J. H., *English linguistics. An introductory reader,* Glencoe, Illinois: Scott Foreman, 1970

10 Lyons, J., *An introduction to theoretical linguistics,* London: Cambridge U.P., 1968

11 Robins, R. H., *A short history of linguistics,* London: Longmans, 1967

12 Schlauch, M., *The gift of tongues,* London: G. Allen & Unwin, 1943

II *Language, culture, and mind*

In this section I list books which, from one standpoint or another, examine language as an aspect of society, behaviour, or the mental activity of the individual. Some, like *Brown, 13,* or *Landar, 18,* contain much of the general doctrine of linguistics, and might have been listed in the previous section, but for their authors' evident concern with some object beside and beyond linguistics; e.g. human behaviour and thought, and the structure of human culture. These are good survey-manuals for the student interested in the role of language in society, culture, and thought. *Hymes, 17,* and *Saporta, 20,* are collections of papers relating language to anthropology, sociology, psychology, etc. They are fairly advanced, and Hymes in particular is not a beginner's book, though it assembles valuable statements by Levi-Strauss, Pike, Malinowski, Firth, Sapir, and Whorf, among others. *Church 15,* and *Vygotsky, 23,* are largely concerned with language-acquisition and with the development of thought, cognition, and perception through language. *Whorf, 24,* develops the thesis that thought and perception are conditioned by language; *Hall, 16,* examines the importance and complexity, in our communications, of the cultural context which constitutes 'the silent language'. *McLuhan, 19,* is the first and least blatant of his books expounding the importance of media; this is devoted to the 'print culture', its affect on our attitudes and thinking, and the way it is now being invaded and subverted by the 'electronic culture' of later media. *Tucker, 22,* is not to be confused with a similar title by McLuhan; it considers the press, advertising, television and radio, and 'pop' music, as shapers and reflectors of popular communication. *Skinner, 21,* puts forward a behaviourist theory of language-acquisition which has been sharply criticised by N. Chomsky. *Chomsky, 14,* expounds in fairly intelligible style his opposing philosophy of a human linguistic competence which is innate, capable of generating grammatical sentences which the individual has never before heard or uttered, and thus not dependent on the response to stimuli, recurrences, analogies, etc. Chomsky is the founding father of 'transformational grammar' (see under VIII below).

13 Brown, R. W., *Words and things,* New York: Free Press of Glencoe, 1968

14 Chomsky, N., *Language and mind,* New York: Harcourt, Brace & World, 1968

15 Church, J., *Language and the discovery of reality,* New York: Random House, 1965

16 Hall, E. T., *The silent language,* New York: Doubleday, 1959

17 Hymes, D. (ed), *Language in culture and society. A reader in linguistics and anthropology,* New York: Harper & Row, 1964

18 Landar, H., *Language and culture,* New York: Oxford U.P., 1966

19 McLuhan, M., *The gutenberg galaxy; the making of typographical man,* London: Routledge, 1962

20 Saporta, S. (ed), *Psycholinguistics: a book of readings,* New York: Holt, Rinehart & Winston, 1961

21 Skinner, B. F., *Verbal behaviour,* New York: Appleton, 1957

22 Tucker, N., *Understanding the mass media. A practical approach for teaching,* London: Cambridge U.P., 1966

23 Vygotsky, L. S., *Thought and language,* (ed. and transl. Eugenia Hanfmann and Gertrude Vakard) Cambridge Mass.: M.I.T., 1966

24 Whorf, B. L., *Language, thought and reality; selected writings of Benjamin Lee Whorf, ed. J. B. Carroll*, Cambridge Mass. and New York: M.I.T. and Wiley, 1956

III *Linguistic change and the history of English*

Histories of English are plentiful; among them, *Baugh, 25,* still seems to me to hold pride of place. However, *Strang, 28,* may set a new pattern. Her book takes as a central assumption the relationship between the structure of society (in particular the urbanisation of English society) and the structure of language; furthermore, it adopts the novel but sensible procedure of reading our linguistic history backwards, from the present day to Anglo-Saxon times. *Foster, 27,* is listed here because it pays attention to changes taking place in present-day English. *Bloomfield and Newmark, 26,* attempts to provide a background of linguistic theory against which the phenomena of change in language may be more readily understood. *Sturtevant, 29,* is a veritable ancient, having first been published in 1917; but it continues to be a useful text for the student, and this recent re-issue makes it the more readily available.

25 Baugh, A. C., *A history of the English language,* 2nd ed., London: Routledge, 1962

26 Bloomfield, M. W. & Newmark, L., *A linguistic introduction to the history of English,* New York: Alfred Knopf, 1963

27 Foster, B., *The changing English language,* London: Macmillan, 1968

28 Strang, Barbara M. H., *A history of English,* London: Methuen, 1970

29 Sturtevant, E., *Linguistic change. An introduction to the historical study of language,* Chicago, Illinois: Univ. Chicago Press, 1962

IV *The structure, use, and varieties of present-day British and American English*

English is of course spoken in countries other than Great Britain and the USA; and I have to apologise to Australians, New Zealanders, Canadians, Nigerians, Indians, and others, for not having access to enough information about their varieties of English. My heading covers a mixture of themes, including detailed descriptions of the structure of American and British English, prescriptive or norm-giving manuals of usage, and discussions of social variations in language, including what British linguists call 'register' – i.e. the use of a particular variety of language for a particular social or cultural purpose. *Francis, 31,* and *Marckwardt, 36,* describe American English; Francis' book contains a chapter on American dialects by R. I. McDavid. Further to this, there are articles on regional and social varieties of American English in *Anderson & Stageberg, I, 1,* and *Hogins & Yarber, I, 8.* These papers may perhaps help to supply the unavoidable deficiencies of my chapter 5, where I have been forced to confine my discussion to regional and social stereotypes of British English. *Quirk, 37,* is an excellent general introduction to the study of contemporary British English, and like most British writings gives due weight to the arbitration of 'usage' and social conditioning. *Strang, 38,* is more detailed and technical. This second edition of her book includes accounts of 'register' and dialect, as well as a good deal of current linguistic theory. From the many books of prescription and reference at my disposal (it is with regret that I pass by names like Fowler, Partridge, and Vallins), I have selected *Gowers, 32,* and *Graves and Hodges, 33.* Both are concerned, of course, with standards of correctness in written English. Gowers represents an attack on the institutional jargon of government departments; Graves and Hodges provide interesting technical comments on the composition of selected passages. The case against an inflexible standard, often irrationally imposed, is made in *Halliday McIntosh & Strevens, 34,* particularly in chapter 4. This book is a general exposition of Firthian linguistics, and has a coverage which would make it an appropriate item in more than one section of this bibliography. *Joos, 35,* is also concerned with variety in language, and distinguishes between five styles of English, i.e. the intimate, the casual, the consultative, the formal, and the frozen, each style having its own criteria of usage. *Dean & Wilson, 30,* is a very useful collection of articles by various hands. It gives a good deal of space to the theme of usage, but contains much of wider interest and can be listed with *Anderson & Stageberg, I, 1,* and *Hogins & Yarber, I, 8,* as a good general introduction to language.

30 Dean, L. P. & Wilson, K. G. (eds), *Essays on language and usage,* 2nd ed., New York: Oxford U.P., 1963

31 Francis, W. N., *The structure of American English,* New York: Oxford U.P., 1958

32 Gowers, Sir E. A., *The complete plain words*, London: Cape, 1954

33 Graves, R. & Hodges, A., *The reader over your shoulder. A handbook for writers of English prose*, London: Cape, 1943

34 Halliday, M. A. K., McIntosh, A., & Strevens, P. A. D., *The linguistic sciences and language teaching*, London: Longmans, 1964

35 Joos, M., *The five clocks. A linguistic excursion into the five styles of English*, New York: Harcourt, Brace & World, 1967

36 Marckwardt, A. M., *American English*, New York: Oxford U.P., 1958

37 Quirk, R., *The use of English*, 2nd ed., London: Longmans, 1969

38 Strang, Barbara M. H., *Modern English structure*, 2nd ed., London: Arnold, 1970

v *The phonetics of British and American English*

Many of the books listed in the foregoing sections contain information about the forms and functions of speech-sounds. During recent decades there has been some revision of opinion as to the place accorded to phonology – the study of the relationship of speech-sounds to linguistic functions – in linguistic theory. It used to be regarded as having fundamental importance, the establishment of a phonological basis of a language being prior to a description of its general structure. Nowadays, there is a general tendency to give priority to grammatical structure and to treat phonology as the study of the realisation or interpretation of grammatical forms. However, these problems belong to general linguistics, and to the theory of grammar. The two manuals listed here are convenient guides to the phonetic substance, so to speak, of British and American English. *Gimson, 39*, warrants particular recommendation; this book has all but superseded Daniel Jones' classic *An Outline of English Phonetics* as the standard text on the phonetics of present-day British English. Part I of Gimson's book, entitled *Speech and Language*, may be found useful as an introduction to general phonetics; this 2nd edition also includes some observations on current attitudes to Standard English.

39 Gimson, A. C., *An introduction to the pronunciation of English*, 2nd ed., London: Arnold, 1970

40 Thomas, C. K., *The Phonetics of American English*, New York: Ronald Press, 1958

VI *Grammatical theory and grammars of English*

Of late, the term 'grammar' has assumed a virtual equivalence to 'linguistic theory'; or at any rate has come to denote the primary task of linguistic investigation. Consequently, various 'grammars', having much in common, but also having distinctive emphases and methodologies, have emerged during recent decades; e.g. *IC (Immediate Constituent) grammar, tagmemic grammar, transformational (transformational-generative) grammar, Stratificational grammar, System and structure (Systemic, Scale and category) grammar.* Each of these is really a general type embodied in various applications, so that one might more appropriately speak of 'transformational grammars', 'systemic grammars', etc. Accounting for their relationships and differences would require more space than I can afford here. Chapter 8 of *Robins, I, 11,* will supply the necessary historical perspective. In my list I include two short books, i.e. *Mittins, 43,* and *Whitehall, 47,* which represent a modern yet fairly conservative approach to English grammar. These works will serve for purposes of comparison with other items. For students and teachers of English, *Fries, 42,* is a landmark of structuralist *(IC)* grammar. *Roberts, 44,* may be said to represent a movement away from that landmark in the direction of transformationalism. The transformationalist position is very clearly explained in *Thomas, 46.* System and structure grammars are the product of the Firthian school of linguistics; they lay emphasis on situation and the varied application of language, and so may be of particular interest to students interested in, for example, the sociological applications of language, or the study and comparison of literary texts. The linguistic philosophy of this school is set out in *Halliday, McIntosh & Strevens, IV, 34. Sinclair, 45,* is a product of the school, but the book is in the nature of a pilot text and does not embody the latest developments in 'systemic' theory. An introduction to system and structure grammars, by my colleague Miss H. M. Berry, is currently in preparation. The principles of tagmemic analysis (a theory first developed by Kenneth Pike) are expounded in *Cook, 41.* Readers approaching this text after acquainting themselves with systemic and transformationalist grammars will notice that tagmemics has points of similarity with both theories.

In fact there is a good deal of common ground in current grammatical theory, and the likelihood is that this will expand as time goes by; perhaps all that is now happening is a process of restoring, repairing, and re-aligning the knowledge of the past.

41 Cook, W. A., *Introduction to tagmemic analysis*, New York: Holt, Rinehart & Winston, 1969

42 Fries, C. C., *The structure of English*, New York: Harcourt, Brace & World, 1952

43 Mittins, W. H., *A grammar of modern English*, London: Methuen, 1962

44 Roberts, P., *English sentences*, New York: Harcourt, Brace & World, 1962

45 Sinclair, J. McH., *A course in spoken English, 3. Grammar*, London: Oxford U.P., 1965

46 Thomas, O., *Transformational grammar and the teacher of English*, New York: Holt, Rinehart & Winston, 1965

47 Whitehall, H., *Structural essentials of English*, New York: Harcourt, Brace & World, 1956

VII *Some versions of semantics*

We can define semantics as the study of meaning, but that still leaves us with the problem of settling the meaning of meaning. Semantics, in other words, is a term capable of a variety of definitions, and a study susceptible to a variety of approaches. *Ullman, 51*, summarises the position of studies in the subject at a fairly recent date, but does not reflect the current attempt to integrate the 'conceptual' approach of traditional semantics with a general theory of linguistic descriptions. *Leech, 49*, represents just such an attempt to put semantics on a descriptive footing; it considers three areas of meaning in present-day English, i.e. time, place, and modality. *Salomon, 50*, is an excellent general text for the student seeking a 'popular' introduction to the subject. *Hayakawa, 48*, is a well-known essay in so-called 'general semantics', i.e. in the description of the individual's attempts to engineer his experience through language-stratagems prompted by his judgements, attitudes, and cultural environment. Mention of the book can generally be guaranteed to bring a frown to the academic brow, there being many who are suspicious or resentful of its publicist techniques; but the layman ought not to be deterred from reading a socially valuable book.

48 Hayakawa, S. I., *Language in thought and action*, 2nd ed., London: G. Allen & Unwin, 1965

49 Leech, G. N., *Towards a semantic description of English*, London: Longmans, 1969

50 Salomon, L. B., *Semantics and common sense*, New York: Holt, Rinehart & Winston, 1966

51 Ullman, S., *The principles of semantics*, 2nd ed., Glasgow: Glasgow University Press, 1957

VIII *Style in language*

A good deal has been written about literary style. Most writings on the subject proceed from the assumption that style is a property of the author's personality ('the style is the man'), and so are averse to linguistic theories of style, which can look like (but seldom are) attempts to reduce personal art to abstract pseudo-science. *Fowler, 53*, and *Sebeok, 55*, are collections embodying a variety of approaches, mainly linguistic, to the subject. *Enkvist, Spencer & Gregory, 52*, attempts to provide a theoretical basis in linguistics for the discussion and study of style. *Leech, 54*, is a detailed study, and, I think, succeeds in showing how linguistic techniques may help us to perceive and define specific features of poetic style. Much work is currently being done on linguistic theories of style, but there is an understandable tendency for the investigator to relate his theory to the grammatical model in which he happens to have been instructed. Consequently we may have to wait for some time for the emergence of a unified stylistic theory. Until that time, each analyst of style will presumably go on devising his own apparatus.

52 Enkvist, N. E., Spencer, J., & Gregory, M., *Linguistics and style*, London: Oxford U.P., 1967

53 Fowler, R. (ed), *Essays on style and language. Linguistic and critical approaches to literary style*, London: Routledge, 1966

54 Leech, G. N., *A linguistic guide to English poetry*, London: Longmans, 1969

55 Sebeok, T. A. (ed)., *Style in language*, Cambridge, Mass.: M.I.T., 1966

Index